FORD MADOX
AND THE CI

International Ford Madox Ford Studies Volume 4

For information about the Ford Madox Ford Society,
please see the website at:
www.rialto.com/fordmadoxford_society

Or contact:
max.saunders@kcl.ac.uk
or:
Dr Sara Haslam S.J.Haslam@open.ac.uk
Department of Literature, Open University,
Walton Hall, Milton Keynes, MK7 6AA, UK

IFMFS is a peer-reviewed annual series. Guidelines for contributors, including
a full list of abbreviations of Ford's titles and related works, can be found by
following the links on the Society's website. Abbreviations used in this volume
are listed from p. 247

FORD MADOX FORD
AND THE CITY

Edited by

Sara Haslam

Amsterdam - New York, NY 2005

The Ford Madox Ford Society

Ford Madox Ford, 'Portraits of Cities', and quotations from unpublished letters and manuscripts, © Michael Schmidt 2005

Cover illustration: James Abbott McNeill Whistler, 1834-1903, 'Nocturne – Blue and Gold: Old Battersea Bridge' (1872-5). Oil on Canvas, N01959/119. The painting was presented to the Tate by the National Art Collections Fund in 1905, the year of Ford's *The Soul of London*. © Tate, London 2005

Illustration on this page: Ford Madox Brown, 'Work', 1852. The painting is discussed on pp. 42-3.
© Birmingham Museum and Art Gallery

Title page illustration: Ford c.1915, pen and ink drawing.
© Alfred Cohen, 2000

The paper on which this book is printed meets the requirements of "ISO 9706: 1994, Information and documentation - Paper for documents - Requirements for permanence".

ISBN: 90-420-1717-1
©Editions Rodopi B.V., Amsterdam - New York, NY 2005
Printed in The Netherlands

[I]t is only the great cities that offer us the chance to bathe in humanity. And to the general man all the world over, it is only humanity that is really and vitally fascinating.

Ford Madox Ford, 'The Fascination of London' (1909)

CONTENTS

SECTION 2: 'THE BL—DY WORLD'

SECTION 3: FORD'S 'PORTRAITS OF CITIES'

GENERAL EDITOR'S PREFACE

Max Saunders

Ford Madox Ford has as often been a subject of controversy as a candidate for literary canonization. He was, nonetheless, a major presence in early twentieth-century literature, and he has remained a significant figure in the history of modern English and American literature for over a century. Throughout that time he has been written about – not just by critics, but often by leading novelists and poets, such as Graham Greene, Robert Lowell, William Carlos Williams, Gore Vidal, A. S. Byatt, and Julian Barnes. His two acknowledged masterpieces have remained in print since the 1940s. *The Good Soldier* now regularly figures in studies of Modernism and on syllabuses. *Parade's End* has been increasingly recognized as comparably important. It was described by Malcolm Bradbury as 'a central Modernist novel of the 1920s, in which it is exemplary'; by Anthony Burgess as 'the finest novel about the First World War'; and by Samuel Hynes as 'the greatest war novel ever written by an Englishman'.

During the last decade or so, there has been a striking resurgence of interest in Ford and in the multifarious aspects of his work. As befits such an internationalist phenomenon as Ford himself, this critical attention has been markedly international, manifesting itself not only in the United Kingdom and the U. S. A., but in Continental Europe and elsewhere. Many of his works have not only been republished in their original language, but also translated into more than a dozen others.

The founding of the International Ford Madox Ford Studies series reflects this increasing interest in Ford's writing and the wider understanding of his role in literary history. Each volume will normally be based upon a particular theme or issue. Each will relate aspects of Ford's work, life, and contacts, to broader concerns of his time. Thus the first, *Ford Madox Ford: A Reappraisal*, explored his less familiar books. The second investigated *Ford Madox Ford's Modernity*. The third, *History and Representation in Ford Madox Ford's Writings* traced his interest in history throughout his career, with specific emphases on the tudor trilogy, the first world war, and the 1930s.

This fourth volume considers the significance of the city in Ford's œuvre. He was born in Merton, Surrey, which in 1873 would have seemed more of an outer suburb than it does now. Apart from his decade or so of living on the Romney Marsh with Elsie Martindale, and collaborating with Joseph Conrad, Ford spent most of his life in London until he joined the army in 1915: first in Hammersmith as he was growing up, and later mostly in Kensington, when he founded the *English Review* and lived with Violet Hunt. *The Soul of London* (1905) was Ford's first major success. It was republished in 2003 in a fine edition of *England and the English*, also edited by Sara Haslam, the editor of the present collection. Over the last few years *The Soul of London* has emerged as one of Ford's most discussed texts: seen both as a classic instance of literary Impressionism, and also as an anticipation of pre-war London Modernism. He continued to write about London all his life; and about half of this volume is necessarily devoted to it. In addition, it covers not only the other major cities in which Ford lived – Paris and New York – but also the idea of the city, whether as a facilitator of the arts, or an image of despair or desire. The volume closes with three of the essays on American cities Ford was writing in his last years. Still relatively unknown, these engaging 'portraits' demonstrate the continuities of his experiments in representing the city, transforming it into image and narrative.

The series is published in association with the Ford Madox Ford Society. Forthcoming and projected volumes will be announced on the Society's website, together with details of whom to contact with suggestions about future volumes or contributions. The address is: **www.rialto.com/fordmadoxford_society**

INTRODUCTION: TELLING THE CITY

Sara Haslam

A guide to London writing published by Waterstone's in 1999 includes a section on Ford Madox Ford. He finds himself sandwiched between Conan Doyle and Gissing, both of whom are well-known explorers of London's secrets and vices, perhaps better-known than Ford. And yet his inclusion in this guide is justified, more so than is appreciated by the section editor who claims that Ford 'never really wrote about the city of his birth again' (after 1905 and *The Soul of London*).[1] Not so. Throughout Ford's career, when he wrote about cities, it was most often London that he took for his subject or its background. He also loved, lived in and wrote about, for example, Paris and New York, but it was the English capital that he found to be 'the final expression of the Present Stage'.[2] Generalizations are and can be made about 'the city' in Ford, or 'the city' as modernist construct. When such abstract notions become concrete in his work it is often the shapes of London that are assumed.

Urban Energy

The view from a palace window in an early Ford tale is, we are told, 'very fine'. 'A dark wood grew in the foreground', and 'far away over the tree-tops were the blue hills, behind which the sun was just preparing to retire'.[3] Though Ford was certainly not averse to telling stories, and even fairy stories, of the country (the subtitle of *The Brown Owl* is *A Fairy Story*), it is his stories which draw at least some of their energy from urban sources for which he is best-known. In *A Call* (1910) and *The Good Soldier* (1915), for example, that energy springs from the chaotic potential in communications offered by the city, and is manifested in illicit sexual liaisons, or confessions, in its diverseness rendering ambiguous things characters know and say. Affective to a lesser degree, but still present in *Parade's End* (1924-8), that energy is associated with institutions for government, commerce, or education, or generated by the crowd. On Armistice Day in London Valentine Wannop is 'jostled by the innumerable crowd', having been 'deafened by unceasing shouts'. She is overwhelmed, and considers that this vocal energy has assumed a form, 'like life'. Once she escapes the crowd, silence appears 'like Death' instead.[4] In *The Soul of London*, uniquely, that energy is the end-product of London's assimilation, or 'digestion', of its visitors from many lands, along with all their individual histories and stories. The vital force that is the result of this quasi-biological process is named by Ford as 'the Modern', whose spirit is 'extraordinary and unfathomable' (*EE* 12). It manifests itself in part as speed, and focuses the minds of the city's inhabitants upon the future at the expense of the past:

> London, with its sense of immensity that we must hurry through to keep unceasing appointments, with its diffuseness, its gatherings up into innumerable trade-centres, innumerable class districts, becomes by its immensity a place upon which there is no beginning. (*EE* 9-10)

'The Modern' promises pleasure too. 'So appealing' is the 'ragout of tit-bits' Ford has just described that we might be justified in identifying an anticipatory dash of futurism in his fulsome prose. (Futurism's Manifesto, published in 1909, exalted speed, 'aggressive action', and crowds.[5]) The city in Ford, then, on this first approach seems to be the locus of a force for progressive challenge and change: its energy is liberating, vital, exciting, always new.

Fairy tales for Ford were rural affairs – think for example of the anti-city parts of *A Call*, during which Kitty is cured as well as, more obviously, *The Brown Owl*, or *Ladies Whose Bright Eyes* – but G. K. Chesterton published what he called a 'London fairy tale' in 1904, a year before the appearance of *The Soul of London*. *The Napoleon of Notting Hill* is set in the future, towards the end of the twentieth century, but it is plain that Chesterton is using his first novel to comment in part on contemporary city life. In contrast to Ford's representation of the city, that comment is mostly to do with what Chesterton perceives as the pernicious lack of energy affecting city dwellers. This is not for want of trying to obtain it. The Honourable James Barker, a key official in the Government, in an early London scene explains the 'modern intellect' to the ex-President of Nicaragua. Thinking of the wider world (as ruled from the English capital) and anticipating Ford's striking image of the digestive body of London, Barker states that the 'moderns believe in a great cosmopolitan civilisation, one which shall include all the talents of all the absorbed people'.[6] Varied and exciting energies should result. But the ex-

President suggests instead that Nicaragua's unique talents have dissipated since its unsuccessful struggle for independence and subsequent 'absorption'. And London, gaining nothing from this process, has lost all life-force. 'I see blank well-ordered streets', muses the revolutionary Adam Wayne, 'and men in black moving about inoffensively, sullenly. It goes on day after day, day after day, and nothing happens [...] Its stillness is terrible' (*Napoleon* 79). Passages like this, argues Bernard Bergonzi, dramatically evoke the 'silence of modernity', and mean that *The Napoleon of Notting Hill* 'conveys a sense of its era': Chesterton's interpretation of the dominant spirit of the age. Bergonzi quotes from George Steiner as he discusses this spirit, relating it to the 'Great Ennui' of the nineteenth century (*Napoleon* xx). In so doing, he gives form to a vision of the Modern, and the role of the city in that vision, that is diametrically opposed to what we know so far of Ford's. The city urges forward movement in Ford's writing, expression, and variety. In Chesterton's, it induces stupor, nightmare, and colourlessness – until, that is, someone tries to build a road through Notting Hill (you'll have to read the novel to find out why).

Despite the evident contrasts in approach to the urban displayed by these two contemporary writers (manifested too, of course, in city writing by Eliot, James, Woolf and others[7]), I have chosen to introduce Chesterton because of the particular way in which he encourages interrogation of the sense of excitement and vitality we have identified in Ford. In fact, Chesterton's protagonist foresees the end of the 'silence of modernity', and as *The Napoleon of Notting Hill* develops, his version of London begins to sound more like Ford's. Revolution comes to the city; boroughs assert their independence and resist the contemporary scourge of urban degeneration simultaneously. London finds energy, a necessary stage in its evolution and progress. More interestingly, and more confusingly, Ford's London can also sound like the city of nightmares that characterizes the beginning of Chesterton's novel.

One powerfully drawn scene from *The Soul of London* depicts what occurs when urban energy turns bad, and turns in on itself. Individuality and order are lost. The 'chaotic crowd' comes to form part of an 'apparently indissoluble muddle of grey wheel traffic, of hooded carts, of 'buses drawing out of line, of sticky mud, with a pallid church wavering into invisibility towards the steeple in the weeping sky'. Pre-figuring some ghastly First World War landscape, terror and injury result as a horse is drawn down into the mess; frantically struggling, rolling its eyes after a fall, it then lies still (*EE* 15). This busy street points away from pleasure and excitement and towards psychological torment and death. And Ford comes back to this idea. Post-war, he uses the London road to represent the fissure between appearance and the new reality to soldiers' shell-shocked, 'smashed', minds.[8] Elsewhere in Ford's autobiography, it is a London of 'physical gloom' that infects his memory as he writes. He remembers a London in which it was 'always winter', never spring. Most of all, he remembers the dark, both inside and out. 'A City whose streets are illuminated only by the flicker of rare street-lamps seems darker than one not lit at all', he reflects, and 'the corners of rooms are always filled with shadows when the sole illuminant is a dim oil-lamp'.[9] In both external and internal filmic examples, the meagre light serves only to make one more aware of the power of the dark it cannot dispel. It forced the Pre-Raphaelites, Ford thought, away from realism, away from the 'life that was around them' to the stories of Launcelot and Guinevere for rejuvenating light and colour.[10] Perhaps that's where Ford might have followed them more permanently, as he did briefly though notably in the jewelled scenes of the *Fifth Queen* trilogy (1906-8), *Ladies Whose Bright Eyes* (1911), and *The Young Lovell* (1913).[11] Yet he didn't. Why not?

The Modernist City

Ford's comrade and collaborator, Joseph Conrad, found a way of reading the dark that oppressed Ford, particularly the kind of dark that gathered in the city. *The Secret Agent* was published in 1907. In its preface, Conrad details the tale's genesis:

> Then the vision of an enormous town presented itself, of a monstrous town more populous than some continents and in its man-made might as if indifferent to heaven's frowns and smiles; a cruel devourer of the world's light.[12]

So far, Conrad sounds more like the bleaker side of Ford, and Chesterton, in his conjuring (and, notably, the thing these contemporary texts all share is the notion of the suffocating über-town). But Conrad's vision does not stop there; he goes on in his preface to investigate the reaches of the city dark, and finds that, in this monstrous town, there was 'room enough' to place any story, 'depth enough for any passion', and 'variety enough' for any setting

(10). It's a story teller's dream, in other words, a riot of potential for plot, motive and setting. And more particularly, it's a modernist story teller's dream – in his more famous preface to *The Nigger of the 'Narcissus'* (1897), Conrad set it out as the task of the modernist novelist to bring the light of at least a 'passing glance' into each 'dark corner of the earth'.[13] If darkness, and people, proliferate in the city, then here is the place to discover a tale to tell. Ford knew this instinctively by the time of *The Soul of London*. But for him there is also evidently something about the way stories of the city emerge, and the form that they take as they do so, that provokes anxiety, and worse. In one highly potent combination of source and subject matter, Ford remembers that his nurse 'had come into contact with more murders and deaths by violence than any person I ever met' (*RY* 61), and perhaps as a consequence, blood, guts and misery loom large overall. Conrad may have had the stronger stomach. I think, though, that the anxiety has more to do with form. A visual clue is provided in this respect by the pallid church and its invisible steeple in *The Soul of London*, pointing who knows where into a generally poisonous sky. In this murky London, where such experiences of occluded or truncated vision are common, the 'order' that has been lost is partly that of narrative. Ford's nurse found a Ripper victim and stood watching a man run off into the fog. Following the intervention of his mother, an impressed and horrified Ford didn't get to hear, and therefore couldn't write about, what happened next (*RY* 62).

In 1937 the urban historian Lewis Mumford asked 'what is a city?'. To his mind, one of the most satisfactory definitions had been provided by John Stow, who Mumford called 'an honest observer of Elizabethan London'. Stow writes that

> Men are congregated into cities and commonwealths for honesty and dignity's sake, these shortly be the commodities that do come by cities, commonalities and corporations. First, men by this nearness of conversation are withdrawn from barbarous fixity and force, to certain mildness of manners, and to humanity and justice [...]. Good behaviour is yet called *urbanitas* because it is rather found in cities than elsewhere.[14]

Mumford himself recognized that such a definition could not easily be applied to contemporary cities. He put it down to their sheer size, for when social interaction must largely be on the basis of anonymity, that 'nearness of conversation' does not have the same genial effect. Stow's vision was also dramatically removed from the realities of the modern city as Ford both saw it, and used it in his fiction and non-fiction. Good behaviour is usually lacking, especially in good soldiers; nearness is a yet larger and more problematic issue.[15] The realities of that modern city receive treatment at the start of *The Soul of London*; for the young provincial, a first impression of the city will refract into a sense of his own 'alone-ness' (*EE* 9). By the time of *A Call*, that impression might, more damagingly, involve a fear of being discovered as an adulterer. *Parade's End*'s London provides an empty space for the more mature, though still emotionally complex, re-unification of Tietjens and Valentine (significantly it's in an eighteenth-century house – a temporary refuge from the twentieth-century world). It then promptly fills it up with shell-shocked and dependent ex-soldiers who need to talk to their father-figure. Their need for conversation (also Tietjens' 'desperate' need (*PE* 659)) conflicts with Valentine's desire to make love to a different persona which Tietjens polymorphously presents. Rather than the force for moral good so praised by Stow, conversation in this London is fractured by interruptions caused by broken minds – and they have been broken by the very barbarity from which a city was historically conceived as a refuge. Conversation is fractured by memories too, as well as distance (crucial conversations in *A Call* and *Parade's End* take place via telephone), and, more simply, the lack of an interlocutor. Such conversation emphatically does not point towards increased 'mildness of manners', but it is a critical part of the way in which the modern city must tell its stories all the same.

The fractured narrative of conversations is one onto which the grander narrative of the city can be mapped. A narrativising of the city (which might be compared with an attempt to re-order it) is a clear aim of *The Soul of London*. Chapter 1 views London 'from a distance', introducing it to us through the eyes of a stranger as though it were a character at the start of a novel. Slightly nearer to the hub of the action in chapter 2, we are treated to a description of 'roads into London', used to display discrete areas of the city characterized by their proximity to the Thames, or the railway, or major roads. The following two chapters detail aspects of life within London, and, progressing as though in narrative time, we are presented with an analysis of death in the city in the final chapter. The form Ford adopts here might be explained by his understanding of the fact that humanity likes 'a story to have an end' (*EE* 61). Ultimately, however, despite what humanity may like, the narratives that the city is shown to enact resist any sense of progression. London has 'no beginning', after all. If London has no beginning, then the stories and the conversations generated by urban life don't either; they are short, fragmented, and characterized by difficulty (coming out of the dark, being mis-heard or misunderstood). And nor can they find an end. Both Henry James and Ford include examples of short stories in their London writing, stories which they remember precisely because they had no end, framed as they were by the moving window of a train or a cab.[16] After one potentially violent scene witnessed from a train Ford writes that 'the evening papers reported no murder in Southwark' (*EE* 41): so one didn't occur then, or did it? (As suggested by that steeple and the 'weeping sky', perhaps the end might not have been one we wanted to hear.)

There may be no beginning to the stories the city has to tell, and no end either. But there is variety, and excitement, to counter the anxiety as to this formlessness that Ford undoubtedly feels. Such variety, and excitement, is found by the youthful Ford, exultantly eavesdropping on the housemaid's stream of cockney gossip with his mother, or awestruck by the extraordinary stories told in pidgin English by Borschitzsky, his music master.[17] Later, he finds it in other places, in his club, say, 'in a room which is supposed to be blessed with silence, – in a club whose members are all supposed to be British born', where people are not silent, and people are not British born but are German, and Irish, and French and are then 'in touch with a spirit of cosmopolitanism' (*EE* 329). More importantly for our present purposes, such people have a wealth of histories to offer, a verbal 'texturology' to complement that more concrete version de Certeau finds in the urban skyline.[18] Following on from Conrad, then, Ford finds some light in the city's shadow-side, some energy too.

I suggested earlier that Chesterton's London begins to look like Ford's energized version, as revolution comes in *The Napoleon of Notting Hill*. Having deviated into the ways in which Ford's London can instead seem to function like Chesterton's, I want now to return to the former idea because of what it seems to suggest about urban evolutionary progress. Chesterton's heroes find energy in *The Napoleon of Notting Hill* when they take up revolutionary cudgels against the notion of the greater city of London.[19] Their aim is to realize the borough-state, with mini city walls, separate spheres, even passports perhaps. His energetic London is, in other words, a throwback, an attempt at control and finiteness amidst the riot of urban sprawl (and its darkness is not mined for stories, but is used to provide cover for murder (*Napoleon* 110-1)). Although Mumford realized that the spread of the city 'meant the inevitable dissipation of its humanity' (17), he argued that better planning as to the social relations and social functions of the city was necessary to combat this. He would certainly not have called for intra-city walls. And neither, of course, would Ford. He would have taken himself off somewhere noisy, with a notebook and pen, to listen, wait and write.

The Volume
This collection includes three of Ford's own essays on the city, two of which ('Boston' and 'Denver') are published here for the first time. The thirteen essays by both established and new American and European scholars[20] provide a wide variety of analytical contexts for Ford's city writing, reflecting developments in Ford studies (for example in the amount of attention given to Ford's poetry) but also in contemporary criticism on the subjects of Literature and the City, and Modernism, as indicated by the descriptions given below. The volume can also be seen as a contribution to debates about Englishness, and nationality more generally too. It is hoped that this volume will be of use to scholars with interests in these wider fields as well as to those who already work in the area of Ford studies.

The critical essays have been divided into two sections: 'London' and 'The Bl—dy World'. (Ford titled Part IV of the autobiographical *Return to Yesterday* 'The Bl—dy World'. In it he describes the misery of his various European cures from 1903 to 1906, but New York at least is treated with great affection!) There may be links based on technique, genre and content between essays in different sections, but for the reasons I described at the beginning of the introduction they make most sense categorized in this way.

Ford lived and worked in London, Paris and New York. He lived in Germany too, and wrote about it, most famously in *The Good Soldier*. None of the essays in this current volume is on Ford's involvement with German life and culture, but one fairly recent example, by Gene Moore, was published in 2002. Moore discusses Ford's fictional and factual representations of Germany, and the time he spent mostly in smaller German towns: Boppard, Telgte, Gießen.[21] Ford also stayed in Carcassonne, and as Paul Skinner argues in the final critical essay of *Ford Madox Ford and the City*, the place embedded itself deep in his writer's mind. Size isn't everything when it comes to Ford and the city. London, Paris and New York may figure prominently, but Ford has notions of the city as a space for imaginative play which are often powerfully realized in his treatment of lesser urban sprawls.

At the end of the volume, in a third section, I have included three examples of Ford's city writing, as mentioned above. 'Boston', 'Denver' and 'Take Me Back to Tennessee' (on Nashville) take the form of short, impressionistic essays, intended for a book to be called *Portraits of Cities*, though it was never completed. These provisional chapters were all written as Ford was living and traveling in the United States in the late 1930s.

(1) London

Ways of seeing the metropolis, from street level, or from a higher plane, and an interest in perspective, link the first five essays in this section. Impressionism features to a large degree, and the main work explored in most cases is *The Soul of London*. Nick Freeman places Ford in a tradition of developing impressionism, and reads the emergence of *The Soul of London* autobiographically, economically and in contrast to other contemporary London writings. Prominence is granted in this first essay to narrative structure and genre in city writings, an issue to which both Angus Wrenn and Sita Schutt return. Wrenn's analysis of London perspectives in Ford concentrates on Ford's earlier influences, Madox Brown among them. A reading of the angles of elevation in Brown's famous painting 'Work' (1852-65) leads to a consideration of views of London provided by various forms of transport; both, in turn, are linked with social class. A comparative reading of Stoker, Conan Doyle (also considered by Freeman) and Ford allows Schutt to investigate perspectives associated with nationality in London writings. Extents of assimilation, marginality and criminality are shown to be linked both with ways of seeing London and ways of constructing modernist narratives. Is London knowable, limitable, assimilable? Answers to this question vary according to whether you are a Stoker, a Conan Doyle, or a Ford.

Max Saunders's essay considers impressionism as particularly a metropolitan phenomenon, and shows the progression, in Ford, from the ideas of the Impressionists into Modernist concerns with urban space, time, energy and technology. Ford's agoraphobic illness from 1904 is linked with his contemporary experiences of crowded city space as well as that of, in one famous example, Salisbury Plain. Saunders' conclusion examines the continuing importance of the city in Ford's writing. Brian Groth's Ford looks forward from contemporary London in a utopian vision – in the essay 'The Future in London' (1909). Developing ideas introduced by Wrenn, and furthered by Schutt and Saunders, Groth notes the importance of views from transport in Ford's utopia, including 'airships', not invented when *The Soul of London* was written. A second London essay dating from 1936 is read as a corrective vision of the city which looks very different due to where Ford himself stood at this time of his life, as well as to contemporary European politics.

Chapters six and seven of this section are dedicated to the non-prosaic London in Ford introduced by Saunders. The London we are treated to by Colin Edwards' reading of *Mr Bosphorus and the Muses* is a riot of theatrical effect, a 'giddying vortex of pleasure and distaste' to which Edwards builds up by comparison with Ford's other writing of the 1920s – choreographed scenes of City Burlesque pep up *Parade's End*. Though Edwards' analysis includes biographical suggestion (this is Ford's 'Last of England'), he focuses on ways the city is given voice and realized by this text: modernist dance-styles, tableaux featuring widows at pawnbrokers', prostitutes, cockney paupers, lecherous, gin-sodden Londoners. This is partly about class: Edwards argues Ford is drawing attention to 'opposing registers' but is also, more simply, enjoying the show. The final essay in the section takes us from drama to poetry, and opens with a useful account of critical acclaim for Ford's modernist poems. However, Ashley Chantler also argues for the importance of Ford's less well-known, early poems, both in terms of what they have to say about the development of Ford's modernism, and in ways more widely applicable to contemporary 'literary meditations' too. Ford's first city poem is set in Paris (and in this sense Chantler's essay forms a bridge to the next section of the volume), but even in this case Chantler finds connections with fin-de-siècle London poems by the likes of Dowson and Symons. Contextual, comparative readings continue to define the essay, as does close attention to the poems themselves.

(2)   'The Bl—dy World'

Continuing the focus on Ford's poetry, Joseph Wiesenfarth's essay, 'Coda to the City', begins with a challenge to the supremacy of Ford's best-known poem, 'On Heaven'. Contemporary praise by Ezra Pound, in particular, offered in extravagant terms, Wiesenfarth argues, made 'On Heaven' 'carry more freight than Ford intended'. He wants to redress the balance, praising 'Coda' as Ford's 'best poem altogether'. Set in Paris, the poem tells the story of two lovers, a writer and a painter. They represent civilization against the various threats that mass against them – political, barbarous, temporal threats too. In this way, Wiesenfarth's essay can be compared with the second in this section, by Elena Lamberti. The city in Lamberti's essay is sometimes a real place, but is more often a virtual site for debating the extent and nature of Ford's 'republic of letters'. When the two coincide, it is Paris that Ford idealizes (ultimately over London: contributors offer different assessments throughout this volume of Ford's preferred city), finding London post-war a 'lost city' but in Paris a place for poets and writers to found a productive community. Lamberti argues that Ford strives in the end for a transnational culture, one that enacts itself beyond the boundaries imposed by nationality, and, particularly, 'the inherent individualism of the English man of letters'. Exploring Ford's Paris in more detail, Caroline Patey investigates the transnational potential offered by sites such as the Quai d'Anjou, a liminal Parisian space that was home to the *transatlantic review*. She reads the island location as echoing and informing the publishing aims of the review – aims which sought to disrupt and challenge boundaries between nationalities, genres, and ages – as well as its logo. Patey appreciates the complexity of Ford's visions of this city, relating them to his attention to the past, and writers such as Flaubert and Turgenev, to his engagement with the brilliant present of Picasso and Braque, and to the particular way in which Paris fostered the talents of the women artists he admired and wanted to promote: Stein, Bowen, Rhys, Djuna Barnes and Gwen John among them.

As Robert McDonough's essay shows, impressionism was not only a characteristic of Ford's early career, or of that associated with modernism, but of his writing into his fifth decade. Focusing on *New York is Not America* (1927), but making recourse to 'On Impressionism' (1914), McDonough shows that impressionism, and by extension anecdote, infused Ford's writing style throughout his writing life. His analysis of this book contributes to an understanding of the import-ance of this city to Ford. Such an outcome is taken up and developed by Michele Gemelos in the fifth essay of the section, in which she argues for the varied importance of Ford's writing about New York.

Such writing helped Ford to develop his notions of the relationship of the individual to the city, his thinking about national identity, and his concept of the 'republic of letters'. Gemelos reads *An English Girl* as an exemplary text in a final section of her essay, which also provides contextual and comparative analysis of other New York writing, by W. T. Stead, H. G. Wells, and Henry James.

In the final critical essay of the volume, Paul Skinner's analysis of Carcassonne as figurative, imaginative, and psychological as well as actual cityscape, will perhaps encourage readers to revisit their reactions to earlier essays. In some ways, as he argues, this and only this is Ford's ideal city. Skinner takes his title from *The Good Soldier* (and offers the only detailed treatment in the volume of Ford's most famous work) when Dowell muses that 'I just wanted to marry her as some people want to go to Carcassonne'. What follows is a quest for Carcassonne, for what it may have stood for, for the resonances of the place in life, in thought, in experience. It's a key, this place, as Skinner pursues it, to the Fordian *oeuvre*, and it makes sense to go there 'if only in imagination' as this part of the volume comes to a close.

(3)   Ford's Essays

The three city essays by Ford which complete the volume are introduced by an editorial note providing further bibliographical and contextual information.

'Boston' is an essay in the Fordian style in that it concerns itself with what he represents as the two-sidedness of this city: religious and scholarly; wealthy and poor; beautiful and forbidding; reactionary and progressive. It's also characteristic, some would say, in its attention to the gastronomic delights of the port in which 'in short, the lobsters were the best' Ford had ever eaten. Food features less in 'Denver', and Ford's observations are less prominent too: this essay is largely an historical sketch, tracing as it does the birth of the city in gold rushes, with their 'horrors, hysterias, crowd-madnesses, pestilences'. Nonetheless, those observations are powerful when they come, and treat the ghostliness of the city, and the imagined suffering of those in the gold rush camps that encircled it. There is humour too: the Ford party tries in vain for three weeks to raise a game of poker! 'Denver' is also a lament for the colourful past inhabitants of the city, now chased away by the tourists and the sugar beet farmers: the Ute braves, the

Mexicans, the 'gold-washers' themselves in their dancing saloons, and the buffaloes. The primitive beauty of the New Mexican Art in the museum indicates the severity of this loss. Finally, 'Take Me Back to Tennessee', the longest of the three essays, is a detailed account of the geography of approach to the city of Nashville, and an exuberant tale of the monuments to three significant figures from its formative past. Ford's companion of the 1930s, Janice Biala, is named in this essay (she provided the illustrations when it was published in *Vogue*) and for this and other reasons the tone is different from that of the previous two unpublished essays. When he and Biala encounter typically Southern political and racial tensions, the relaxed note to Ford's impressionism vanishes altogether. A 'quiet place of reflection' is disturbed by what Ford first of all terms 'magnificent specimens of the Aryan Quinquagenarian type'. Later, having learned who these figures are, he and Biala leave, suffused by anxiety and in a hurry to be a long way away. Ford concludes the essay by suggesting that it is the legacy of Southern artists such as the Fugitives that will outlast the city's monuments, and provide not only its best memorial, but also its strongest claim to be 'the Athens of the South'.

NOTES

1   *Waterstone's Guide to London Writing*, ed. Nick Rennison, Middlesex: Waterstone's Booksellers Ltd, 1999, p. 76. Ford was born in Merton, Surrey, on 17 December 1873.

2   Ford Madox Ford, *England and the English* [1907], ed. Sara Haslam, Manchester: Carcanet, 2003 – hereafter cited as *EE*, p. 13. This edition collects *The Soul of London* (1905), *The Heart of the Country* (1906) and *The Spirit of the People* (1907).

3   Ford Madox Ford, *The Brown Owl*, London: T. Fisher Unwin, 1892, pp. 6-7.

4   Ford Madox Ford, *Parade's End* [1924-8], London: Penguin, 1982 – hereafter cited as *PE*, p. 645.

5   In *Modernism: An Anthology of Sources and Documents*, ed. Kolocotroni *et al*, Edinburgh: Edinburgh University Press, 1998, p. 251.

6   G. K. Chesterton, *The Napoleon of Notting Hill* [1904], ed. Bernard Bergonzi, Oxford: Oxford University Press, 1998 – hereafter cited as *Napoleon*; pp. 22-3.

7   On this see, for example, John Mepham, 'London as Auditorium: Public Spaces and Disconnected Talk in Works by Ford Madox Ford, Patrick Hamilton and Virginia Woolf', *London in Literature: Visionary Mappings of the Metropolis*, ed. Susana Onega and John A. Stotesbury, Heidelberg: University of Heidelberg

Press, 2002; Caroline Patey, 'Londonscapes: Urban Anxieties and Urban Aesthetics in James, Ford and Conrad', *Inter-Relations: Conrad, James, Ford and Others*, ed. Keith Carabine and Max Saunders, Maria Curie-Skłodowska University, Lublin, 2003, pp. 53-67; and Michael Neal, '"Infinite Miles of Unmeaning Streets": Exhaustive and Tentative Surveys of Early Twentieth-Century London – An Essay', *EnterText*, 2:3 (Summer 2003); see: http://www.brunel.ac.uk/faculty/arts/EnterText/23pdfs/neal.pdf

8   Ford Madox Ford, *It Was the Nightingale* [1933], New York: Ecco Press, 1984, p. 63.

9   Ford Madox Ford, *Return to Yesterday* [1931], ed. Bill Hutchings, Manchester, Carcanet: 1999 – hereafter cited as *RY*, p. 62.

10   Ford Madox Ford, *Ancient Lights and Certain New Reflections*, London: Chapman and Hall, 1911, p. 37.

11   Powerful examples include the following from the less well-known of these texts. In the first, from *Ladies Whose Bright Eyes*, Sorrell arrives at Salisbury cathedral:
       The immense pillars were painted a strong blue, and the little pillars running up them were bright scarlet; the high windows through which the sun fell were all in violent, crude and sparkling colours, and these colours, thrown down, seemed to splash a prismatic spray all over the floor. ([1911], London: Constable, 1931, pp. 233-4)
     In the following extract from *The Young Lovell*, the protagonist has just returned to view, after his travels with the white goddess of fantasy:
       He considered the sleeve of his scarlet coat that was very brave, being open at the throat to shew his shirt of white lawn tied with green ribbons. He saw that the scarlet was faded to the colour of pink roses. He looked before him and, on a green hill-side, he was aware of a great gathering of men and women bearing scythes whose blades shone like streaks of flame in the sun. (London: Chatto & Windus, 1913, pp. 52-3)
     Both examples seem to me to owe a great debt to the Pre-Raphaelite use of colour and tone.

12   Joseph Conrad, *The Secret Agent* [1907], Harmondsworth, Middlesex: Penguin, 1974, p. 10.

13   Joseph Conrad, *The Nigger of the 'Narcissus'* [1897], Harmondsworth, Middlesex: Penguin, 1970, p. 12. It pointedly isn't the task of the philosopher, according to both Conrad and Ford, as Elena Lamberti discusses in her essay in this volume.

14   Quoted in Doreen Massey, John Allen and Steve Pile eds, *City Worlds*, London and New York: Routledge, 1999, p. 15.

15   This might be said to shed more light on Ford's desire to write about Tudor London – his fictional subject in 1905-6. The prominent note at the outset of *The Fifth Queen* is Udal's belonging to London, through various networks, in direct contrast to the opening of *The Soul of London*. But even Ford would be hard pushed to say it resulted in 'mildness of manners'.

16   Henry James, *English Hours* [1905], ed. Alma Louise Lowe, London: Heinemann, 1960, p. xvii; *EE*, pp. 40-1.

17   Ford Madox Ford, *Mightier Than the Sword*, London: George Allen & Unwin, 1938, p. 244; *RY* 66.

18 Taken from Michel de Certeau's description of the Manhattan skyline ('a texturology where extremes coincide'), as seen from the 110th floor of the World Trade Centre. Quoted in Massey *et al.* eds, *City Worlds*, London and New York: Routledge, p. 7.

19 In a recent essay on Chesterton Patrick Wright states that this novel 'is said to have inspired Michael Collins in the struggle for Irish independence'. The essay is otherwise concerned with Chesterton's concept of Englishness, which, according to Wright, is founded on phobias, largely an 'apprehension of alien threats'. 'Last Orders', the *Guardian,* 9 April 2005, *Review*, 4-6.

20 Three of the essays, by Brian Groth, Paul Skinner, and Joseph Wiesenfarth, are based on papers given at the third British conference on Ford, 'Ford and the City'.

21 Gene Moore, 'Ford and Germany: The Question of Cultural Allegiance', *Modernism and the Individual Talent*, Jörg Rademacher ed., Münster: Lit Verlag, 2002, pp. 148-155.

NOT 'ACCURACY' BUT 'SUGGESTIVENESS': IMPRESSIONISM IN *THE SOUL OF LONDON*

Nick Freeman

> If a city hasn't been used by an artist not even the inhabitants live there imaginatively.
>
> Alasdair Gray, *Lanark* (1981)

In *Love and Death* (1975), Woody Allen sagely remarks that 'objectivity is subjective'. His comment bewilders the hapless Diane Keaton, but it would certainly not have surprised Ford Madox Ford. Ford has often been challenged on the grounds of inaccuracy and misrepresentation, and his opponents have been eager to see his response as no more than a cad's bluster. Declarations such as the dedicatory letter to *Ancient Lights* (1911) cause particular annoyance:

> This book [. . .] is full of inaccuracies as to facts, but its accuracy as to impressions is absolute [. . . .] My business in life, in short, is to attempt to discover, and to try to let you see, where we stand. I don't really deal in facts, I have for facts a most profound contempt. I try to give you what I see to be the spirit of an age, of a town, of a movement. This cannot be done with facts.

Those of a Gradgrindian disposition, inhabitants of what Ford termed 'our terrific, untidy, indifferent empirical age'[1] have little sympathy with this approach, but such selective treatments of the past do have their merits, as Simon Nowell-Smith reminds us. '[Ford's] imaginative inventions are often more plausible than the conscientious efforts at recollection of more sober historians', he writes in the context of reminiscences of Henry James.[2] Ford's attitudes are not simply those of an inveterate (self-) deceiver. They should instead be seen as an aspect of the English *avant garde*'s suspicion of Victorian empiricism, a reaction that drew upon Paterian relativity, impressionism and Wilde's witty rejections of the distinction between truth and falsehood. Ford is far from being the only writer of the early twentieth century to adopt this stance, although his tendency to employ it in his autobiographical writing has prompted considerable criticism.

This essay will focus on the ways in which Ford's 'accuracy as to impressions' helped to shape his response to the English capital in *The Soul of London* (1905). It will also consider the similarities of approach that link Ford's writing about the city to the work of Edwardian contemporaries such as Henry James and G. K. Chesterton. The representation of London was a surprisingly contested issue during the *fin de siècle*, and Ford was one of a number of writers who used the metropolis as a testing ground for radical theories of perception and recall. He was one of the more successful prose impressionists of the era, and his experiments would have far reaching consequences for his work as a whole.

The Soul of London is a transitional book. It is both original and 'Fordian' while yet belonging to a slew of works in the late nineteenth and early twentieth centuries that engaged with the spirit of London in sundry quasi-essentialist ways. It was, on paper at least, traditional enough in its concerns to be commercially successful. However, its impressionistic perceptions of the metropolis were more in line with the radicalism of writers such as Arthur Symons than the stolid certainties of London's contemporary historians W. J. Loftie and Walter Besant. Besant had died in 1901, but his writing on London remained influential until after the First World War, serving as a continual provocation to more innovative commentators on city life.

Ford first envisaged *The Soul of London* as a collaboration with the artist William Hyde, drawing up a prospectus for an illustrated volume that was hawked around London publishers in the autumn and winter of 1902. The book, provisionally entitled 'London in Seven Essays', was to be around 50,000 words in length and feature 30 drawings of 'places and incidents in & around London under all conditions night & day, summer & winter, spring & autumn'.[3] Ford proposed to combine 'perfectly accurate facts of topography' with aesthetic appeal, although having already demonstrated his attitude to 'perfectly accurate facts' in *The Cinque Ports* (1901), prospective publishers may have wondered quite what he had in mind.

A book that paired discursive metropolitan essays with illustrations was hardly a new idea in itself. Gustave Doré and Blanchard Jerrold had published the successful *London: A Pilgrimage* in 1872, the year before Ford was born, and Hyde had already collaborated with Alice Meynell on *London Impressions* (1898). Ford however would develop and refine the subjective sketch that Jerrold had called 'a touch and go chronicle' into a more coherent aesthetic and perceptual strategy.[4] It was this new attitude to city writing that delayed publication of Ford's work until May 1905. Constable and John Murray both rejected his proposal, nominally on the grounds that there were numerous books on the capital currently in circulation. It seems unlikely that either firm would have been unduly alarmed by adding a conventional volume to this number, but Ford's 'impressionism' made them uneasy about the book's potential sales. Ford was equally unsuccessful in attempting to sell the serial rights to the *Daily Telegraph* in April 1903, for then as now, the paper was rarely sympathetic to radical initiatives.[5] Although Ford enlisted the influential literary agent J. B. Pinker in his cause, it is telling that it would be a new publishing firm, Alston Rivers, rather than established companies, which would finally issue the book. Even then, 'London in Seven Essays' appeared without illustrations and was retitled *The Soul of London*.[6]

As the *Fifth Queen* trilogy, his biography of Ford Madox Brown, and studies of Holbein and D. G. Rossetti demonstrate, Ford was certainly capable of researching a project in relatively traditional ways. However, research was a time-consuming commitment for a writer in perennial financial difficulties, and in the case of London, it erected a barrier between subject matter and its lived experience. While Ford was privileging the recording or invention of experience over factual or historical detail, Henry James was providing him with an object lesson in the perils of 'accumulation'. Since 1903, James had been working on 'London Town', a study of the capital for which Macmillan had offered him £1,000, his largest ever advance. Initially optimistic, James soon found himself overwhelmed by his material. Cowed or simply bored by the works of Besant and others – many of the books he acquired while researching 'London Town' were not even cut, much less studied – James was also swamped by his decades of metropolitan experience.[7] He was, he later told A. C. Benson, 'so *saturated* with impressions that I can't take in new ones'.[8] By 1903, James had been a travel writer for the best part of four decades, and while he constantly revised existing work, his methods were firmly established. His problem was that while these methods worked brilliantly in brief essays, he had become the man who knew too much where London was concerned.

Ford, by contrast, was still learning about the city and about his own literary practices. Unconstrained by contractual obligations, and so committed to presenting his own impressions that secondary reading was an irrelevance, he was free to tackle London in ways that James could no longer countenance. James was sixty in 1903, but Ford was a mere thirty, and although he knew London well, he was not yet as encumbered as James by decades of life in the capital. As a young writer still making his name, Ford was also free of 'the master's' twin burdens of reputation and expectation. He did not have to try to adapt his technique as a travel writer to an extended study of London because that technique was still at an early stage of evolution. This meant that he was highly flexible and untroubled by any inconsistencies of approach when moving from sociology to impressionism to clubbish anecdote.

Ford's inconsistency, even occasional vagueness, was bolstered by the example of Walter Pater. In the conclusion to *Studies in the History of the Renaissance* (1873), Pater had argued that 'Failure is to form habits', and that to 'acquiesce' 'in a facile orthodoxy . . . of our own' was to prevent 'testing new opinions and courting new impressions'.[9] There was nothing facile about James' orthodoxies, but 'London Town' struggled nonetheless with an apparent need to 'make theories about the things we see and touch'. Ford had no such aims, seeking instead to capture the moods and atmospheres of the city, the 'feel' of contemporary London rather than its complex history. His personality, status and commercial needs harmonized very effectively in planning the book. Openly disdaining writing about 'Dr Johnson's chair' unless such detail 'cast light upon modern London',[10] he sought instead 'a picture of a place as its author sees it' (*SL* 4). In essence, he placed all historical concerns at the service of individual perception, echoing Pater's claim that 'experience' is no more than 'a swarm of impressions'.[11]

Ford's relationship with the demands of the marketplace was an uncomfortable one throughout his career. On one hand, his pursuit of innovation and his recognition of excellence in others often made him unwilling to compromise his artistic ideals for commercial purposes. On the other, as a writer who lived by his pen and whose tastes and problematic domestic circumstances necessitated a regular income, Ford needed to keep a keen eye on literary fashion and its commercial implications. A book about London offered an opportunity both for radical experiment and for financial reward. Ford had neither the time nor the inclination for the 'encyclopaedic, topographical, or archaeological' (*SL* 3), phrasing that reiterates his dedication to *The Cinque Ports*, a book which was to be 'neither archaeological nor topographical, nor even archaeological-topographical'.[12] Instead, he self-consciously proclaimed his own subjectivity and modernity. 'To use a phrase of literary slang,' he wrote, 'I have tried to "get the atmosphere" of modern London' (*SL* 3). Ford spoke of human beings 'melt[ing] as it were, into the tide of humanity as all these vapours melt into the overcast skies' (*SL* 3), imagery that suggests Karl Marx's evocation of modernity, where 'all that is solid melts into air'.[13] He sought to produce 'A really ideal book' (*SL* 3), and clearly invested considerable imaginative effort in his London project. Not only would it bring him his first experience of being 'boomed', but it was also the clearest statement so far of his impressionist ethos.

Impressionism is notoriously difficult to define, existing in philosophy and art as well as in literature. It is unlikely that many writers of Ford's generation were interested in revisiting the debates of Hume and Berkeley, being drawn instead to Pater's world of 'impressions unstable, flickering, inconsistent, which burn and are extinguished with our consciousness of them'.[14] Pater's impressionism focused on 'know[ing] one's impression as it really is', in the process openly embracing subjectivity.[15] By 1889 he was arguing that 'in persuasive writers generally', 'there is an appeal to catch the writer's spirit, to think with him'. This, he suggested, has become 'an expression no longer of fact but of his sense of it, his peculiar intuition of a world'.[16] Such beliefs are central to Ford's 'peculiar intuitions' of the English metropolis and to much of his fiction.

Impressionist art, like Pater's *Renaissance* a product of the late 1860s and early 1870s, was another potent influence on the young writers of the *fin de siècle* but one that defied easy definition. The *Oxford Dictionary of Art* notes that it was:

> not a homogenous school with a unified programme and clearly defined principles, but a loose association of artists linked by some community of outlook and banded together for the purposes of exhibiting [. . . .] It is dangerous to lay down rigid criteria for defining so individualistic a group of artists and the Impressionist movement must rather be described in terms of very general attitudes and techniques from which numerous exceptions must be noted.[17]

Impressionism's complex history will not be recapitulated here, but two important points should be noted. The first is that while impressionist painting, a term covering a disparate range of artists from Manet to Whistler, was winning over progressive British art critics and had a number of distinguished British and Irish practitioners, it had yet to make great inroads into wider public consciousness. Perhaps the suspicion of impressionism engendered by the Whistler vs. Ruskin trial of 1878 remained. Durand-Ruel's 1905 exhibition of impressionist art, probably the greatest ever to be staged in Britain, attracted considerable interest but no paintings were sold. As Ford was writing *The Soul of London*, Claude Monet was in his Giverny studio finishing the series of London pictures he had begun on the fifth-floor of the Savoy Hotel early in 1901. These would appear between 1902 and 1904, and now seem, as Kenneth McConkey has argued, 'central to the modernist project'. Monet, he suggests, is 'a name for a set of procedures' that offer complex meditations on time, space and memory rather than the quasi-objectivity of realist art.[18] Such radicalism was, however, far removed from the popular taste of Edwardian Britain, and anyone hoping to exploit impressionist techniques for financial gain had to tread carefully, finding some way of combining artistic innovation with more familiar and accessible modes of expression.

The second point is that literary impressionism, of the kind chiefly associated with Pater and his followers, had begun to develop in both 'elite' and 'popular' directions during the 1890s. Arthur Symons, whose devotion to Pater's ideals had led him to dedicate his first volume of poems to his idol in 1889, exemplifies this dual evolution. The notorious conclusion to *The Renaissance* was often misread as a licence for excess under the auspices of *carpe diem*, but it also offered a memorable formulation of the transitory nature of experience: the 'short day of frost and sun' that Monet painted on the Savoy balcony three decades later. The fascination with what Robert Browning had termed 'the instant made eternity' led Symons to produce vivid vignettes of urban life in which fleeting sensation replaced realist detail.[19] His poems recorded the illumination of a girl's face in the sudden flare of a match or the erotic memories prompted by a favourite perfume, allowing the pleasures of the moment to over-ride any didactic elements. Such approaches spread quickly through poetry to the quintessential 1890s' art form, the short story. The techniques demonstrated in the fragmentary, invariably inconclusive work of *fin de siècle* impressionists such as Henry Harland, Ella d'Arcy and Frederick Wedmore would lead eventually to Joyce's *Dubliners* (1914), Katherine Mansfield's *Bliss, and other stories* (1918) and the early fiction of Virginia Woolf.[20]

At the same time, the complexities of the impressionist style that would connect Henry James in particular to wider investigations of the nature of time in philosophy and science, had a more popular element that frequently surfaced in journalistic writing.[21] Impressionist concerns with the recording of the brevity of experience encouraged openly subjective accounts of everyday living. The print culture of the 1890s, ever hungry for material, saw hundreds of short prose accounts of city life that recorded and often celebrated defiantly quotidian experiences. As Gissing's *New Grub Street* (1891) had demonstrated so graphically, the war between art and commerce was intensifying at a rapid pace, with the first casualty being traditional notions of literary art. The years since the first Education Act of 1870 had witnessed a steady increase in what intellectuals saw as downmarket newspapers and periodicals aimed at a 'semi-educated' readership. In such a world, the popular press assumed ever greater power and importance, and *The Soul of London* deplores the influence of the newspaper on Londoners' conversation, criticizing the ways in which it has assumed the book's cultural centrality and the church's erstwhile monopoly on the sermon. However, the media would play a vital role in the dissemination of radical theories such as impressionism. Armed with impressionist ideas (often perpetuated in a deliberately popular manner), those who like Symons deemed the newspaper 'the plague, or black death, of the modern world' were able to retain a measure of intellectual credibility while yet meeting the demands of the marketplace.[22]

In this way, initially sophisticated theories drawn from the European *avant garde* began trickling down to a reading public of widely varying educational levels, perhaps allowing, in time, for a greater appreciation of contemporary artistic movements. Ford, like Symons and other *fin de siècle* writers, oscillated between the elite productions acclaimed by his peers (*The Good Soldier* is the obvious example) and less ambitious, often ephemeral work that offered a blending of 'high' and 'popular' discourses. The proposed serialization of *The Soul of London* is a case in point. Had the work appeared as a series of individual, if loosely linked, essays, its radical content would have been diffused. Ford could not have guaranteed that it would be read in its entirety, and it might have seemed merely another journalistic account of metropolitan wandering, a type of writing with which the reading public was becoming familiar at the turn of the century.

Impressionism allowed writers to investigate the experience of temporality, an increasingly complex topic following the standard-isation of the measurement of world time, as Stephen Kern has shown.[23] It allowed too an intellectually legitimate way for them to valorise their own perceptions and emotions: cynically speaking, it meant in extreme cases that 'impressionist' approaches could allow a writer or more particularly, a writer forced into the drudgery of journalism, to evade charges of mere egotism or lazy research. However, its most important consequence for Ford in *The Soul of London* was its recognition that life did not play by the rules of the Victorian novel. Why then should literature?

Nowhere is this demonstrated better than in the experience recounted in 'Roads into London'. Whether or not Ford actually witnessed this incident is unimportant: it is a quintessentially urban moment that is a consequence of the book's recognition of the Modern, and could not have happened without modern technology, in this case, the delayed train. Ford peers out of his railway carriage:

> I looked down upon black and tiny yards that were like the cells in an electric battery. In one, three children were waving their hands and turning up white faces to the train; in the next, white clothes were drying. A little further on a woman ran suddenly out of a door; she had a white apron and her sleeves were tucked up. A man followed her hastily, he had red hair, and in his hand a long stick. We moved on, and I have not the least idea whether he were going to thrash her, or whether together they were going to beat a carpet. At any rate, the evening papers reported no murder in Southwark.
>
> Incidents even so definite as these are more or less the exception, but the constant succession of much smaller happenings that one sees, and that one never sees completed, gives to looking out of train windows a touch of pathos and of dissatisfaction. It is akin to the sentiment ingrained in humanity of liking a story to have an end. (*SL* 42-43)[24]

For a brief moment Ford seems about to achieve, albeit in a more limited way, the panoramic vision of the city granted to Eugène de Rastignac in *Le Père Goriot* (1835) as he gazes down on Paris at the book's conclusion, but modern transport systems, and indeed modern cities, do not allow for Balzacian set pieces. The incident is (hopefully) inconsequential in itself, but represents a marked change in sensibility from the comforting certainties of many other London writers. Obviously, impressionistic travel books obey or devise very different codes from those of detective stories, but a comparison between *The Soul of London* and the fiction of Conan Doyle is revealing nonetheless. In 'The Red-Headed League' (1892), Sherlock

Holmes boasts that 'it is a hobby of mine to have an exact knowledge of London', and throughout his investigations, this knowledge stands him in good stead.[25] However, one of the many reasons why Sherlock Holmes is not Ford Madox Ford, aside from the unlikely prospect of Ford claiming an 'exact knowledge' of anything, is that Holmes' knowledge of London is practical and based upon surface detail. Holmes can often derive greater significance from that detail than the police, Watson, or the reader of the stories, but for Ford, surface detail is just the start. Holmes' enthusiasms are always bounded by the needs of his criminal investigations, but Ford's are limited only by the ingenuity of his perceptions. Holmes' observations solve mysteries, provide answers, explain the seemingly inexplicable. For Ford however, observation encourages endless reflection on history, the self, and the processes of change and alteration that deny stasis to both the city and the individual.

In this respect, Ford's London book shares something of its outlook with James' abortive 'London Town'. In the preface to the New York edition of *The Golden Bowl* (1907), James portrayed himself and the photographer, A. L. Coburn, as critics who sought to 'recognize . . . with the last fineness' the significance of the urban vistas they explored.[26] For Holmes, the 'last fineness' is the concluding detail of crucial importance in the solving of a mystery – the dog that does not bark in 'Silver Blaze'. For James and Ford however, the last fineness is an endlessly renegotiable terrain to be played out and re-explored through memory and even syntax as well as through the original encounter with the thing perceived. One should reiterate here the differing obligations of genre – unsolved or unsolveable detective puzzles have little appeal beyond the True Crime shelves of public libraries. Even so, it is salutary to imagine Holmes, Ford and James stalking through London at the same time, or to note that Conan Doyle's *His Last Bow* appeared in 1917, the year Eliot's Prufrock pondered the irresolvable mysteries of 'Streets that follow like a tedious argument / Of insidious intent'.[27]

Until Ford's rationalisations at the end of the train incident, his account of events seems oddly like that of one of Holmes's clients or perhaps even Dr Watson himself. The registration of detail that seems as though it might be significant if only it could be interpreted correctly – does the man's hair suggest a choleric disposition? Is he an Irish immigrant? Does he belong to the Red-headed League? Is the red and white colour scheme in any way symbolic? – the reading of newspapers, even the fondness for travel by train, all are recognisable ingredients of a Conan Doyle story. However, the unfulfilled expectation and the admission of the limits of his own knowledge provide the incident with precisely the 'pathos and dissatisfaction' that Ford identifies. Holmes made his creator a rich man through meeting the human need for narrative closure, but writers such as Ford and James asked instead awkward questions concerning our perception of the metropolis. These continue to reverberate through a twenty-first century world of unsolved and unreported crime, arbitrary identity and casual disappearance.

The search for the 'last fineness' was widespread in the writing of Ford and his contemporaries, who found it incompatible with doctrines of objectivity. In 'The Decay of Lying' (1891), Oscar Wilde's Vivian awaits the day on which 'Facts will be regarded as discreditable': Wilde even managed to espouse such iconoclasm in the dock at the Old Bailey.[28] Ford's dedication to *The Cinque Ports* had embraced not 'accuracy' but 'suggestiveness' (*CP* vi), and his 'profound contempt' for facts is demonstrated throughout his work. Anticipating James' reference to 'the fatal futility of Fact' in the 1909 preface to *The Spoils of Poynton*, Ford was able to proclaim the modernity of his perceptions as well as making a wider point about the pace and concomitant mystery of urban life. G. K. Chesterton was also prepared to suggest that a writer could only engage with London once he had discarded an allegiance to objectivity and empiricism. In *The Club of Queer Trades* (1905), Rupert Grant is invariably led astray by his 'cold and clear reasoning' but saved by the intuitive insights of poetry.[29] Meanwhile, his brother Basil coolly maintains that facts 'obscure the truth', and only by entertaining the irrational and unsubstantiated can one hope to make sense of modern London. 'Do you really admit', Basil cries in 'a kind of despair', 'are you still so sunk in superstitions, so clinging to dim and prehistoric altars, that you believe in facts? Do you not trust an immediate impression?'[30] Arthur Symons was another writer who argued strongly for the primacy of impressionism, prefacing the revised edition of *London Nights* (1897) with a critic-baiting espousal of subjectivity:

> I do not profess that any poem in this book is a record of actual fact. I declare that every poem is the sincere attempt to render a particular mood which has once been mine, and to render it as if, for the moment, there were no other mood for me in the world.[31]

His essay, 'Fact in Literature' (1904), encapsulated a position very similar to Ford's own in maintaining that 'Facts are difficult of digestion, and should be taken diluted, at infrequent intervals. They suit few constitutions when taken whole'.[32] Such remarks show that impressionist sympathies could be witty, as well as earnest.

Ford's deployment of impressionist strategies has another important consequence in that it allows him to distance himself from writers of the preceding (or indeed his own) generation whom he saw as tainted by Victorianism. Ford later professed to dislike the poets of the 1890s, 'Dowson, Johnson, Davidson and the rest', terming them 'just nuisances, writing in derivative language uninteresting matters that might have been interesting matters had they been expressed in the much more interesting medium of prose'.[33] However, the absence of Symons from this list, and the heavy influence of Symons and Davidson on Ford's 'Finchley Road' in *Songs from London* (1910) suggests that their effect on him was more profound than he cared to admit. It is also ironic that Symons, like Ford, hoped that enthusiasm for modern European art was one means by which he might escape being stifled by English provincialism. It may be that Ford's impressionism is another example of what Linda Dowling has termed the 'parthenogenesis of the *avant garde*', an elective genealogy that highlights the appealing uncles and cousins while drawing a veil over parents the child too closely resembles.[34] In view of the fact that Symons was also planning an impressionistic book on the capital at the same time as Ford was publishing *The Soul of London*, one must treat the convenient divisions of literary history, 'late Victorian' and 'modernist' with caution if not outright scepticism. Identifying with a new aesthetic system of French origin (which had, nonetheless, English guiding spirits in Constable, Turner, and Pater, figures spared the worst associations of 'high' Victorianism) allowed Ford and other artistic radicals to advertise their modern sympathies. It also allowed them to tone down impressionism's more precious prose effects for commercial purposes, again breaking from associations with 1890s' decadence, a break expressed with habitually snide elegance by T. S. Eliot in his essay on Symons in *The Sacred Wood* (1920).

The Soul of London shows Ford's ability to balance and synthesize competing discourses to great effect. It has elements of impressionism and a modish distrust of objectivity, but is still prepared to use the techniques of Mayhew, though without his ameliorative ambitions. It concludes with a symbolist vision reminiscent of *Heart of Darkness*, 'London writing its name upon the clouds' (*SL* 170), but frequently reverts to middle-of-the-road clubbish anecdotalism. It theorises in far-sighted ways about the spread of the city, the measurement of its limits, and the processes by which immigrants become 'Londonised', but it also has few qualms about deploying 'local colour' in the style of less radical Edwardian writers. Although Alston Rivers' chosen title implies an old fashioned essentialism about the city, a topic of considerable interest to reviewers, the book itself is a signal of changes to come in Ford's work and in twentieth century writing as a whole. As such it is fascinating snapshot of Ford's development, and a work whose wider significance has yet to be fully acknowledged.

NOTES

1   Sondra J. Stang, ed., *The Ford Madox Ford Reader*, Manchester: Carcanet, 1986, p. 221.
2   Simon Nowell-Smith, *The Legend of the Master* (1947), Oxford: Oxford University Press, 1985, p. 8.
3   This information is drawn from letters of William Hyde to Ford [Hueffer] in the Rare and Manuscript Collections, Carl A. Kroch Library, Cornell University. The sequence commences on 26 August 1902 and ends on 26 September 1904, and does not include Ford's replies. The 'Prospectus' is undated but seems to have been drafted prior to initial approaches to publishers in late 1902. My thanks to Barry Johnson for bringing these papers to my attention. When Hyde's drawings were eventually used in the omnibus volume, *England and the English: An Interpretation* (1907), only 16 of the proposed 30 drawings appeared.
4   Gustave Doré and Blanchard Jerrold, *London: A Pilgrimage*, New York: Dover, 1970, p. 16.
5   Hyde's letters reveal the extent of Ford's market research. He planned to approach Bell's, A. & C. Black (who published the influential guide to London edited by A. R. Hope-Moncrieff), Heinemann, Longman, Cassells, Macmillan and Dent. First choices for serial rights were the *London Magazine* (of course) and the *Pall Mall Magazine*.
6   Hyde's role in the proceedings remains unclear. As he was as impecunious as Ford in 1903 and 1904, he may have decided to sell individual drawings rather than waiting for publishers to offer a contract for a set of 30.
7   John L. Kimmey, 'The London Book', *Henry James Review* (1979), 65-78.
8   James referred to his brimming 'bucket of impressions' in his preface to *The Princess Casamassima* (1907). His fear of saturation was recorded in Benson's diaries. H. Montgomery Hyde, *Henry James at Home*, London: Methuen, 1969, p. 226.

9   Walter Pater, *The Renaissance* (1893 edition), ed. Adam Phillips, Oxford: Oxford University Press, 1986, p. 152.

10 Ford Madox Ford, *The Soul of London*, ed. Alan Hill, London: Everyman, 1995 – henceforth *SL*, p. 4.

11 Pater, p. 151. The 1893 edition has the less evocative 'group of impressions'.

12 Ford Madox Hueffer, *The Cinque Ports*, Edinburgh and London: William Blackwood and Sons, 1900 – henceforth *CP*; p. v.

13 Karl Marx and Friedrich Engels, *The Communist Manifesto* (1848), ed. David McLellan, Oxford: Oxford University Press, 1992, p. 6.

14 Pater, p. 151.

15 Pater, p. xxix.

16 Walter Pater, 'Style' (1889), *Essays on Literature and Art*, Jennifer Uglow ed., London: Dent, 1973, p. 71.

17 'Impressionism', *Oxford Dictionary of Art*, ed. Ian Chilvers & Harold Osborne, Oxford: Oxford University Press, 1988, pp. 249-250.

18 Kenneth McConkey, *Memory and Desire: Painting in Britain and Ireland at the Turn of the Twentieth Century*, Aldershot: Ashgate, 2002, p. 251.

19 Robert Browning, 'The Last Ride Together', *Men and Women* (1855).

20 Wedmore was the first English art critic to write at length on French Impressionism. His article 'The Impressionists' appeared in the *Fortnightly Review* in January 1883.

21 For detailed consideration of James' engagement with physics and philosophy, see Peter Rawlings, 'Grammars of Time in Late James', *Modern Language Review*, 98:2 (April 2003), 273-84.

22 Arthur Symons, 'A New Guide to Journalism', *Saturday Review* (8 August 1903), 165.

23 Stephen Kern, *The Culture of Time and Space 1880-1918*, Cambridge, MA.: Harvard University Press, 1983.

24 The use of a fleeting vision from a railway carriage reappears in a number of early twentieth century works – the experience seems in many ways to signify and encapsulate modernity. See, for instance, Virginia Woolf's 'The Mark on the Wall' from *Monday or Tuesday* (1921), in which the speaker notes how she has been separated from the former occupants of her house, 'torn asunder, as one is torn from the old lady about to pour out tea and the young man about to hit the tennis ball in the back garden of the suburban villa as one rushes past in the train'. *The Mark on the Wall and other short fiction*, ed. David Bradshaw, Oxford: Oxford University Press, 2001, p. 3.

    One might cite too the impressionistic matrimony evoked by H. G. Wells in *The History of Mr Polly* (1910), where Polly's wedding ceremony is 'blurred and hurried, like the momentary vision of a very beautiful thing seen through the smoke of a passing train'. *The History of Mr Polly*, ed. Norman Mackenzie, London: Dent, 1993, p. 88.

25 Arthur Conan Doyle, 'The Red-Headed League', *The Adventures of Sherlock Holmes* (1892), *The Penguin Complete Sherlock Holmes*, London: Penguin, 1981, p. 185.

26 Henry James, *The Golden Bowl*, London: The Bodley Head, 1907, p. 12.

27 'The Love Song of J. Alfred Prufrock' in T. S. Eliot, *Complete Poems and Plays*, London: Faber, 1969, p. 13.

28 Oscar Wilde, 'The Decay of Lying: An Observation' (1891), *The Complete Works of Oscar Wilde*, London: Harpercollins, 1994, p. 1090.
29 G. K. Chesterton, 'The Eccentric Seclusion of the Old Lady', *The Club of Queer Trades*, London: Penguin, 1986, p. 103.
30 Chesterton, 'The Painful Fall of a Great Reputation', *The Club of Queer Trades*, p. 33.
31 Arthur Symons, *London Nights*, London: Leonard Smithers, 1897, p. i.
32 Symons, 'Fact in Literature', *Studies in Prose and Verse*, London: Dent, 1904, p. 3.
33 Ford, *Collected Poems*, London: Max Goschen, 1913, p. 23.
34 Ian Fletcher, ed., *Decadence and the 1890s*, London: Edward Arnold, 1979, p. 7. Linda Dowling's comments appear in the introductory essay to her *Aestheticism and Decadence: A Selected Annotated Bibliography*, New York: Garland, 1977.

ANGLE OF ELEVATION: SOCIAL CLASS, TRANSPORT AND PERCEPTION OF THE CITY IN *THE SOUL OF LONDON*

Angus Wrenn

In *The Soul of London* Ford Madox Ford discusses ways in which the modern city is perceived. Ford is at pains to stress that the work, which Alan Hill describes as resembling 'fiction, where the scene is set for characters who never actually appear',[1] is in no sense strictly documentary.[2] Rather he claims that his objective is essentially to evoke atmosphere: 'I have tried to make it anything rather than encyclopaedic, topographical, or archaeological. To use a phrase of literary slang I have tried to "get the atmosphere" of modern London' (*SL* xi-xii).

And Ford emphasizes the 'personality' of London, and in consequence the importance of speaking of it as one might give one's 'impressions' of a personality to one's friends (*SL* xi). Perhaps as a result *The Soul of London* has tended to be overlooked within the field of social science studies of the city in modernity (an important exception is Andrew Lees's essay 'The Metropolis and the Intellectual').[3] Nevertheless the date of *The Soul of London*'s composition (1903-1904) is of quite precise significance as regards developments in the modern London landscape. This is true both in relation to the establishment of certain institutions, such as the London County Council (1888) (*SL* 33) and in terms of the means of transport available in London at the turn of the nineteenth and twentieth centuries. Mode of transport is in fact crucial to the ways in which London is perceived in the period which Ford covers. He denotes as much in the subtitles which he gives to two of the sections of the work: 'London at a Distance' and 'Roads Into London'. The two subsequent sections of the book additionally reflect the importance of social class as a determinant of the mental image of London: 'London at Work' and 'London at Leisure'. By setting *The Soul of London* in the context of the work of some of Ford's contemporaries and successors, which also takes London as its setting, it is possible to see

Ford as both the heir of the nineteenth century (essentially James and Conrad), and as a pre-1914 precursor, especially in his emphasis upon fragmentation of perception, of those writers who may be termed the 'high modernists' of the 1920s: Virginia Woolf and T. S. Eliot.

While Ford clearly inherited a musical sensibility and sensitivity from his father Francis Hueffer, which is evidenced elsewhere by his own serious attempts at composition, he also inherited a leaning towards the visual arts from his maternal grandfather Ford Madox Brown. In *The Soul of London* it is everywhere the visual and the painterly which dominate over the auditory and the musical. By reference to the landscape artist's concept of 'angle of elevation', that is to say the height from which a scene is painted or drawn, and the position within the frame given to the horizon and perspectival vanishing point, Ford's strange urban prose-poem can be given a certain unity.

Perhaps Ford Madox Brown's most celebrated painting of the urban landscape, or at any rate of a London scene, is his 1852 *Work*.[4] It depicts a scene of labourers digging a hole in the road in Heath Street, Hampstead. Although the painting is framed in terms of traditional 'classical' perspective, insofar as there is a single vanishing point, multiple points of view are also in operation here, and may be said to be determined by social class and professional status. At first glance a naturalistic slice of random everyday street life, it is in fact almost schematically hierarchical. Arguably the lowest viewpoint of all is that enjoyed by the navvies at work in the hole in the road. Theirs could almost be said to equate to a worm's eye view. Scarcely higher is the angle of elevation enjoyed by the unemployed, who sit at the road's surface, their backs indolently propped against the embankment. This scene is surveyed by two further groups: in the distance, making their way toward the workers come on horseback two sophisticated ladies. Their progress will be complicated by the hole in the road, but this lies ahead of the scene presented. Whether they have as yet even noticed the labourers in the road is unclear. By contrast the two men who stand in the same foreground plane as the labourers are clearly aware of them. Standing at street level, but at a certain distance, propping themselves against the railing, are F. D. Maurice, the great progenitor of Muscular Christianity,[5] and, on the extreme right both literally and figuratively, Thomas Carlyle, the proponent of 'work' as the redemptive and fulfilling quintessence of the Victorian age. These are the two 'labourers of the pen', as it were, whose mental efforts are to be equated with those of the more obvious toilers in the hole in the road. Ford himself, in *The Soul of London*, gives a parallel scene which combines road digging and the labours of the pen (albeit in an administrative and bureaucratic rather than creative capacity):

> Workers in London divide themselves, roughly, into those who sell the labours of their bodies and those who sell their attentions. You see men in the streets digging trenches, pulling stout wires out of square holes in pavements, pecking away among greasy vapours at layers of asphalte, scattering shovelfuls of crushed gravel under the hoofs of slipping horses and under the crunching tyres of wheels. If walls would fall off offices you would see paler men and women adding up the records of money paid to these others. That, with infinite variations, is work in London. (*SL* 68)

This would seem to lend itself to an interpretation of London as a fragmented city, the poor, the manual labourers, being unbridgeably divided from their white collar counterparts. Indeed Ford goes on next to offer an alternative scene which suggests that the pen has the function of determining in the most literal optical terms the view of London which the working and writing classes respectively enjoy:

> It is astonishing how different London looks from one or from the other end. Speaking broadly, the man who expresses himself with a pen on paper sees his London from the west. At the worst he hopes to end with that view. His London of breathing space, his West End, extends from say Chiswick to say Portland Place. His dense London is the City as far as Fenchurch Street, his East End ends with what he calls 'Whitechapel.'
>
> The other sees his London of elbow room extend from say Purfleet to say Blackwall. He is conscious of having, as it were at his back, the very green and very black stretches of the Essex marshes dotted with large solitary factories and small solitary farms. His dense London, *his* City lies along the line from Blackwall to Fenchurch Street. Beyond that, the City proper, the city of the Bank and the Mansion House, is already a place rather of dilettante trifling [. . . .] already a foreign land, slightly painful because it is so strange. That, further west, there may be another enormous London never really enters his everyday thoughts. (*SL* 70-71)

This implies a process of social fragmentation and division. Yet Ford also offers the pen, or more strictly speaking the pencil, as an agent of unification between the classes.

While the labourers in the hole in the road may evoke Madox Brown in the high Victorian era, the image with which Ford follows it seems at first glance to look forward to the modernists of the next two decades. In his description of the scene at Tilbury Docks Ford begins

by placing great stress not upon the human but upon the purely
geometrical perspectival lines of cranes at the docks:

> The vast, empty squares of water lay parapeted, arbitrary and dim in their
> eternal perspectives; the straight lines of the water, the straight lines of the
> parapets, of the bottoms of the goods sheds, of the tops, of the gray corrugated
> roofs, all dwindled together into the immense and empty distances. (*SL* 68-69)

Up to this point the description, with its emphasis upon the
geometrical, might be seen to anticipate the images of the Vorticists to
be made famous over the next two decades. *In the Hold* (1913-1914)
by David Bomberg (Tate Gallery, London) comes particularly to
mind, choosing as it does the same dockside subject as Ford at
Tilbury, and also employing a strictly geometrical and abstract
technique. However Ford then proceeds to dissolve the hard-edged,
proto-Vorticist vision in favour of a blurred, watercolour conception
perhaps closer to the Impressionists, to Whistler, or even to Turner:

> The rows of four-footed, gaunt, inactive cranes, painted a dull rust colour, and
> the few enormous steamers at the inner ends of the quays – all these things
> were wetted, fused and confused in their outlines, beneath a weeping sky in
> which a drapery of clouds had the look of a badly blotted water-colour
> painting, still wet and inefficient. (*SL* 69)

Rather than making his rendering of the scene at Tilbury a paean of
praise to physical labour, Ford surprisingly focuses (with the
concentration of the telephoto lens years before its invention) on a tiny
detail. Among all the dockers he homes in on their foreman: 'He dived
into another small office. He was the chief officer of the liner that was
coaling and he had a pencil behind his ear' (*SL* 69).

Not only does Ford choose for attention a figure who is set apart
by function, and arguably social class, from the manual labourers, but
he even focuses in on a single feature 'a pencil behind his ear'. That
detail, which would surely elude the naked eye in normal
circumstances, now becomes the very focus of Ford's attention:

> He was uniting as it were the labours of the men shovelling in the buckets of
> coal, of the men uttering melancholy wails as they swung-in a white boat, of
> the men hooking up long planks for the painters to sit on, and of the painters
> themselves on the upper decks. With that pencil he controlled all their labours,
> as if he were twisting them into an invisible rope which passed through that
> tin office and up, far away into town where other pencils and other pens
> recorded these things on large pages, digested them into summaries and
> finally read them out to Boards of Directors. (*SL* 70)

Ford's implications here are ambiguous. On the one hand he seems to be suggesting that the modern city is thoroughly alienated and alienating – as shown by the apparent insignificance of the pencil and the enormity of the labours it controls, together with the 'other pencils and other pens' which process information for management. In one sense the fragmentation and alienation are complete in that here the pencils and pens have been divorced from human hand and seem to be going about their work unaided. At the same time Ford is suggesting that there is a unity, of sorts, but of questionable moral value. This is identified in the reference to 'Boards of Directors', a phrase which so closely echoes Ford's collaborator at this date, Joseph Conrad. The latter's *Heart of Darkness* (1899) is also set in the same area of the estuary to the east of London. Moreover one of Marlow's select audience on the *Nellie*, for his tale of physical danger and labour in Central Africa, is the 'Director of Companies',[6] a figure who is distinguished from, yet also shown as sharing an apparent affinity with, the manual workers (sailors): 'it was difficult to realize his work was not out there in the luminous estuary, but behind him within the brooding gloom' (*Heart of Darkness* 47). In *Heart of Darkness* it is capitalistic commercial interest, represented by the ivory trade, which links and also compromises all. Perhaps in Conrad the dubious link forged was between the developed and undeveloped, exploited worlds. Ford's image of oppression carried out in the name of capitalism seems to focus instead on the links which exist between the different social classes within London itself: 'Those invisible ropes – they are strong enough in all conscience – seem to be the only tie between these two classes of workers, between these two great camps set one against another' (*SL* 70). Ford at once views London as a city divided by class and as a city paradoxically, and almost miraculously, unified by knowledge, brain rather than brawn. While that link might be far from benign, it is nonetheless a link, as opposed to none at all, as opposed to a dissolution into total social fragmentation.

Elsewhere in *The Soul of London* social analysis comes again to the fore, and once again it is expressed in terms of the very optical perception of the city itself. As suggested, Ford perceives modes of transport as key in determining the individual's perception of the city. Despite his opening caveat Ford does allow in the historical development of transport in London, while insisting that his strict remit is always modernity. The oldest mode of transport into London which he considers is by river, but Ford pays this relatively little attention regarding it as, by 1900, an anachronistic form. Here he does make recourse to history in identifying the rise of horse transport and horse carriages in the eighteenth century as a factor which transformed the life of the capital, by bringing about the commercial demise of some forty thousand boatmen who hitherto provided the easiest means of crossing from one bank to the other of the Thames, in days before the building of the modern bridges (*SL* 48). In the medieval era, and even into the early modern period, Ford alludes to social class, when he contends that the most common form of transport around the city employed by royalty was the litter: 'when Queen Elizabeth went abroad on land she was carried in a litter by her gentlemen' (*SL* 48). Since the monarch or aristocrat inevitably enjoyed a higher angle of elevation than that of his bearers (who were by the same token inevitably of lower rank) this form might be said to constitute the *locus classicus* of the notion that angle of elevation and mode of transport are traditionally determined by social class.

If this is the extreme case, and offered as purely historical by Ford in 1903, elsewhere he shows that modes of transport at the turn of the twentieth century are in a period of transition, and with them traditional social hierarchies. Thus, in his concern to focus upon the modern, Ford finds the notion of entering London on foot as anachronistic as the approach along the Thames by boat or the use of a litter: 'It is a long time since I have come into London on foot, so long that I have forgotten what it feels like. Indeed, I fancy that the proceeding is no longer modern, and is in consequence illegitimate to my purpose' (*SL* 43). To bear this out Ford cites two thoroughly marginalized groups, tramps and gipsies, who still come in to London on foot (*SL* 43), but the inclusion of the latter leads him to some surprising conclusions, concerning both class and point of view. Ford observes that the gipsy inside the caravan, while not enabled literally to look down on the urban scene through which he is passing, nevertheless enjoys a privileged view of the city because he always sees it from the view point of his own, moving home:

> I fancy, however, that looking at things through the small square of a back window, being at home in the middle of strange things, the sense too of being very aloof from the rest of the world must make one's point of view rather a special one. One would become more or less of a foreign observer. (*SL* 44)

Ford then proceeds audaciously to suggest that there is an aesthetic community between the age-old gipsy and the quintessentially modern, sophisticated cosmopolitan globetrotter, arriving in London by Pullman car after a journey from some foreign city, perhaps as far-flung as St Petersburg: 'Your foreigner, reaching his London in a Pullman car, has been during his whole journey in an hotel, very much like one of his own hotels, not very much unlike his own home' (*SL* 44-45). Hence the socially marginalized and the socially elevated are seen as on a par by Ford. Elsewhere too changes in mode of transport may reinforce social hierarchies or work to break them down.

In 1903 the motor-car was still a very new invention, and the ultimate social status symbol of affluence and success. Thus Henry James, by this date suffering ever declining sales, said he could hope to afford no more expensive a vehicle than a new wheelbarrow, while Rudyard Kipling, the greatest popular success of the day, would make a great scene arriving in Rye with a motor-car and chauffeur.[7] Yet if in the most literal, physical terms the motorist, perched higher up, enjoys a superior point of view to that of either the walker, the boat traveller, or the bicyclist (*SL* 41), in other respects Ford sees the motorist's vision of the city as fundamentally flawed:

> It is not so much that the speed is very great, there is always the statutory limit, a sort of nightmare; but the motorist is too low down as a rule, the air presses against the eyes and half closes them; he has a tendency to look forward along the road, to see more of vehicles and of pedestrians than of the actual country or the regiments of buildings. He grows a little aloof, a little out of sympathy; he becomes more intent about keeping a whole skin on himself and on his car than about the outer world. (*SL* 38-39)

Paradoxically, in the London of the early twentieth century, it is a much more democratic form of public transport, the electric tram, which enjoys, in Ford's analysis, the most privileged view and psychological experience of London:

> What the automobile is to the comfortable classes the electric tram is becoming to the poorer. It is a means of getting into town. It does not, however, produce the same psychological effects. For one thing, the speed is not so great, and you have not the least anxiety as to what you may choose to run into; if you want to see things you are at a greater height, your range of sight is much longer. You may pick out upon the pavement any strange object [. . . .] You pick them out from a distance and watch them for a minute or two; you may look down at passing, you may look round. (*SL* 39-40)

Again this leads Ford to an image of a crane seen from a tram which is redolent of the Vorticists in its emphasis upon abstract, geometrical patterns and perspectives rather than human interest:

The other day I saw from the top of an electric tram, very far away, above the converging lines in the perspective of a broad highway of new shops, a steam crane at work high in the air on an upper storey. The thin arm stretched out above the street, spidery and black against a mistiness that was half sky, half haze; at the end of a long chain there hung diagonally some baulks of wood, turning slowly in mid-air. They were rising imperceptibly, we approaching imperceptibly [. . . .] Looking back I could see down the reverse of the long perspective the baulks of timber turning a little closer to the side of the building, the thin extended arm of the crane a little more foreshortened against the haze. Then the outlines grew tremulous, it all vanished with a touch of that pathos like a hunger that attaches to all things of which we see the beginnings or the middle courses without knowing the ends. It was impressive enough – the modern spirit expressing itself in terms not of men but of forces, we gliding by, the timber swinging up, without any visible human action in either motion. No doubt men were at work in the engine-belly of the crane, just as others were very far away among the dynamos that kept us moving. (*SL* 40-41)

The reference here to the pathos of the uncompleted sight anticipates Ford's description of London viewed from the train, which comes at the end of the chapter and is surely the best known passage in *The Soul of London*. The angle of elevation from the train is placed at the apex of the hierarchy of modes of transport into London. Indeed Ford mentions that from the train he looks down upon one of the other forms of transport, a bus in a street (*SL* 60). The train passenger enjoys the most elevated, but also the most alienated, point of view: 'One sees, too, so many little bits of uncompleted life. As the train pauses one looks down into a main street, and all streets look the same from a height' (*SL* 60). The bus or tram passenger might not be in control of the point of view, but s/he is sufficiently close to recognize the individual streets through which s/he passes. The train passenger, by contrast, experiences only distant, incomplete sights, without the illumination of speech or sounds overheard to give full meaning to them:

> Perhaps the comparative quiet fosters one's melancholy. One is behind glass as if one were gazing into a museum; one hears no street cries, no children's calls. And for me at least it is melancholy to think that hardly one of all these lives, of all these men, will leave any trace in the world. (*SL* 60)

The association of angle of elevation, transport, social class and perception, is also to be found in at least two contemporary works of Ford's friend and precursor Henry James. In *The Wings of the Dove*, the heroine Milly Theale, learning that for all her wealth, she is doomed to die, dismisses her carriage, her normal transport, and elects to walk on her return from Sir Luke Strett's Harley Street consulting rooms. The gesture is made as an assertion of her common humanity with the London poor, who for social and economic reasons have also met a dead end in life:

> she went into it further now; this was the real thing; the real thing was to be quite away from the pompous roads, well within the centre and on the stretches of shabby grass [. . . .] here were wanderers anxious and tired like herself; here doubtless were hundreds of others just in the same box. Their box, their great common anxiety, what was it, in this grim breathing-space, but the practical question of life ? They could live if they would; that is, like herself, they had been told so: she saw them all about her, on seats, digesting the information, recognising it again as something in a slightly different shape familiar enough, the blessed old truth that they would live if they could. All she thus shared with them made her wish to sit in their company.[8]

James's *The Golden Bowl*, published in the year in which *The Soul of London* was finished, also begins with a walk through London. Amerigo is an Italian Prince and would normally take a carriage, but perhaps symbolically this walk stands for his last act of independence before marriage. For he is making a marriage of convenience to an American heiress in order to pay off his inherited debts. Elsewhere James informs the reader that Amerigo's perception is both physically and metaphorically (socially) elevated:

> below a certain social plane, he never saw [. . . .] One kind of shopman was just like another to him [. . . .] He took throughout always the meaner sort for granted – the night of their meanness, or whatever name one might give it for him, made all his cats grey. He didn't, no doubt, want to hurt them, but he imaged them no more than if his eyes acted for every relation. [9]

In another age, as prince, he would have been borne on a litter, like Ford's Elizabeth I, literally over the heads of others. Modern financial realities (the rise of the mercantile (American) classes, and the decline of his own) force him to walk. Yet his vision remains elevated, in the sense of what he excludes from consideration.

In two modernist works which Ford may be said to anticipate, T. S. Eliot's *The Waste Land* (1922) and Virginia Woolf's *Mrs Dalloway* (1925), angle of vision is also bound up with social class in the perception of the city. In *The Waste Land* Eliot, writing in the wake of the First World War, describes the crowd of city workers as resembling the dead in Dante's *Divine Comedy*, with their vision fixed on the ground:

> A crowd flowed over London Bridge, so many,
> I had not thought death had undone so many.
> Sighs, short and infrequent, were exhaled,
> And each man fixed his eyes before his feet.[10]

Whether Tiresias, who is blind, enjoys any angle of elevation at all is perhaps questionable, but Eliot describes him as 'I who have sat by Thebes below the wall/ And walked among the lowest of the dead' (*Waste Land* ll 245-6). Elsewhere the viewpoint is that of the canal bank, 'fishing in the dull canal/ On a winter evening round behind the gashouse' (ll 189-90), and again in 'The Fire Sermon' similarly low, from the river Thames '"By Richmond I raised my knees / Supine on the floor of a narrow canoe"' (ll. 194-5).

In *Mrs Dalloway*, the heroine, upper-class Clarissa Dalloway, walks through Westminster, having made the gesture that she would 'buy the flowers herself'.[11] In the post-First World War era the affluent no longer travel exclusively by carriage. Nevertheless, servants still exist who would, in normal circumstances, take on Clarissa's self-imposed task. Yet Clarissa's decision, like Milly Theale's and Prince Amerigo's, to transgress her class enables her to come into contact, at street level, with other social strata.[12] Both Clarissa, whose daughter has been presented at Court, and the humbler Septimus Warren Smith contend as pedestrians with the same motorised London traffic. There is moreover a powerful affinity between Septimus's shell-shocked hallucination of the trenches of the Western Front in Regent's Park and the image which Ford, with uncanny prescience, gives in 'London at Leisure' describing the proximity, but also the distance, between the rich in the gentlemen's clubs and the unemployed lying idle on the lawns of Hyde Park below:

> And if you desire a sight, equally impressive, of London at leisure, go down Piccadilly to Hyde Park Corner on a pleasant summer day. On the right of you you have all those clubs with all those lounging and luxuriating men. On the left there is a stretch of green park, hidden and rendered hideous by recumbent forms. They lie like corpses, or like soldiers in a stealthy attack, a great multitude of broken men and women, they, too, eternally at leisure. They lie, soles of boots to crowns of heads, just out of arm's reach one from the other for fear of being rifled by their couch-mates. They lie motionless, dun-

coloured, pitiful and horrible, bathing in leisure that will never end. There, indeed, is your London at leisure; the two ends of the scale offered violently for inspection, confronting and ignoring steadily the one the other. For, in the mass, the men in the windows never look down; the men in the park never look up. (*SL* 141-2)

This vision anticipates the scene of Septimus's hallucination in Regent's Park, which had earlier served as the site for the doomed Milly Theale's expression of common suffering with the poor. Woolf also offers a certain sense of unification between disparate elements – Clarissa, driven to despair within her conventional upper-class marriage, parallels Septimus, driven all the way to suicide by shell-shock and the insensitivity of the medical profession. Furthermore Ford himself was emerging from a nervous breakdown, characterized by agoraphobia, when he wrote *The Soul of London*. The urban setting allows 'random' interaction – Peter Walsh is passing by as Septimus undergoes his hallucination – but also compels individuals to continue about their business without empathizing, as if committed to tramlines, or like Ford's train passenger viewing London as if behind a glass case. The classes in the modernist world of the 1920s are still kept apart, although society is also altering, in the wake of World War One and in response to continuing technological change. And finally Woolf almost takes up Ford's idea, expressed before the First World War, that written language has the power to unify the fragments of disparate urban experience. Ford's uncompleted vision from the train in Southwark of a man rushing out after a woman into their backyard emphasizes the fragmentary nature of vision in this context, exacerbated by the lack of sound to accompany the vision:

> The other day, too, we were moving rather slowly. I looked down upon black and tiny yards that were like the cells in an electric battery. In one, three children were waving their hands and turning up white faces to the train; in the next, white clothes were drying. A little further on a woman ran suddenly out of a door; she had a white apron and her sleeves were tucked up. A man followed her hastily, he had red hair, and in his hand a long stick. We moved on, and I have not the least idea whether he were going to thrash her, or whether together they were going to beat a carpet. (*SL* 61)

These fragments of human experience, of partial vision, are given unity (or not) by the written word. In this case the answer to the 'uncompleted life' (*SL* 60) which gives rise to 'a sense of some pathos and of some poetry' (*SL* 60) is provided by a form of writing scarcely less banal than the company reports which made sense of the experience of workers digging in the road, or dockers at Tilbury Docks: 'At any rate, the evening papers reported no murder in Southwark' (*SL* 61).

In *Mrs Dalloway* the fragments of the day (and of the novel) are united in part by the spoken word – the conversation overheard by Clarissa at her evening party:

> Sinking her voice, drawing Mrs Dalloway into the shelter of a common femininity, a common pride in the illustrious qualities of husbands and their sad tendency to overwork, Lady Bradshaw (poor goose – one didn't dislike her) murmured how, 'just as we were staring, my husband was called up on the telephone, a very sad case. A young man (that is what Sir William is telling Mr Dalloway) had killed himself. He had been in the army.' Oh! Thought Clarissa, in the middle of my party, here's death, she thought. (*Mrs Dalloway* 240)

But the fragments of Septimus Warren Smith's and Clarissa's lives have also already been linked earlier in the day, and by means of absolutely modern facts of urban experience. So modern that Ford could not have included both of them in his 1905 *The Soul of London*. The first, the car, Ford might have been expected to anticipate – the backfiring of a limousine (presumed to be royal) startles Clarissa (who takes it initially for 'a pistol shot in the street outside' (*Mrs Dalloway* 26) while she is shopping in Bond Street), and the same noise serves to trigger Septimus's hallucinations of the trenches. However the other example of modern technology, or indeed mode of transport, which appears in *Mrs Dalloway* and serves to unify the fragments, while also involving the written word, is a form which the Wright brothers had only just invented in 1903, the year Ford started *The Soul of London*. Both Clarissa and Septimus react to the sight of an aircraft flying over London. Clarissa and Septimus, along with the rest of the population of London free to look up at the time, are united in their focus upon an aircraft which is spelling out with its trail an advertising slogan for 'Kreemo Toffee'. The royal limousine, modern day successor to the litter on which Ford says Elizabeth I was borne, which had previously held everyone's attention, is now quite forgotten: 'and the car went in at the gates and nobody looked at it' (*Mrs Dalloway* 26).

The aircraft enjoys an angle of elevation unknown to Ford in 1903, a bird's eye view, all-encompassing, verging upon authorial omniscience, in its ability to see the whole of London at once, in an aerial panorama, and Woolf's parallel narratives of Clarissa and Septimus are for a moment allowed to intersect, like two trails in the sky overhead. Clarissa is later to seek her own moment of 'elevation' as she contemplates her own suicide from an upper window on the evening of her party, prompted by the news that Septimus (unknown to her by name) 'had thrown himself from a window' (*Mrs Dalloway* 241). As an advertising slogan 'Kreemo Toffee' may be still more banal than either the company reports or the evening newspaper articles alluded to in *The Soul of London*. Yet for Septimus, the war invalid, the aircraft, with its word appearing between clouds, which as yet he cannot understand, nevertheless serves as evidence that he is overseen by omniscient, perhaps heavenly, at any rate otherworldly, forces:

> So, thought Septimus, they are signalling to me. Not indeed in actual words; that is, he could not read the language yet; but it was plain enough, this beauty, this exquisite beauty, and tears filled his eyes as he looked at the smoke words languishing and melting in the sky and bestowing upon him, in their inexhaustible charity and laughing goodness, one shape after another of unimaginable beauty and signalling their intention to provide him, for nothing, for ever, for looking merely, with beauty, more beauty! Tears ran down his cheeks.
>
> It was toffee; they were advertising toffee, a nursemaid told Rezia. (*Mrs Dalloway* 27)

If only in Septimus's own tragic terms, as with the evening newspaper headline and the company reports in *The Soul of London*, the written word here makes some sense of the individual's fragmented experience of the city. Crucially, it is Ford, writing non-fiction (albeit in an impressionistic cast), before the social cataclysm precipitated by the First World War, who points the way for both Eliot and Woolf and anticipates their imaginative response to the modern city.

NOTES

1   Ford Madox Ford, *The Soul of London* (1905), ed. Alan Hill, London: Everyman, 1995, p. xx.
2   Ford Madox Hueffer, *The Soul of London*, London: Alston Rivers, 1905 – hereafter cited as *SL*, p. xi.
3   Andrew Lees, 'The Metropolis and the Intellectual', *Metropolis 1890-1940*, ed. Anthony Sutcliffe, London: Mansell, 1984, p. 88.
4   Birmingham Museum and Art Gallery. The painting is illustrated on the verso of the title page of this volume.

5   The *Edinburgh Review* (Jan. 1858) gave the following definition of this movement: 'It is a school of which Mr Kingsley is the ablest doctor, and its doctrine has been described fairly and cleverly as "muscular Christianity". The principal characteristics of the writer whose works earned this burlesque though expressive description, are his deep sense of the sacredness of all the ordinary relations and the common duties of life, and the vigour with which he contends for the great importance and value of animal spirits, physical strength and a hearty enjoyment of all the pursuits and accomplishments which are connected with them.'

6   Joseph Conrad, *Heart of Darkness* (1899), Harmondsworth: Penguin, 1995 – hereafter cited as *Heart of Darkness*; p. 47.

7   'Wharton said she had bought her car on the proceeds of her last novel'. HJ: 'With the proceeds of my last novel I purchased a small go-cart, or hand-barrow, on which my guest's luggage is wheeled from the station to my house. It needs a coat of paint. With the proceeds of my next novel, I shall have it painted.' Percy Lubbock, *Portrait of Edith Wharton*, (1947), pp. 69-70, quoted in Philip Horne, *A Life in Letters*, London: Allen Lane, 1999, p. 482.

8   Henry James, *The Wings of the Dove* (1902), New York: Norton, 1978, pp. 153-4.

9   Henry James, *The Golden Bowl* (1904), Harmondsworth: Penguin, 1993, p. 114.

10 T. S. Eliot, *The Waste Land* (1922), *Collected Poems*, London: Faber and Faber, 1977 – hereafter cited as *Waste Land*; ll. 62-5.

11 Virginia Woolf, *Mrs Dalloway* (1925), Oxford: Oxford University Press, 1998 – hereafter cited as *Mrs Dalloway*; p. 3.

12 Note however 'Clarissa's Invisible Taxi' in John Sutherland, *Can Jane Eyre Be Happy?*, Oxford: World's Classics, 1997, pp. 215-24, where it is argued that the time scheme of the novel implies that Mrs Dalloway must have returned home by taxi rather than on foot.

'CLOSE UP FROM A DISTANCE': LONDON AND ENGLISHNESS IN FORD, BRAM STOKER AND CONAN DOYLE

Sita A. Schutt

> What can be seen designates what is no longer there. . . . You see here there used to be. . . . Demonstratives indicate the invisible identities of the visible: it is the very definition of a place.
>
> *Walking in the City*, Michel de Certeau

Famous turn-of-the-century depictions of London do not necessarily bring to mind Bram Stoker's *Dracula* (1897). Yet Stephen Arata's reading in 'The Occidental Tourist: Dracula and the Anxiety of Reverse Colonialism'*,* foregrounds notions of identity, invasion and Englishness, which tally with similar themes to be found embedded in Conan Doyle's detective narratives (1886-1926) – and Sherlock Holmes stories *do* famously represent London – notably in the description of criminals and foreigners. Anxiety about the influx of foreigners into the English metropolis, their gradual assimilation, the threat or bonus this might pose to native inhabitants, as well as the alternately elusive or fixed identity of the city to be found in these narratives, serve as useful points of comparison with Ford's 1905 work, *The Soul of London*.

England Ltd
London, in Conan Doyle's and Bram Stoker's narratives, is characterized both by notions of the archaic and of the modern. That is, the amalgam of the past, through the fantasy of the fixed and historical identity of certain parts of the city, and the possible future (represented by science and technology), create for the reader a distinct sense of both London and 'Englishness'.

Dracula and the Sherlock Holmes series were both, and are still, bestsellers, whereas Ford's literary investigation is not a 'popular' fiction. Yet in *The Soul of London* Ford explores the idiosyncratic, the fragmented, the effect of technology on ways of perceiving – or gaining multiple impressions of – the city, and occasionally also, notions of crime and the criminal. As a personal and journalistic inquiry into English identity and the city, however, Ford's work articulates what is perhaps only implicit in the two fictional texts: an historic investigation of national identity, as well a modernist recognition of the impossibility of capturing the true spirit of the place, if not of the age whilst – in a sense – doing exactly that.

Ford may write of London as 'illimitable', but there are ways in which all these texts juggle with representations of 'limitability', notably in how the boundaries of identity are constructed: what is it to be English in London, how can one distinguish the native from the stranger and what dangers circulate around these labels?

London, in all three authors' work, is represented as a magnet not just for the provincial English. 'Foreigners' are as attracted to the capital city where they are seen alternately as threatening if not downright criminal, or as safely assimilated and tamely 'Londonised'. In reaction to this we also find that representations of national characteristics grow stronger alongside this influx of 'strangers'. Bram Stoker's and Conan Doyle's heroes protect London and celebrate the particular virtues of being 'English'. In *Dracula* this is achieved through the triumph of a London solicitor and his wife over a foreign aristocrat, and is indicative of a new type of Englishness, as represented by the growing professional middle class. In *The Soul of London*, Ford's authoritative presentation of the differing angles from which 'Englishness' can be understood, offers a more inchoate perception of national identity, which thereby also becomes more pervasive.

The superlative 'Englishness' that emerges from all three authors' texts might be explained by their actual 'foreignness' or, rather, their 'un-Englishness'. Ford, half-German, describes himself as a 'man of no race with few ties',[1] Bram Stoker was Irish, Conan Doyle, Scottish (with Irish antecedents) – none of them from central London and not obviously or comfortably 'English'. All are, in some way, both strangers to and intimate with the 'Englishness' that they depict. It is this outsider position, in part, that contributes to the creation of an 'insider' perspective.

Definitions of Englishness are produced, then, through the writers' 'attempted' totalisation of the city through its textual rendition. In other words, a project of narrative 'assimilation' is undertaken in which the constituents of London are explained which mirrors the apparent assimilation of an increasingly varied population.

Yet the homogeneity achieved by one aspect of this totalisation is superficial. London as an imagined 'whole' is, in fact, represented in fragments, whether obviously, as in *The Soul of London* or through the 'seriality' of short detective stories or through the glimpses we get, almost as though through train windows, of London in *Dracula*, in between the Transylvanian travelogue.[2] The fragmented, fragmenting representations of the metropolis whose energy and power are both exhilarating and alarming, in each case either generate plot, or indicate the possibility of plot. That is, the city creates criminals for Sherlock Holmes to catch as surely as 'London' is the ultimate destination of the voracious Count Dracula. In Ford, we witness, also often literally through train windows, tantalizing glimpses of lives that would lead to a fully blown story if that were the narrator's intention. Yet in Ford the 'fragmented' approach is far more schematized and deliberate, and takes on many more forms than simply the witnessed snatches of possible dramas.

Assimilation: the Consumption and Digestion of the Monstrous?
In the author's preface to the American edition of *England and the English* (1907), Ford recounts his investigation aboard a transatlantic liner as to the statistics of the foreign population in New York. People give him various replies:

> One told me [. . .] three and a half million Jews. Another said that there were two million Germans [. . . .] every Londoner is aware that he lives amongst an immense body of foreigners [. . . .] I suppose we, as Londoners, exaggerate in these matters more than do most New Yorkers [. . . .] I know whole districts of London where all the signs in the shop windows are incomprehensible to me.[3]

Yet for all this marked difference, the effect of habitation, as he goes on to describe it in the first chapter of *The Soul of London*, through a metaphoric process of digestion, renders these aliens into natives. Their eventual conversion into the London product occurs through a process of assimilation in which the foreigner is transformed by 'the most potent of all juices' (*SL* 12) and slowly but surely digested 'into the singular and inevitable product that is the Londoner' (*SL* 12). When in Dickens's novels, London is variously personified, it is almost always a London of parts. The 'unifying' power of London that Ford creates through this metaphor instead recalls Balzac and his depictions of Paris, notably in *The History of the Thirteen* when desire and gold whip up the entire population of Paris into a frenzy of appetite in which the city is characterized as a feeding monster. Ford's European literary influences may well account for the quasi-organic power he attributes to London, describing it as 'anaesthetically' (*SL* 12) able to convert its inhabitants into one type of legible product and as destroying 'all race characteristics' (*SL* 12). The foreigner becomes more or less fully, or at least well 'translated', not into 'English' but into 'London'. For example:

> You may watch, say, a Berlin Junker, arrogant, provincial, unlicked, unbearable to any other German, execrable to anyone not a German, turning after a year or two into a presentable and only just not typical Londoner; subdued, quiet in matters of collars, ties, coat, voice and backbone, and naturally extracting a 'sir' from a policeman. London will do all this imperceptibly. And, in externals, that is the high-water mark of achievement of the Modern Spirit. (*SL* 13)

The intervention of the law in this extract, in which the city is seen as a site of operation and transformation, relates to themes of identity, of invasion, and in a sense of masquerade, that we find in *Dracula*.

What is 'monstrous' in *Dracula* is less the vampiric, assimilative identity of the Count, but his desire to pass unnoticed in London, a prerequisite to his conquest of that city. Although, of course, it is the conjunction of the two that render him so sinister.

The Count wishes to improve his English conversation with Jonathon Harker because

> a stranger in a strange land, he is no one; men know him not – and to know not is to care not for. I am content if I am like the rest, so that no man stops if he sees me, or pause in his speaking if he hear my words, to say 'Ha, ha! a stranger!'[4]

Jonathon Harker's horrified reaction to this is compounded by the fact that not only is Dracula studying English conversation and intonation, but he is also learning the English Bradshaw's Guide by heart, studying various maps of London and atlases of England. That Count Dracula might elicit a 'Sir' from a policeman is a really rather disagreeable prospect and one Harker makes no bones about:

> Then I stopped and looked at the Count. There was a mocking smile on the bloated face which seemed to drive me mad. This was the being I was helping to transfer to London, where, perhaps for centuries to come, he might, amongst its teeming millions, satiate his lust for blood, and create a new and ever widening circle of semi-demons to batten on the helpless. The very thought drove me mad. A terrible desire came upon me to rid the world of such a monster. (51)

Dracula is terrifying because he threatens the English social fabric through territorial acquisition which takes the form of his desire both to be assimilated and to assimilate. By the same token, he threatens English manhood. Harker nearly faints when he sees him in Piccadilly Circus: not simply because of his presence, which is bad enough, but also because he is ogling pretty girls; a day-time activity which serves as the disturbing reminder of his night-time proclivities. Yet Count Dracula only desires what Ford articulates as desirable, not so much for the foreigner in question, but for the native population – and indeed for what Ford calls for to serve the interests of the future of the city, at the end of *The Soul of London*:

> If a fitted race can be bred, a race will survive, multiply and carry on vast cities. If no such race arrive the city must die. For, sooner or later, the drain upon the counties must cease: there will be no fresh blood to infuse. (*SL* 104)

It is interesting that in a climate of anxiety with regard to foreign invasion and suspicion of the 'foreign population' (including those arriving from the colonies), Ford celebrates, however optimistically, the increasing diversity of the native population. Although perhaps the danger of this, as perceived by other journalists and writers at this time, is contained by the consequences of assimilation as Ford describes them. But the safety net of strangers becoming 'Londoners' is rendered less secure by a narrative that presents the city as a plotless 'text' to be variously explored, whose signs (including its population) can be interpreted differently depending on where you are looking from, or who you are, with parts that even the author finds 'incomprehensible'. The fear of foreign sexual potency, implicit in Dracula's take-over of London, remains only marginal to Ford's call for a 'fitted race', although I suppose that implicit in obtaining a policeman's polite acknowledgement must be the assumption of docile sexual mores.

Ford recognizes that:

> One may sail easily round England, or circumnavigate the globe. But not the most enthusiastic geographer [. . .] ever memorised a map of London. Certainly no one ever walks round it. For England is a small island, the world is infinitesimal amongst the planets. But London is illimitable. (*SL* 15)

Yet Dracula's attempted conquest of London, in contrast, takes the form of the possibility of complete knowledge. He attempts the 'memorisation' of London. He evidently does not succeed – the foreigner's knowledge of 'maps' is never then as good as the native inhabitants' experience – yet his uncanny power to infiltrate the city, find his way round, and buy property in its wealthiest parts, is alarming. He nearly makes London 'limitable' but in fact, through his supernatural powers, ultimately represents something of its illimitability and 'vastness'. His defeat at the end of the novel thus also serves to control something of the sense of alarm generated by the 'out-of-controlness' of a city growing so rapidly – it would seem – with the help of foreign agencies.

Conan Doyle's criminally populated London might also ultimately be seen as assimilable, and limitable. The London that Sherlock Holmes deciphers for us is an eminently chartered London. Under his keen eye, every by-pass, every underground exit in the sprawling metropolis – from aristocrat's secret boudoir to criminal window-ledge – is recorded, and leaves the reader with a very specific map of London. As Colin Watson points out,

> The London of Holmes commends itself at once and unconditionally [. . . .] It is a city where every crime is soluble and whose vices are sealed within narrow and defined areas. It is a cosy place. It is, for as long as a hawkeyed man broods in Baker Street, a safe place. It does not exist. It never did. But Doyle managed to build it in the minds of his readers.[5]

If Ford writes of the 'sepia tinge' that makes the spirit of the age unfathomable, reflecting the illimitability of London, then in Conan Doyle's narratives that sepia tinge signifies the opposite: the nostalgic colouring of something indescribably familiar, safe and circumscribed. Sherlock Holmes as perspicacious detective does 'fathom' the city: the detective really 'notices' and therefore he alone, in a sense, creates this London, enabling others to 'see'. The 'sepia tinge' of the Sherlock Holmes stories defines and delimits a sense of London and of Englishness that is fixed, whereas the 'sepia in water' (*SL* 12) of Ford's colouring represents the swirl and flux of a still-wet aquarelle. Conan Doyle's London is an imaginary place, which, as Watson states, never existed; yet it continues to be solidly associated with 'Edwardian' London to most readers.

Yet 'seeing' through the city, in Sherlock Holmes's case, serves to cover up a different kind of blindness, for frequently (although certainly not always) the foreigner is suspect: the King of Bohemia is morally despicable, Mormons are fatally vindictive, and Englishmen who have been abroad too long begin to poison their daughters with exotic snakes. If not wholly 'criminal', the stranger represents danger, is certainly not agreeably 'assimilated' and rather than eliciting 'Sir' from policemen, is better-off arrested by them. Although many Englishmen and women also turn out to be guilty, when they are appraised at the end of the story, they are found to have betrayed their country, either literally because they were spies, or figuratively, because somehow they have behaved in way considered 'unEnglish'. In *The Bruce-Partington Plans* (1908) for example, Sir Walter Valentine is arrested and imprisoned:

> 'Everything is known, Colonel Walter,' said Holmes. 'How an English gentleman could behave in such a manner is beyond my comprehension. But your whole correspondence and relations with Oberstein are within our knowledge.'[6]

Walter Valentine betrays his class as well as his country, a double outrage then, and one which serves to reinforce the underlying chivalric order that determines Sherlock Holmes's judgments, which frequently remain separate from the law. As David Trotter notes, quoting Sir Charles Dilke in 1868:

> Love of race, among the English [. . .] rests upon a firmer base than either love of mankind or love of Britain, for it reposes upon a subsoil of things known: the ascertained virtues and powers of the English people.[7]

Chivalric values have their place in both Bram Stoker and in Ford. Yet the onset of modernity, specifically of technological advances in locomotion and elevation, provide a link here with the second half of this discussion. From the 'subsoil of things known' we shall leap to the literal and figurative abstractions that occur in all three writers, with regard, in the first place, to physical perception.

Modernity Through Fragmentation/Systematization

Michel de Certeau in 'Walking in the City' writes of New York as viewed from the 110th floor of the World Trade Center and of the desire that artists have always had to picture the whole, if possible, from above:

> Medieval or Renaissance painters represented the city as seen in a perspective that no eye had yet enjoyed [. . . .] To what erotics of knowledge does the ecstasy of reading such a cosmos belong? Having taken a voluptuous pleasure in it, I wonder what is the source of this pleasure of 'seeing the whole' of looking down on, totalising the most immoderate of human texts?[8]

De Certeau's approach seems to be an apt one when considering Ford for although he uses 'height' as part of the totalising perspective and Ford uses distance, both share the *fantasy* of an attempted totalisation. The 'pleasure' that this project inevitably provokes is very much in evidence in Ford's account although his text consists of an attempted totalisation made up of fragments. London, he writes, is a place of 'innumerable class districts' (*SL* 10). In his visits to and accounts of these little 'districts', and the various forms of travel with which he experiments, Ford creates both complete and incomplete cameos.

What you see is a function of where you are positioned, and Ford places himself in various modes of transport, reporting alternatively from inside a motor car, on top of a bicycle, an electric tram, or, closer, with the 'eye of a bird that is close to the ground' (*SL* 16), noting the difference in impressions at different speeds. This 'kaleidoscopic' imagery contributes to 'the modern spirit'. Ford's dizzying or acrobatic accounts, punctuated by moments of tranquility, contemplation and repose are echoed in how the detective patrols the modern city (nose down to the ground or watching from a window), and in how the team of vampire chasers sets about catching Dracula.

We receive, thereby, a composite photograph of the whole. Instead of creating one 'text' Ford creates a series of short stories, or impressions of potential short stories. 'London is a thing of these "bits"...' (*SL* 22). Upon seeing a couple from a train window – a man with red hair brandishing a stick following a woman wearing a white apron – he comments, 'I have not the least idea whether he were going to thrash her, or whether together they were going to beat a carpet' (*SL* 40). He does give the story a footnote, and thus a sense of possible ending, by adding that 'the evening papers reported no murder in Southwark.'

The incomplete, he writes,

> gives to looking out of train windows a touch of pathos and of dissatisfaction. It is akin to the sentiment ingrained in humanity of liking a story to have an end. And it is the 'note' of all roads into London. (*SL* 41)

In the Sherlock Holmes stories we are given completed stories where plot is paramount and endings always in evidence. The crime that might be, in the story of the carpet-beating couple, is precisely what Sherlock Holmes would track down and resolve, although it wouldn't necessarily be the obvious one of murder – no doubt such a story would end in the discovery of a narrowly averted international conspiracy, complete with German barbers. The 'fragmented' in Sherlock Holmes remains, on the whole, relegated to structure (the short story or, within this, the incidental) and the 'modern spirit' is obvious mostly in the treatment of systems, technology and science. Although the detective and his vision – the way he and only he sees patterns in apparently disconnected events – creates an interesting parallel to Ford's notion of the 'visible world'.

In Ford, the visible is in a sense framed by the invisible, thereby ensuring a form of suspense or at least of the lack of (re-)solution: London provokes and evokes a background both to the mysterious and the incidental. In the Sherlock Holmes stories, it does so with the addition of a *dénouement*.

Yet there is a more disturbing element which is never fully articulated in these 'family' stories. The crimes are, in fact, often more grotesque and alarming than their solutions would suggest, and although the stories lock away bad foreigners and celebrate the English powers not only of detection but of justice, they acknowledge the romance of the criminal story, the strangers' mesmerizing story-telling powers, and the city's endless absorbing capacity to receive, generate and accommodate the exotic. That is, in other words, Sherlock Holmes's London though represented ultimately as cosy, contained, knowable and safe, partakes – through the grotesque and sinister elements that are never fully developed or acknowledged – of some of unknowable 'illimitability', the vastness, danger and mystery of Ford's London.

Dracula, of course, is wildly exotic and as a narrative we can speak of its 'fragmented' quality primarily in terms of structure. The story is told, to borrow from Ford, as a series of 'little bits' – that is, one moment a diary, the next a newspaper cutting, the next a rendering of scientific observations into a phonograph. The fearful tale is not only recounted from various vantage points, but it covers so much (literal) ground, that it has been referred to as a travel narrative:[9] its sweeping breadth from sheer mountain tops in the Carpathians to the reading rooms in the British Museum give it a breathlessness and even a kaleidoscopic quality akin to the movement and changing vistas present in Ford's journeys in and around London. Ford, in fact, also circulates metaphorically much farther afield than simply the English countryside. He mentions, at one point, those 'ruined temples' that become 'little pieces of London' (*SL* 24) and describes the sense of an extended 'Englishness' present through the perusal of the latest

English books and journals: 'the stores and the circulating library make London extend to Jubbulpore...' (*SL* 24).

Ford writes 'we talk of the Londoner [...] but there is none' (*SL* 89-90): as quickly as he creates London subjects he then erases them. This, in a sense, creates a kind of 'vanishing point' narrative: 'close-ups' swiftly merging into the distance. Yet within this there is also a sense of contained journey that perhaps best defines the Englishness of this period, one which both Bram Stoker and Conan Doyle in their various ways helped to construct or celebrate, albeit as a fondly imagined quality that none, in a sense, really themselves 'owned'. The following quotation refers to passengers in a railway carriage, and 'trains', perhaps as much as London, are common to all three authors' works. In Ford's words, taken from *The Spirit of the People*, then:

> It is not – the whole of Anglo-Saxondom – a matter of race but one, quite simply of place – of place and of spirit, the spirit being born of the environment. We are not Teutons; we are not Latins; we are not Celts or Anglo-Saxons in the sense of being descendants of Jutes or Angles. We are all passengers together, carving or not carving our initials on the doors of our carriage, and we all vaguely hope as a nation to jolly well get somewhere [. . . .] But, in a dim way too, we do hope that we shall jolly well get somewhere where they sell ginger-beer. (*SP* 255-6)

The sense of journey here, the anticipation of passage, rather than of arrival, recalls Huysmans' *Against the Grain*, but is also thoroughly post-modern. The inscription of the individual through the 'carving of initials' yet the assumption of unity implicit in a common taste or desire goes beyond Empire and war. Dracula's longevity as a 'vampire' continues to exist in heterotopic relation to the urban, though not necessarily to London in particular. Sherlock Holmes is imbued with the spirit of a non-existent address in Baker Street, but Ford's paragraph on 'getting somewhere where they sell ginger beer' could apply to a description of the package-holiday brigade waiting in the Gatwick departure lounge. Perhaps it is less 'London' that is a thing of these 'bits', than England. 'Close-up from a distance' as aptly describes the lot of third and more generation immigrants in London, the 'trouble' with having shop signs in a 'foreign' language, or the problem of 'assimilation' which has hit the world almost more brutally since the collapse of the twin towers from which de Certeau imagines the Renaissance artists' ideal perspective.

Yet rather more comfortingly than the towering perspective of a world-view that exists only retrospectively, Ford's London is still a

London we can recognize. In contrast, Conan Doyle's and Bram Stoker's London, no less familiar, is firmly fixed in the past. It is a London of bygone times, fired and cast, one might say, with a particular sense of urgency: Mina and Jonathon Harker, and Sherlock Holmes, defend the city from the immediate perils of the crook and the opportunist. Ford's London, projected more speculatively, results in a qualitatively different kind of defense: a 'protection' of the *nature* of London that endures due to the way his evocations both anticipated and encompassed the passage of time.

NOTES

1 Ford Madox Ford, *England and the English*, ed. Sara Haslam, Manchester: Carcanet, 2003, p. 325. Hereafter separate volumes cited in quotations refer to this edition: *The Soul of London* (*SL*), *The Heart of the Country* (*HC*) and *The Spirit of the People* (*SP*).

2 In my final section I discuss this idea in more detail.

3 This Author's Note is reprinted in *England and the English*, Haslam ed., pp. 327-36; pp. 328-9.

4 Bram Stoker, *Dracula*, Oxford: Oxford University Press, 1999, p. 20.

5 Colin Watson, *Snobbery with Violence: English Crime stories and their Audience*, London: Methuen, 1987, p. 24.

6 Conan Doyle, 'The Bruce-Partington Plans', *The Complete Short Stories*, London: John Murray, 1928, p. 997.

7 David Trotter, *The English Novel in History 1896-1920*, London: Routledge, 1993, p. 154.

8 Michel de Certeau, *The Practice of Everyday Life*, Berkeley & L.A: University of California Press, 1984, p. 92.

9 Stephen D. Arata, 'The Occidental Tourist: Dracula and the Anxiety of Reverse Colonisation', *Dracula: New Casebooks*, ed. Glennis Byron, New York: St Martin's Press, 1999, p. 129.

FORD, THE CITY, IMPRESSIONISM AND MODERNISM

Max Saunders

Introduction

'I personally regard the great city with horror': 'it is for me a hideous shadow, continually brooding on the horizon [. . .]'.[1] When Ford wrote these words, at the end of the nineteenth century, he was in the first of his country phases, living the simple life on the land. He never completely lost that sense of the possibilities of the city for ominousness. But, as he wrote in 1915: 'this country and the rest of the civilised world have long since accepted the fact that modern life is almost inevitably urban life'.[2] Ford himself was to live much of his life in great cities, where he became a crucial figure in Anglo-American urban modernism, first in London, then after the war in Paris and New York. I shall argue that his writings about the city, and particularly London, are not only an important part of his own work, but crucial for Modernist literary aesthetics. Most of this chapter considers his first successful book, *The Soul of London*. It also outlines how London figures in his other works, especially *A Call*, and some of the poems in *Songs from London*.

Impressionism and the City

Impressionist London – Monet's scenes of fog on the Thames; Whistler's Thames *Nocturnes* – lies behind the modernist London of Ford, Conrad, and Eliot. The art historian Richard Brettell distinguishes two major divisions within Impressionism.[3] First, 'Transparent Impressionism', where painters produce 'what appear to be impressions of visual reality'. Monet is the 'canonical' figure here; 'the subject of the painting is the entire visual field in front of the painter rather than clearly separate forms in illusionistic space'. Second, 'Mediated Impressionism', in which painters followed the lead of Degas or Renoir. For them: 'visual reality is conceived not as a vibrant coloured field, but as a social world in which the figure and its various 'grounds' must be analyzed to be understood'.

In Ford's *The Soul of London* we find both modes, the Transparent and the Mediated. Ford seeks to aestheticize the city into a vibrant coloured field; but the social world, and the demand for analysis, keeps creeping back in. This oscillation, produced by an urban crisis of aestheticism, ushers in Modernism. Ford's London is not the same as Conrad's in *The Secret Agent,* or Eliot's in 'The Waste Land'. But it does help us see how they arrived at their visions of the city.

Relativity in the City: Space

The *Soul of London* was written in 1903 and early 1904, out of the agoraphobic depression into which Ford was then falling. Though some of his worst agoraphobic attacks occurred in the country, on places like Salisbury Plain, he was struck by the German term 'Platz Angst', in which 'Platz' can mean 'space' but also town or square.[4] As in the Greek term 'agoraphobia', there is a sense in which what is denoted is a fear of the city, or of what the city has done to space – which is presumably why the period sees such concern with agoraphobia. Ford didn't visit America until 1906, after he had written *The Soul of London.* But he would have already known of the skyscrapers for which New York was famous, and which had transformed city space.[5] And he knew them first hand when he was writing his *Songs from London* from early 1907. The agoraphobic dimension of *The Soul of London* is thus more than the expression of a private crisis. Ford's engagement with the modern city (his subtitle is *A Survey of a Modern City*) and its aesthetic implications were representative of a more general concern; and of a shift away from Impressionism. In 1908 Wilhelm Worringer's *Abstraction and Empathy* sought to relate modernist geometric form to agoraphobia, or space-shyness; an idea which was restated for Anglo-American modernists by T. E. Hulme.[6]

But as early as 1905 Ford was already registering how the city transforms and disturbs our sense of space and reality; as in the beautiful and defamiliarising description in *The Soul of London* of a hailstorm. It begins with an estranging expression of agoraphobia:

> Suddenly space exists: it is as if a red torch were shaken in the air and quenched. That is lightning, a reminder of the outside world that we have half forgotten [. . . .] the blackness descends once more, the hail, the colourlessness of all the world. The houses once more look like clouds.

And indeed it is impossible, without an effort, to dissociate in our minds the idea of London from the idea of a vast cloud beneath a cloud as vast [. . . .] London itself is at times apt to seem unreal.[7]

And it ends with that vision of an 'Unreal city', which leads directly to 'The Waste Land'.

Crowds

Spatial anxiety in the city is of course inseparable from the idea of the crowd. City squares are no less menacing when full than when empty. Like Pound, Eliot, and Lewis, Ford wrote about the experience of crowds. And like theirs, Ford's crowds invoke human mortality. That image of the *cloud*, that recurs in the *Soul of London* and elsewhere in Ford, is more than a Transparent Impressionist rendering of London fog. It is a Mediated Impression: the cloud of the dead; the dead *crowd* of past inhabitants. In the book's closing sentence, it is 'A cloud – as it were of the dust of men's lives' (*SL* 176). (Compare Eliot: 'A crowd flowed over London Bridge, so many / I had not thought death had undone so many'.) Pound's famous haiku 'In a Station of the Metro' has been compared to Ford's vision of the crowd at the Shepherds Bush Exhibition. Both men wrote about these experiences around 1913-14, which has generated discussion of whose came first. But Ford had already written of a comparable experience in 1907 – before he met Pound:

> The other night I was going eastward upon the top of a 'bus. It was just outside the Tottenham Court-road Tube Station. In front of us was a tongue of deep shadow, the silhouetted forms of 'bus-tops, dray-tops, drivers' hats, all in a pyramidal mass of darkness, and a stimulating, comfortable, jangling confusion. Before us was a blazing haze of golden light, on each side the golden faces of innumerable people, lit up by the light that streamed from shop-windows, and up along the house fronts the great shafts of light streamed heavenwards. And the gloom, the glamour, the cheerfulness, the exhilarating cold, the suggestion of terror, of light, and of life . . .
>
> It was not Romance – it was Poetry. It was the Poetry of the normal, of the usual, the poetry of the innumerable little efforts of mankind, bound together in such a great tide that, with their hopes, their fears, and their reachings out to joy they formed a something at once majestic and tenuous, at once very common and strangely pathetic.
>
> But of that I find little in the work of living novelists, and less or nothing in the work of living poets.[8]

This was two years after *The Soul of London*, and suggests what Ford had been trying to achieve there, as well as in his poems (as we shall see). At the end of the first paragraph the Transparent Impressionism modulates into the Mediated, analytic kind.

Georg Simmel: 'The Metropolis and Mental Life'

A key figure addressing the sociological impact of the city was Georg Simmel, who in 1903 published a seminal essay 'Die Grosstadt und das Geistesleben', translated as 'The Metropolis and Mental Life'.[9] There's no evidence Ford knew of Simmel. But their ideas about the psychological effects of modern city life are remarkably congruent.

For Simmel the central problem is the maintenance of the individual's independence against society, culture and technology – as in Ford's image of the 'great tide' of mankind, which while it binds together humanity in a mass, also threatens to drown the individual. Simmel notes the rapidity of incessant stimuli, which intensify the individual's emotional life. 'The stimuli are in the form of a contrast between present impressions and past impressions'.[10] The number and frequency of impressions is greater in the metropolis than in small towns. This suggests that, even when it is concerned with natural landscape, Impressionism is a metropolitan phenomenon – which concurs with Bretell's account of Mediated Impressionism.

Simmel's metropolis as commercial/financial centre conduces to norms of impersonality (calculation, precision, punctuality).[11] These correspond to three of Ford's cardinal aesthetic anxieties: statistics (which he loathed); accuracy (he founded his impressionism on a profound contempt for facts, but an accuracy of his impressions); and time, which his narratives characteristically fragment and shift around.

Personality

'Impersonality' – like 'personality' – is a key term in Ford's critical lexicon. Indeed one could argue that it is this combination that locates him on the cusp of the transition from aestheticism to modernism – with James, Wilde, and Yeats, say. Paradoxically, Ford's approach to London, his attempt to see as an individual what is too massive to be visualized, is to imagine it as like a person. (Hence the titles of all three volumes of the trilogy comprising *England and the English: The Soul of London; The Heart of the Country; The Spirit of the People*.) This is a trope at once familiar and de-familiar:

> Most of us love places very much as we may love what, for us, are the
> distinguished men of our social lives [. . . .] We are, all of us who are
> Londoners, paying visits of greater or lesser duration to a Personality that,
> whether we love it or very cordially hate it, fascinates us all. And, paying my
> visit, I have desired to give some such record. (*SL* 3)[12]

'Let us go and make our visit', says Prufrock, in Eliot's poem
famously comparing a city evening to a person: a patient etherized
upon a table.

Unsurprisingly, Ford's attempts to read London's personality or
'character' are baffled by its multiplicity and incoherence. Indeed, it's
the sheer impersonality that characterises urban life. 'For, sooner or
later, the sense of the impersonality, of the abstraction that London is,
will become one of the most intimate factors of his daily life' (*SL* 8-
9). And this was Simmel's point too. It's characteristic of Ford's skill
to arrive at the familiar industrial conception of alienation in such a
way as to make it seem surprising.

Social Space and Technology
In an ingenious essay Philip Horne discusses Ford's novel of 1909-10,
A Call, set in London and perhaps the first novel to be preoccupied
with the telephone. Horne argues that: 'The telephone [. . .] casts
reality into doubt'. Ford has his hero plagued by 'the unreal sounds of
voices on the telephone'.[13] Horne notes that 'Ford is also alive to the
telephone's potential for psychological disturbance and intimate
intrusion'. And he reminds us that it was in 1910, too, that Virginia
Woolf was to say, notoriously, 'human character changed'. The
telephone also changes the social conception of space. Ford's
repressed characters often inhabit a world of 'silence and loneliness'
that appears purgatorial. The telephone might seem to offer the
consolation of some form of connexion and contact, albeit somewhat
vicarious. But it presents paranoid possibilities, since its noise and
communication can be intrusive (as when Robert Grimshaw disturbs
Etta Hudson as she is about to seduce Dudley Leicester; and menacing
and disturbing, since Grimshaw recognizes his friend Leicester's
voice, but Leicester, surprised in a compromising situation, is too
flustered to know who has caught him out). Of course you can
persecute people by 'phone in the country too, but it is no accident
that this early novel is set in the metropolis, since the 'phone's
invasiveness is yet one more example of modern metropolitan life
making inroads on our private space. Communal apartment blocks,

public transport, public baths, public houses, public places for eating, resting (such as on park benches), recreation. . . .

Impressionist artists like Monet and Whistler incorporate images of engineering – cranes, bridges, ships. But they make them seem timeless; part of a seamless aesthetic realm connecting medieval Japan with modern cityscapes. They return design from technology to aesthetics. But Ford is clear how technological change changes our perception, our experience, what Simmel calls our mental life:

> The other day I saw from the top of an electric tram, very far away, above the converging lines in the perspective of a broad highway of new shops, a steam crane at work high in the air on an upper storey. The thin arm stretched out above the street, spidery and black against a mistiness that was half sky, half haze; at the end of a long chain there hung diagonally some baulks of wood, turning slowly in mid-air. They were rising imperceptibly, we approaching imperceptibly. A puff of smoke shot out, writhed very white, melted and vanished between the housefronts. We glided up to and past it. Looking back I could see down the reverse of the long perspective the baulks of timber turning a little closer to the side of the building, the thin extended arm of the crane a little more foreshortened against the haze. Then the outlines grew tremulous, it all vanished with a touch of that pathos like a hunger that attaches to all things of which we see the beginnings or the middle courses without knowing the ends. It was impressive enough – the modern spirit expressing itself in terms not of men but of forces, we gliding by, the timbers swinging up, without any visible human action in either motion. (*SL* 29-30)

Fragmentation and Bafflement
Just as Transparent Impressionism is baffled by our curiosity, the result of Mediated Impressionism is again bafflement. Urban fragmentation multiplies our ignorance; makes us aware of all the uncompleted lives, the people, the stories, about which we can only wonder. Narrative attempts to mediate impressions into story. But there are too many fragments of too many stories to tell or to read. The problem of *reading* London is of course related to the problem of reading *in* London:

> You cannot in London read a book from day to day, because you must know the news, in order to be a fit companion for your fellow Londoner. Connected thinking has become nearly impossible, because it *is* nearly impossible to find any general idea that will connect into one train of thought: 'Home Rule for Egypt', 'A Batch of Stabbing Cases', and 'Infant Motorists'. (*SL* 88)

If this sounds entirely negative about modern urban consciousness, we should note that all the things Ford is lamenting are also good descriptions of his best techniques, as developed with Conrad. In A. S. Byatt's marvelous description of his method: 'he wanted precise, clear images to happen, and next to the precise, clear images, spaces in which you guessed and intuited'.[14]

> One is behind glass as if one were gazing into the hush of a museum; one hears no street cries, no children's calls. And for me at least it is melancholy to think that hardly one of all these lives, of all these men, will leave any trace in the world. One sees, too, so many little bits of uncompleted life. As the train pauses one looks down into a main street – and all streets are hardly recognizable from a height. A bus is before the steps of a church, a ragged child turns a catherine wheel in the road, and holds up her hand to the passengers. Suddenly a blue policeman steps into the roadway. The train moves on. (*SL* 42)

Relativity in the City: Time

This rapt contemplation of the fragmentary is characteristic of Ford's impressionism. But – as in a crucial passage from *The Soul of London* – it also reveals Ford Madox Hueffer as a precursor of J. Alfred Prufrock. In it Ford moves from the speed of city life, to a freezing of time:

> "It takes a good deal out of you," this leisured life of display. You rush more or less feverishly, gathering scalps of one sort or another [. . . .] But each of these things sinks back into the mere background of your you. You are, on the relentless current of your life, whirled past them as, in a train, you are whirled past a succession of beautiful landscapes [. . . .]
>
> You carry away from it a vague kaleidoscope picture – lights in clusters, the bare shoulders of women, white flannel on green turf in the sunlight, darkened drawing rooms with nasal voices chanting parodies of prayers, the up and down strokes of fiddle bows, the flicker of fifty couples whirling round before you as with a touch of headache you stood in a doorway, a vague recollection of a brilliant anecdote, the fag end of a conversation beneath the palms of a dimmed conservatory, and a fatigue and a feverish idea that if you had missed any one of these unimportant things you would have missed life [. . . .] And, the breaks being less marked, the life itself is the more laborious and less of a life. For it is in the breaks, in the marking time, that the course of a life becomes visible and sensible. You realise it only in leisures within that laborious leisure; you realise it, in fact, best when, with your hands deep in your trouser pockets, or listless on your watch-chain, you stand, unthinking, speculating on nothing, looking down on the unceasing, hushed, and constantly changing defile of traffic below your club windows. The vaguest thoughts flit through your brain: the knot on a whip, the cockade on a coachman's hat, the sprawl of a large woman in a victoria, the windshield in front of an automobile. You live only with your eyes, and they lull you. So Time becomes manifest like a slow pulse, the world stands still; a four-wheeler takes as it were two years to crawl from one lamp-post to another,

and the rustle of newspapers behind your back in the dark recesses of the room might be a tide chafing upon the pebbles. That is your deep and blessed leisure: the pause in the beat of the clock that comes now and then to make life seem worth going on with. Without that there would be an end of us.

For, whether we are of the leisured class, whether we are laundry-women, agricultural labourers, dock labourers, or bank clerks, it is that third state that makes us live. Brahmins would call it contemplation; the French might use the word *assoupissement*. It would be incorrect to call it reverie since it is merely a suspension of the intellectual faculties; it is a bathing in the visible world: it is a third state between work and amusement – perhaps it is the real Leisure. (*SL* 80-81)[15]

This temporal paradox is central to Impressionist art, which freezes time in order to suggest its processes; and it can be traced back to, say, Pater's celebration of the 'exquisite pauses in time' composed by the School of Giorgione: pauses in which, 'arrested thus, we seem to be spectators of all the fulness of existence, and which are like consummate extract or quintessence of life'. But what Pater goes to the Renaissance to get, or Whistler to Japan, Ford finds in the city.

Impressionist reverie seeks to act as a salve for the anxiety over uncompleted lives, fragmentary perceptions, the sense of acceleration. (E. M. Forster's Margaret Schlegel shares Ford's earlier horror of the city: 'I hate this continual flux of London [. . . .] eternal formlessness'.[16]) The pause in the beat of the clock converts time into space; turns fragments of narrative into vision; into a composition for calm contemplation. There are two problems that make for bafflement again, though. It can't be done for long; it's a slow pulse, rather than no pulse, which would be death. (And would the sight of completed lives be any less melancholy than uncompleted ones?) But even while it is done, the frozen space becomes itself transparent. The visible items, taken out of their narrative contexts, acquire a semantic and emotional charge that incites analysis and understanding, mediating the impressionism and bringing it back to narrative.

Urban Poetics

This is very much the basis of Ford's poetry and poetics too. 'I want the poetry of cafés, of automobiles, of kisses, and of absinthe', he wrote in 1914.[17] That was precisely the poetry he had been writing – in both verse and prose – since 1905: an innovative, and innovatively theorized, poetry of the city: one that was to have a profound influence on Pound and Eliot, and the modernist imagination in general. Ford's writing in *The Soul of London* doesn't quite feel like that modernism. At this stage Ford can't stop himself from discoursing about the fragmentary renderings, mediating them and explaining their connotations. Those are the parts Eliot and Pound excised.

But Eliot's purgatorial townscapes had developed Ford's perception about the human expressiveness of the concrete objects of urban detritus. Instead of taking what might seem the safe option of writing about 'the comfrey under the hedge', Ford advocates a poetry contemplating 'the portable zinc dustbin left at dawn for the dustman to take': 'the ash-bucket at dawn', he argues, 'is a symbol of poor humanity, of its aspirations, its romance, its ageing and its death'.[18]

Edwardian London is thus in part an anti-Romantic venue for Ford, as it was for Eliot too. His poems dealing with London present an aggressive contrast between a hackneyed past of feudal palace, tiny town, or dead lovers walking in the countryside on the one hand, and on the other, the Edwardian underground stations of North West London – Finchley Road and Kilburn. (It won't be a revelation to readers of *The Good Soldier* or *Parade's End* that Ford writes well about trains and stations.)[19] The hackneyed nature of the fantasy past is Ford's point, though. Stylistically it will no longer serve. He writes in the poem 'The Three-Ten':

> *But see, but see! The clock marks three above the Kilburn Station,*
> *Those maids, thank God! Are 'neath the sod and all their generation.*[20]

Thank God, presumably, because it's time to say goodbye to poetic clichés of love in country lanes.

But at this point in the argument, the value of the city has changed. It isn't merely negational, to undermine or cancel an earlier style. For it offers a style of its own; a style of disillusion (Simmel notes that metropolitan impersonality fosters a blasé attitude), demoralization, squalor, and above all for Ford, mortality. It's the clock at Kilburn Station that tells Ford the time of death of the past lovers. The ending of the other poem about underground stations – 'Finchley Road' – is oddly haunting.[21] After fantasizing about the kind of feudal aristocratic life his lover should have had, he returns to the present and the city:

> *But here we are at Finchley Road,*
> *With a drizzling rain and a skidding 'bus*

And the twilight settling down on us.

You don't have to spell out the contrast. It's enough just to say 'here we are' – the cityscape's character is self-evident. But again it's not quite just that it negates the feudal fantasy. That image of 'the twilight settling down on us' is more than just the last touch of gloomy realism. It registers the gloom as almost physically oppressive. This is negative about the reality of the modern city, certainly; but it sees that reality as an opportunity for modern poetry; as an expressive resource. The city twilight, imaged as something between a burial and a blanket, is more evocative than the fantasy alternative.

This was very much the nub of Ford's poetics, as has been shown in a fine essay by Joseph Wiesenfarth: the precise use of observations to render a personal vision.[22] But it is essentially an urban poetics, that Ford repeatedly needs to define against a conventional rural romanticism.[23]

The City in Ford's Subsequent Writing
It is probably because cities feature only slightly in *The Good Soldier* that their importance to him hasn't been grasped. Yet London is central to his other Edwardian novels of contemporary metropolitan life, such as *Mr Apollo* and *Mr Fleight*; and very important in later fiction such as *The Marsden Case* and *Parade's End*. It also looms large in his discursive and reminiscential books such as *Women & Men, Ancient Lights, Return to Yesterday,* and *It Was the Nightingale.* New York and Paris are vital in this last book too, as they are in later novels such as *When the Wicked Man* and *Vive Le Roy*; and again in other books such as *A Mirror to France*, and *Great Trade Route*.

In a century of increasing urbanization, wouldn't something similar be true for any novelist? Can a twentieth-century writer avoid the city as at least an occasional background? Such objections are true as far as they go. But Ford went further, as can be seen in two concluding instances of how important the city was to his imagination. First, despite all his agrarian activities, he explicitly conceived of city life as the principal modern subject. In the preface he wrote for an edition of Conrad's *The Sisters* in 1928 he says that Conrad:

> regarded the writing about normal terrestrial humanity as the only glorious occupation for a proper man. That is to say, in common with myself, he regarded the writing of novels as the only occupation for a proper man and he

thought that those novels should usually concern themselves with the life of great cities.[24]

He goes on to endorse the latter idea, judging Conrad's urban fictions more highly than his novels of the sea, and speculating about what kind of novelist Conrad might have been had he concentrated on 'the misty problems of the Slav soul amidst the more complicated, strained and subtle psychologies of city streets'.[25]

The second case is the book Ford planned, but didn't complete, and which was to put the city in the foreground. It was to be a companion volume to *Provence* and *Great Trade Route*; and it was to be a book of 'Portraits of Cities', described by Ford and illustrated by Janice Biala, as the previous two books had been.[26] Only one chapter was published: an article about Nashville, described as 'The Athens of the South', which appeared in *Vogue*. [27] This is included in the current volume, as are two previously unpublished typescripts from Cornell about Boston, and Denver. There is also a typescript about the journey between Boston and Denver, in which cities do not figure much.[28]

The scope of the work kept changing, and the changes are described in the editorial note on pp. 211-13 of this volume. But the two books of the trilogy that we do have – *Provence* and *Great Trade Route* – provide glimpses of what the third might have been; and they already touch on many of the cities he proposed to cover. To the end of his life, then, Ford was writing the city. He always believed that to be 'happy though human' (in a phrase from his proposed title for the concluding chapter) we need the city as well as the country. We might note how the working title, 'Portraits of Cities', again plays with representing the city as if human. He wrote that 'Civilized man' was 'man who must live in great cities'.[29] The 'highly cultured civilizations' he valued were, from the days of Athens and Rome, the products of cities. And, as the essays in this volume demonstrate, 'Portraits of Cities' were integral to much of his work. We need to grasp the significance for him of the city, not only in order to be able to understand Ford's own work, but also to understand the role of the city in the history of modernism.

NOTES

1 Ford, 'William Hyde: an Illustrator of London', *Artist*, 21 (January 1898), [1]-6 (p. 4).

2 Ford, *When Blood is Their Argument*, New York & London: Hodder & Stoughton, 1915, p. 203.

3 Bretell, *Modern Art 1851-1929: Capitalism and Representation*, Oxford: Oxford University Press, 1999, p. 18. Also see Robert L. Herbert, *Impressionism: Art, Leisure, and Parisian Society*, New Haven and London: Yale University Press, 1988; and Sylvie Gache-Patin, 'The Urban Landscape', in Richard R. Brettell, Scott Schaefer, Sylvie Gache-Patin and Francoise Heilbrun, *A Day in the Country: Impressionism and the French Landscape*, Los Angeles: L. A. C. M. A., 1984.

4 Ford to Elsie Hueffer, 15 September 1904: Carl A. Kroch Library, Cornell University: quoted in Saunders, *Ford Madox Ford: A Dual Life*, Oxford: Oxford University Press, 1996, vol. 1, p. 176.

5 While he was away, Conrad wrote to the Galsworthys: 'Ford I guess is being now entertained in the skyscraping wigwams of the unpainted savages of the grrreat continent. I hope he'll find the war dances soothing to his nerves'. Letter of 14-15 August 1906: *Collected Letters*, ed. Frederick R. Karl and Laurence Davies, volume 3, Cambridge: Cambridge University Press, 1988, pp. 349-50. One could note that Salisbury Plain too has its skyscrapers, in their Druidic version. By the late 1930s Ford had lived periodically in New York for a decade, and had grown to like the verticality of its city-space. He 'astounded' himself by saying 'Gawd, Give us a skyscraper!' when visiting Denver, which he said 'pressed herself flat down to the plain ... as if in fear of the appalling catastrophes and panics that in those boundless solitudes the skies can produce'. See p. 221 of this volume.

6 See Hulme, *Speculations,* ed. Herbert Read, London: Kegan Paul, Trench, Trubner & Co, 1936, p. 86.

7 Ford, *The Soul of London: A Survey of a Modern City*, London: Alston Rivers, 1905 – henceforth *SL*; pp. 101-2.

8 See for example Ford's Preface to *Collected Poems*, London: Max Goschen, 1913, pp. 15-16. Camilla Haase, 'Serious Artists: The Relationship Between Ford Madox Ford and Ezra Pound', Dissertation: Harvard University, 1984, p. 206, asks which came first: the experience Pound retailed in *Gaudier-Brzeska*, New York: New Directions, 1974, pp 86-87, of coming out of a metro train in Paris – which was to go into his haiku 'In A Station of the Metro'; or his reading of Ford's rendering of the Shepherds Bush exhibition. Certainly Pound referred to Ford's impression in 'Mr Hueffer and the Prose Tradition in Verse': *Pound/Ford*, ed. Brita Lindberg-Seyersted, London: Faber, 1982, pp. 19-20. The two renderings indeed have much in common. But with two such close literary friends, questions of influence and priority are not always clear-cut. Yet Pound's Paris experience presumably came first, since he dates it 'Three years ago', and the essay reprinted in *Gaudier-Brzeska* first appeared as 'Vorticism', *Fortnightly Review*, 96, new series (1 Sept. 1914), [461]-71. This would place it in 1911. Anyway, the poem was first published in 'Contemporania', *Poetry*, 2:1 (April 1913), 1-12; whereas Ford's essays 'Impressionism – Some Speculations' (that were re-worked into the Preface) didn't appear until the August and September

issues of the same magazine. However, Pound might have known this earlier essay of Ford's on what he called 'the poetry of the normal', about the emotions aroused by seeing a crowd from the top of a bus outside the Tottenham Court Road Tube station: 'Literary Portraits.: XXIII. – The Year 1907', *Tribune* (28 Dec. 1907), 2.

9 Georg Simmel, 'Die Grosstadt und das Geistesleben', in *Die Grosstadt. Jahrbuch der Gehe-Stiftung* 9 (1903). Available in English translation in Kurt H. Wolff, *The Sociology of Georg Simmel*, Glencoe, Illinois: The Free Press, 1950. See Giovanni Cianci, 'Three Memories Of A Night: Ford's Impressionism In The Great London Vortex', in *Ford Madox Ford's Modernity*, ed. Robert Hampson and Max Saunders, Amsterdam and New York: Rodopi, 2003, pp. 47-58, on Simmel's relevance to Benjamin and Ford's Modernism.

10 P. A. Lawrence, *Georg Simmel: Sociologist and European*, Sunbury-on-Thames, Middlesex: Thomas Nelson, 1976, p. 35.

11 *Ibid.*, p. 35.

12 Michael Levenson puts this paradoxical effect very well, and rightly sees it as central to Fordian impressionism:

> Ford is so intent on limiting art to immediacy that the attitudes and sentiments of the artist are refined away; no trace of the artistic self remains; there is only what the self perceives. Nonetheless, as Ford continually insists, the work remains an individual and personal expression – simply in virtue of its constituting a distinct point of view, a single egoistic perspective. Ford's impressionism, then, is a *subjectivity in which the subject has disappeared.*

    A Genealogy of Modernism, Cambridge, Cambridge University Press, 1984, p. 119. Also see Caroline Patey, 'Londonscapes', in *Inter-relations: Conrad, James, Ford, and Others*, ed. Keith Carabine and Max Saunders, Lublin: Maria Curie-Skłodowska University/New York: Columbia University Press, 2003, pp. 53-67.

13 Philip Horne, 'Absent-Mindedness: Ford On The Phone', in *Ford Madox Ford's Modernity*, ed. Robert Hampson and Max Saunders, Amsterdam and New York: Rodopi, 2003, pp. 17-34. Ford, *A Call: A Tale of Two Passions*, with an Afterword by C. H. Sisson, Manchester: Carcanet, 1984, p. 156. Also see Sita Schutt, 'The Clitter of Small Sounds: Desire and the Audible in Ford Madox Ford's *A Call: The Tale of Two Passions*', *Ford Madox Ford and 'The Republic of Letters'*, ed. Vita Fortunati and Elena Lamberti, Bologna: CLUEB, 2002, pp. 123-7.

14 A. S. Byatt, on BBC Radio 3, 'Night Waves', 31 January 1996.

15 *The Soul of London*, pp. 120-3 of the Chapter 'London at Leisure'. Compare *Thus to Revisit*, London: Chapman and Hall, 1921, p. 160: 'the quality of attention is in this world so rarely demanded of one that, if into it we are coerced, it cannot but make better men, and better poets, of us'. For a more detailed discussion of this passage see Saunders, vol. 1, pp. 165-9.

16 E. M. Forster, *Howards End*, Abinger Edition, ed. Oliver Stallybrass, London: Arnold, 1973, p. 179.

17 'Literary Portraits – XXXIII.: Mr. Sturge Moore and "The Sea is Kind"', *Outlook*, 33 (25 April 1914), 559-60. Quoted by Joseph Wiesenfarth, 'The Ash-Bucket at Dawn: Ford's Art of Poetry', *Contemporary Literature*, 30:2 (Summer 1989), 240-62 (p. 245).

18 Preface, *Collected Poems* (1913), pp. 16-17.

19 We've already seen the description of Tottenham Court-road Tube Station from the article in 1907. One of his best poems, and best war poems, 'Antwerp', first published with illustrations by Wyndham Lewis, describes Belgian refugees haunting Charing Cross Station in London. 'Pon... ti... pri... ith', *La Revue des Idées* (Novembre 1918), 233-38, gives a haunting Impresssionist account of Waterloo station as soldiers are being seen off to the War: 'Clouds, shadows, pale faces, spirals of violet smoke, out of which loomed the iron columns supporting the station roof – enormous and as if deathly...': translation (from Ford's French) in Max Saunders, ed., Ford Madox Ford, *War Prose*, Manchester, Carcanet, 1999, p. 32. Also see *A Call*, with a crucial scene where lovers part on a station platform, the public space making it impossible for them to reveal their feelings; and compare the station parting (though a country station there) at the end of *The Good Soldier*. For a stimulating account of Ford and trains see Sara Haslam, 'Ford's Training', *Ford Madox Ford's Modernity*, ed. Robert Hampson and Max Saunders, Amsterdam and New York: Rodopi, 2003, pp. 35-46.

20 'The Three-Ten', *Songs From London*, London: Elkin Matthews, 1910, p. xii.

21 Ford's original title for the poem had been 'Castles in the Fog': *Daily Mail* Books Supplement (19 January 1907), 3.

22 Joseph Wiesenfarth, 'The Ash-Bucket at Dawn: Ford's Art of Poetry', *Contemporary Literature*, 30:2 (Summer 1989), 240-62.

23 This is why it doesn't quite work to say with Lowell that pre-Raphaelitism is 'always peeping through Ford's railway stations': Foreword to *Buckshee*: quoted by Wiesenfarth, p. 242n3. It is rather that he's moving in the other direction. In fact his attitude to Pre-Raphaelitism shifts between 1906/7 (when he published an anonymous article, 'The Pre-Raphaelite Brotherhood', *Quarterly Review*, 204 (April 1906), 352-74, and his monograph *The Pre-Raphaelite Brotherhood*, London, Duckworth, 1907) and 1911, when he published 'A 'Molested' Author: Characteristic Letter from Mr. F. M. Hueffer.: Two New Books', *Daily News*, (14 Jan 1911), 7, and *Ancient Lights*.

24 Ford, 'Introduction', *The Sisters* by Joseph Conrad, New York: Crosby Gaige, 1928, p. 3.

25 *Ibid.,* p. 16.

26 Ford to [G. F. J., though Ford gives the initials erroneously as 'E. C.'] Cumberlege of Oxford University Press, 27 Oct. 1936: *Letters of Ford Madox Ford,* ed. Richard M. Ludwig, Princeton: Princeton University Press, 1965, p. 264. See David D. Harvey, *Ford Madox Ford: 1873-1939: A Bibliography of Works and Criticism,* Princeton: Princeton University Press, 1962, pp. 83-4.

27 'Take Me Back to Tennessee', *Vogue* (New York) (1 Oct 1937), 104-05, 134, 138, 140. The typecript, entitled 'The Athens of the South', is at the Carl A. Kroch Library, Cornell University.

28 'Portraits of Cities: I. Boston', TM [carbon], 8 leaves; 'From Boston to Denver', TM [carbon], 19 leaves ; 'Portraits of Cities. Denver', TM [carbon], 7 leaves. Carl A. Kroch Library, Cornell University.

29 'In Praise of Garlic', *Harper's Bazaar* (New York) (Aug. 1937), 104, 126, 129.

FORD'S SADDEST JOURNEY:
LONDON TO LONDON 1909-1936

Brian Ibbotson Groth

The city figures prominently in Ford's writing throughout his career. On the very first page of his first novel, *The Shifting of the Fire*, he wrote 'the air was filled with a mighty hustling that drowned the distant rumble of traffic, never ceasing in this our city'.[1] His interest in the city never ceased; the subject fascinated him right to the end of his life. In what Ford's bibliographer David Harvey says was perhaps the last article he wrote for publication before his death ('A Paris Letter' of 1939), Ford describes the City of Light as it impressed itself upon him in that fateful year.[2]

Ford wrote about numerous cities in his lifetime but it was the book on London, the city of his childhood and youth, which became his first commercially and critically successful work for adults. *The Soul of London* was published in 1905, and dwells almost exclusively on the past and present in England's capital. The future is far less prominent. In 1909, however, Ford published a long essay entitled 'The Future in London' which, even though it appeared and was probably written several years after *The Soul of London*, could perhaps be described as the 'missing chapter' from the 1905 book, especially as it has the same impressionistic, discursive style that Max Saunders feels is typical of *The Soul of London*.[3] 'The Future in London' formed the final chapter in a two-volume work entitled *London Town Past and Present*. W. W. Hutchings wrote the remaining 1110 pages. 'Chapter' is something of a misnomer, however, since 'The Future in London' is really an essay quite independent of and different from the material that precedes it.

Over a quarter of a century later Ford took London as his subject for the last time. This was in a much shorter essay entitled 'London Re-visited', published in 1936 in the December issue of the *London Mercury*. When did he write this essay? Though a cautionary note must always be added when dealing with Fordian facts, biographical evidence largely supports his statement that: 'since July 1916 I have been domiciled elsewhere than in London. That makes just twenty years' (between then and writing the essay),[4] which seems to claim that 'London Re-visited' was written shortly before its publication in 1936. However, in 1936 Ford spent only one month in London, whereas at the very beginning of the essay he tells us he had been back in his childhood city for three months. This would place the writing somewhat earlier than Ford suggests. The three-month time span must refer to the period from March to May 1934 when he took his *de facto* wife Janice Biala to London. They were to return for a month in July 1936. Saunders dates the writing of 'London Re-visited' to around the time of this second visit (Saunders vol. 2, 497), and were it not for the three-month claim this latter stay would neatly confirm the period of 'just twenty years' mentioned in the essay. What probably happened was that Ford combined impressions from both visits and presented them as being from one stay in 1936: it was after all the truth of his impressions not the accuracy of facts that he was about.

Impressions of London vary widely in 'The Future in London' and 'London Re-visited'. The first essay often bubbles with *joie de vivre* about the city which is and is to come; prominent in the second are images of a capital lacking in energy mainly because its inhabitants have such a poor diet. Things get worse: in the dramatic conclusion to 'London Re-visited', Ford exhorts Londoners to abandon the city as if it were a sinking ship, such is his pessimistic view of its future. So between 1909 and 1936 Ford's impressions of his hometown and his predictions for its future shift from those associated with joy and hope, to despondency and despair. Describing this transition – from his view of the London of his youth to that of his old age – as 'the saddest journey' would therefore not seem entirely inappropriate.

As I now examine the two essays in some detail there is one obvious and overwhelming question. Why this major change in Ford's impressions and mood about London? There is more than one possible response. Ford's age could be a reason. He was in his mid-thirties at the time of writing 'The Future in London', but over sixty when 'London Re-visited' was published. Couple this with the pattern of his commercial and critical success. In 1909 Ford had enjoyed several years of excellent reviews and reasonable sales of his books, especially, as noted, *The Soul of London* and then *The Fifth Queen* and its two sequels (1906-8). The period from 1905 to 1909 had also been an extremely productive period for Ford. In all he published an impressive fourteen books during this time. Furthermore, by 1909, as Saunders observes, he was invigorated by his affair with Violet Hunt, whom he had started to see regularly from the summer of 1908, while he was also approaching the height of his powers as a writer (Saunders vol. 1, 289).

Compare this with the mid 1930s. Though he had achieved a measure of romantic happiness with Janice Biala, Ford's personal life was far from untroubled; he was at odds with his teenage daughter Julie and her mother Stella Bowen over Julie's upbringing. Moreover, Ford was periodically ill with gout and insomnia and had been having difficulty getting his work published since the Depression (Saunders vol. 2, 486, 498). His most recent books, *Henry for Hugh* (1934) and *Provence* (1935), had not even found English publishers in 1936.

Such personal and professional matters undoubtedly affected Ford's outlook, but I will argue that Ford's optimism in 1909 and his pessimism in 1936 are also closely tied to his unorthodox theory of history. As H. Robert Huntley has noted, this theory is best explicated in *The Spirit of the People* (1907), though references to it appear throughout his work right up to *Great Trade Route* (1937), at the end of his career.[5] In the *The Spirit of the People* Ford postulates that history is an evolutionary process in which 'the psychology of the civilised world changes – that the dominant types of the world alter with changing, if mysterious, alternations in the economic or social conditions of the races'.[6] Applying this concept of 'dominant types', Ford divides English history into three ages, each ruled by a special personality. Each type controlled and symbolized its age until, as Huntley has observed:

> With the inevitable circling of the years, each of Ford's historical-cultural ages, along with its dominant psychological type, was fated to give way before an ensuing historical epoch with a variant dominant type, a type better fitted to survive, even excel, in the altered historical milieu to follow. (Huntley 36)

And the Ford we meet in 'The Future in London' appears very much as one of the dominant types of his age who is not just surviving but excelling in England's capital. Even in the later essay, he was to describe himself in 1909 as a member of a class acknowledged by deference everywhere he went:

> You see […] in the nice easy old coat of a metropolis of our hot youths and vigorous manhoods you were the ruling class. Because you did not wear

reach-me-downs. You drifted about on your easy affairs all over that great, easy befogged space to a perfect hailstorm of yessir-nosirs. (*LR* 180)

The reader sees the city in 'The Future in London' through the eyes of an optimistic author who feels very much at ease and in control in his metropolis and who is confident enough to make predictions as to how it will be to live in London in the years to come. Ford shows himself to be a forecaster of a certain amount of accuracy, and in addition he alludes to topics that stamp him as something of an early environmentalist.

Yet at the very beginning the essay concerns itself more with London's past than its future. Without showing any of the regret and melancholy for the city's past that sometimes features in *The Soul of London*, Ford nonetheless notes that 'London is being so rapidly and so constantly "made over" that today there are parts of the town in which it is difficult to find one's way'.[7] He remembers maying as a child (i.e. collecting flowers for May Day) where the Olympia Exhibition Centre now stands and is mildly surprised by this. But with a characteristic and optimistic time shift he moves quickly into a consideration of the future, given that he 'may reasonably expect to see a London of three or four decades hence' (*FL* 1095). (An unconsciously poignant statement since he was to die exactly thirty years after 'The Future in London' was published, though in France not London.)

In considering the London to come Ford presents two of what he terms 'sections'. Today we might call them scenarios. One he calls 'the Future Probable' or 'the Future that seems likely', the other is 'the Future Utopian' or 'the Future that we should like' (*FL* 1095). He then goes on to say he will examine each scenario separately, but in somewhat typical Fordian fashion he quickly abandons that plan. What we get is almost exclusively 'the Future Utopian' or 'the Future we should like'. Or perhaps he should have said, 'the Future I should like', since most of what follows is really how Ford would like to see London in the future.

Dominating his examinations are the roads of the capital. If the medieval pilgrims believed that 'all roads lead to Rome', Ford believes the same now applies to London for he writes, 'London is great today because so many roads lead to it'. As if to underline how important he considers roads to be, he adds, 'the chief feature of a city's life is its roads' (*FL* 1095).

But in Ford's Utopian London of the future he also sees 'railroads', as he calls them, as the other lynchpin holding his transport vision together. Displaying the same fascination with trains that Sara Haslam has observed in some of his other works,[8] Ford envisages building 'an extremely efficient railroad with some ten to twenty lines of rails side by side'. Then as if one railroad is no longer enough, an apparently enraptured Ford immediately ups the number to 'four or five railroads radiating from Trafalgar Square'. And quantity would be matched by quality since he proposes that 'along the ten to twenty lines I should send the most efficient, the speediest possible trains. I should make travelling free, smooth and luxurious' (*FL* 1098).

This reference to fast, efficient and luxurious trains brings to mind the sumptuous first paragraph of *Some Do Not . . .* when the main character, Tietjens, a fellow member of Ford's 'ruling class', makes his fateful railway journey from London to the South Coast:

> The two young men – they were of the English public official class – sat in the perfectly appointed railway carriage. The leather straps to the windows were of virgin newness; the mirrors beneath the new luggage racks immaculate as if they had reflected very little; the bulging upholstery in its luxuriant, regulated curves was scarlet and yellow in an intricate, minute dragon pattern, the design of a geometrician in Cologne. The compartment smelt faintly, hygienically of admirable varnish; the train ran as smoothly – Tietjens remembered thinking – as British gilt-edged securities. It travelled fast; yet had it swayed or jolted over the rail joints, except at the curve between Tonbridge or over the points at Ashford where these eccentricities are expected and allowed for, Macmaster, Tietjens felt certain, would have written to the company. Perhaps he would even have written to the *Times*.[9]

Such is the breadth of Ford's vision and optimism, if not his grasp of financial and economic reality, that he proposes not only superb free railways but a veritable spectrum of other transportation as well:

> Along the railways I should set motorways, and, between hedges, moving platforms for pedestrians and those who needed exercise. I should clean out the Thames and set upon it huge, swift and fine express launches. (*FL* 1098)

Ford even predicts that this mass transport by road, rail and water might be supplemented by air travel. 'If we come to airships', he writes, they will glide 'over the Brighton road' (*FL* 1097). Not a bad piece of forecasting made in an essay probably written before Bleriot first flew the English Channel in July 1909.

The speed, comfort and cheapness of getting in and out of central London would mean, in Ford's vision, that people would rather live in places like Alresford, Hampshire though they may still work in London. And the fact that almost everyone would want to live outside the central areas would lead to vast tracts of abandoned residential areas being turned into parklands, galleries, restaurants and the like. A quick look around central London today and one might say that was a reasonably accurate prediction. On the other hand, the status of shops and shopping is only briefly touched upon and does not seem to be a major element in Ford's vision of Utopian London. He does, however, correctly forecast the demise of the street trader:

> 'Shopping' might become more centralised, or it might not; but because of the great distances, the baker shoving his hand-cart full of loaves, the obstructive milk-cart, the dilatory chemist's boy with his box-tricycle – all these slow-going and cumbersome things would vanish from the streets. I presume that either my housekeeper would order the day's supply over the telephone from Alresford, and the things would be blown through a pneumatic tube from the stores in South Kensington, or these stores would have a department in Alresford, in direct underground communication with the central offices. In either case we should be rid of the whole host of sutlers and camp followers who have no business to cumber the streets of our city. (*FL* 1101)

And while these people and what Ford calls their 'hangers-on' live their lives on the outer ring of the city, inner London would be given over to 'sensible people' who would spend their working hours in 'tall, white buildings that hold ten thousand workers apiece' and their breaks in hundreds of acres of 'parks, squares and open spaces' (*FL* 1101). Again, aside from the 'white' of the buildings and perhaps a substitution of 'tens' for 'hundreds' of acres, a pretty accurate forecast.

This then is how Ford describes what an ideal weekday would be like for him and other 'sensible people' in the future:

> My line of rails would make it possible for me to inhabit a bright, joyous little card-house, say in Alresford in Hampshire. I could lunch at my club, stroll in St James's Park and adore the pretty little ducks, return to Alresford to dress and dine, go to a theatre in the Strand and be in bed in Alresford by half-past twelve, much as I do in Kensington today. (*FL* 1100)

Besides improvements in transportation and changes in residential patterns, Ford proposes other measures that would help 'render my Great London of the Future the most attractive city in the world'.

Telephones would be made 'perfect' while the problems of noise, air and what might be termed equine pollution would also be solved (*FL* 1101).

This would be achieved by getting rid of the horse – a 'pestiferous nuisance in the city', petrol driven motor traffic, steam trains and steamships, and replacing them all with electrically driven trains, cars and vessels. Coal fires would also disappear, at least from inner London, as people moved out of the centre taking with them what he calls the 'domestic hearth'. At the same time factories, offices and 'large commercial buildings' would begin to use electric heat (*FL* 1101). Accurate as regards the demise of coal fires, though obviously totally off the mark in respect of petrol driven cars, even if Ford must be considered notable and praiseworthy in desiring their replacement. Remember this wish was expressed in 1909 when motoring was in its infancy.

Ford rounds off his essay with a summary of his Utopian London in the future. The metropolis would be a massive expanse of city stretching in what he envisages as a sixty-mile radius from Dover to Oxford with a 'huge, light, white, inner city filling the greater part of this shallow bowl that is London'. To realize this vision 'London – Great London – would have to be a place not of seven, but seventy millions of imperially-minded people' (*FL* 1102). During the week the workers would pour into this inner city using the vast networks of railroads that would be built. Journeys would be free and quite quick. He envisioned, for example, a trip from Oxford to inner London taking about half-an-hour on what he called 'my non-stop, monorail expresses' (*FL* 1103). This, he says, was about the same length of time it took for him to get from Hammersmith to the City. Furthermore, travellers would become politer and more courteous, Ford thought, since he had found less rowdyness when people travelled in larger groups. Thus there would be 'an immense gain in what is called manners' (*FL* 1106). English football supporters have put this prediction sorely to the test!

People would live outside the inner city, which should not be called 'the suburbs', since Ford thought the prefix 'sub' demeaned and subordinated these residential areas by portraying them as 'temporary shelters for gallant spirits'. Instead he preferred the German term *Vorstadt* for the 'outer ring that greets the traveller before he reaches the heart of the town'. And this vast *Vorstadt* ought to be a garden city. In this way Londoners, who Ford felt largely lacked pride in their capital, would be able to embrace what he called 'an awakened corporate spirit' (*FL* 1109).

Ford's optimism permeates 'The Future in London', especially in respect of his Utopian vision being realized. He really did seem to think that his 'Great London of the Future' could be turned into 'the most attractive city in the world' and made into what he terms 'the Ideal City that all the populations of the world would flock to' (*FL* 1099). The prediction regarding London being the world's most attractive city and an ideal one would probably be disputed by many today. On the other hand, Ford was right in forecasting that England's capital would become a multicultural metropolis. Furthermore, his use of the words 'flock to' gives the prediction great contemporary relevance since one of the key and divisive issues of the British General Election of May 2005 was precisely the size of immigrant populations that should be allowed to enter the United Kingdom. And it is an issue that British politicians and society in general will continue to grapple with in the years to come.

However, despite his strongly optimistic mood in 'The Future in London', Ford concludes his essay on a cautionary note with words that must again be said to ring every bit as true and relevant today as they did in 1909:

> For, after all, the Future of London is very much in our hands. We are the tyrants of the men to come; where we build roads, their feet must tread; the traditions we set up, if they are evil, our children will find it hard to fight against; if for want of vigilance we let beautiful places be defiled, it is they who will find it a hopeless task to restore them. (*FL* 1110)

The overarching optimism of 'The Future in London' is the voice of Edwardian Ford, confident member of the 'ruling class', speaking in the age of *belle époque*, an age shaped and controlled, he felt, by like-minded 'sensible people'. Yet what he hoped and believed about London, its ruling class, and its future was not to endure. In 'London Re-visited', the pendulum of his impressions had swung very much the other way.[10]

Now it is the views of Ford the 1930s expatriate rather than the optimistic Londoner of a younger century that dominate the writing. England's capital no longer appears to him as the 'Ideal City', but 'our poor old charlady amongst metropolitan cites'. It is the 'lower middle classes' who now rule and they define not only England's capital, but also the new era throughout the world (*LR* 177). The old rulers have in Ford's unorthodox view of history been swept aside and new dominant psychological types are in control. The happy, confident Ford who strode around the capital before the Great War and made optimistic predictions about its future, was, he now feels, a case of mistaken identity:

> You see ... in the nice easy old coat of a metropolis of our hot youths and vigorous manhoods you were the ruling class [...] I don't, then, know what claim I had to be called ruling class – I or the people with whom I drifted about. (*LR* 180)

As he has shown in other works, notably the *Parade's End* tetralogy, Ford believed that this pre-war ruling class had been displaced during the Great War by a debilitated, poorly nourished lower-middle class: 'Well, that is all gone and the real lower middle-class, as it were, naked and unashamed, has the ball of the world in its hands' (*LR* 180).

Ford felt that this dominance of the unaspirational, unhealthy lower-middle class in the thirties was everywhere to be seen, not only in London but also in other major large cities he was familiar with such as New York, which he had recently visited, Paris and Buenos Aires. He felt there was uniformity in the architecture of new buildings, the goods offered in shops and the way people dressed. Even the film posters outside cinemas seemed the same. And though the posters in London largely advertised American films, Ford does not adhere to what seems to have been a widely held belief even then that Britain's capital was being Americanised. In fact he holds that if the United States had not existed the situation would have been exactly the same, for it is the tastes of the new rulers rather than their nationalities that have determined the changing appearance of London and so many other cities.

A primary reason for the parlous state of the new rulers, in whom Ford clearly lacked confidence, was, he thought, poor diet. The state of the green vegetables and fruit laid out for sale in the London markets causes him special concern. The first sentence of the essay conveys these worries: 'The quality, the age, the condition, the appearance of the green vegetables and fruits displayed for sale in the London markets, and their paucity and lack of variety, are appalling' (*LR* 177). He goes on to maintain and lament that 80% of the food Londoners eat is from cans and that which is not canned is treated with dangerous preservatives. He compares this unfavourably to the market of his *provençal* home which displays 'sixty-eight varieties of vegetables and salads and nineteen kinds of fruits – each one of them not two hours out of the earth or off the tree' (*LR* 183).

Ford wrote this essay at around the same time he was espousing the merits of the 'small producer' and the philosophy of the kitchen garden in works such as *Provence* (1935) and *Great Trade Route* (1937). And it shows. In these two books, widely regarded as his best work after the *Parade's End* tetralogy, Ford described himself as 'a man with an inspired mission'.[11] This mission was to persuade readers to support and adopt the frugal, altruistic and healthy life of the Mediterranean small producer because 'it is that spirit that could yet save the Western World'.[12] In a world he felt was increasingly being dominated by arid, selfish materialism and acquisitiveness – traits he summed up as 'the eternal nothingness of Northern ideals' (*GTR* 256) – Ford believed that 'only the Estate of the Small Producer [...] can radically restore the face of the World to sanity and health' (*GTR* 174-5).

So the Ford of 'London Re-visited' felt he had the solution for the new rulers if only they would embrace it. In his opinion the portents were not good, however, and consequently these rulers, and by extension the countries they ruled, were at great risk. The lack of fresh vegetables was creating a passivity that was dangerous: 'if they do not have a sufficiency of fresh, real, green vegetables, their digestions must suffer, and so their brains ... and their nerveless fingers must fall from the plough-handles of affairs' (*LR* 183).

Though Ford's justification for his fears may seem mildly humorous and somewhat quirky, there was nothing funny about the reason for his disquiet and fear. There were, he felt, much more sinister dominant types from the lower middle-classes eager and able to assume control if the present poorly nourished rulers weakened and their spirit waned. These were the fascists led by a diet-conscious German Chancellor:

> Mr. Hitler – don't forget that – like the rhinoceros, the gorilla, the bull, the stallion, and all the fiercest beasts of the world, is a VEGETARIAN[13] ... whilst London's vegetable supplies are the worst in the world. (*LR* 183)

Emphasising the import of his dire warning, Ford repeats it two paragraphs later, 'yes, Mr. Hitler *is* a vegetarian ... and a member of the lower Middle Classes who have inherited the earth and the power thereof, at that' (*LR* 183).

It is not by chance that Ford singles out fascism and its German leader as a major concern. As Saunders has noted, from the time he met and fell in love with the Jewish-American painter Janice Biala in 1930,

Ford's political views had shifted to the Left although neither of them was a communist. Ford thought both communism and fascism were 'mass manias'. He became especially concerned about the fate of the Jews in Europe and wrote to newpapers supporting Jewish refugees from fascism and spoke out forcibly against the fascist dictators.[14]

Nothing in 'The Future in London' and 'London Re-visited' better demonstrates the development of Ford's thought on these subjects than the conclusion of each essay. Though in 1909 the young Ford warns against the dangers of tyranny and evil, he feels the future of London can be shaped in a positive way because he trusts the ruling class to which he belongs. They will indeed create the 'Ideal City that all the populations of the world would flock to' (*FL* 1099).

However, by 1936 the author despairs and can only counsel flight from the city towards the warm south: 'down to the land where blooms the olive flower', there to be welcomed 'by a population as kindly as themselves' (*LR* 183). In an extraordinary last few paragraphs of 'London Re-visited', Ford gives up exhorting England's new ruling class and trying to save them. Instead he turns to London's 'two-million-fold' children and urges his companion, 'the depressed expatriate from Manhattan' (more specifically his partner Janice Biala) to assume the role of someone akin to a latter-day Pied Piper. She is to stand atop Primrose Hill, fiery cross in hand, and urge the children of London, and thus its future, to abandon their city. This is the same city he had said he hoped the whole world would flock to in 'The Future in London'. Now the capital's young are told to flee and leave 'the Ruling Classes and the Mother of Parliament Front Benches for Mr. Hitler to plunder and play with' (*LR* 184).

A final telling and sad comparison between the two essays concerns his views on Germany. In 'The Future in London' Ford looks to Germany to enhance London and its future. He hopes that all the architectural improvements he proposes, many of which are modeled on German cities, will instill in Londoners 'an awakened corporate spirit – the spirit of which I have spoken as existing in almost every German city – how much more beneficent that would be' (*FL* 1109).

Yet, when he came to write 'London Re-visited', Germany and the culture of its people were no longer something for Londoners to admire and copy. On the contrary, Germany and its fascist ruler were putting London at terrible risk and represented the supreme danger to its future. Hueffer had definitely become Ford in more than name only.

NOTES

1   Ford Madox Ford, *The Shifting of the* Fire, London: T. Fisher Unwin, 1892, p. 1.
2   David Dow Harvey, *Ford Madox Ford: 1873-1939: A Bibliography of Works and Criticism*, Princeton: Princeton University Press, 1962, p. 270. The article was published in the Winter 1939 number of the *Kenyon Review*.
3   Max Saunders, *Ford Madox Ford: A Dual Life*, 2 vols, Oxford: Oxford University Press, 1996 – hereafter cited as Saunders; vol. 1, p. 197.
4   Ford Madox Ford, 'London Re-visited', *The London Mercury* (Dec. 1936) – hereafter cited as *LR*; p. 177.
5   H. Robert Huntley, *The Alien Protagonist of Ford Madox Ford*, Chapel Hill, CL: The University of North Carolina Press, 1970 – hereafter cited as 'Huntley'; p. 36.
6   Ford Madox Ford, *The Spirit of the People*, London: Alston Rivers, 1907, p. 63.
7   Ford Madox Ford, 'The Future in London', *London Town Past and Present,* vol. 2, London: Cassell and Company, 1909 – hereafter cited as *FL*; p. 1094.
8   Sara Haslam, 'Ford's Training', *Ford Madox Ford's Modernity*, ed. Robert Hampson and Max Saunders, Amsterdam: Rodopi, 2003, pp. 35-46.
9   Ford Madox Ford, *Some Do Not . . .*, London: Duckworth, 1924, p. 9.
10 Ford's changing views of London are also discussed by Elena Lamberti on p. 141 of this volume.
11 Ford Madox Ford, *Great Trade Route*, New York: Oxford University Press, 1937 – hereafter cited as *GTR*; p. 67.
12 Ford Madox Ford, *Provence*, Philadelphia: J. B. Lippincott, 1935, p. 257.
13 The question of whether Hitler was a vegetarian has been much debated over a considerable period of time. There are countless pages on the Internet discussing the subject. The *New York Times* of 30 May 1937 reported somewhat incongruously that Hitler was a vegetarian 'although he occasionally relishes a slice of ham'. *Hitler's Table* Talk, New York: Enigma Books, 2000, pp. 204, 230, 231, 442, 443, 572, 640, records numerous purportedly verbatim conversations with Hitler in the period from 5 July 1941 to 30 November 1944 in which he claims to be a vegetarian. In another conversation Hitler is reported as saying: 'One may regret living in a period when it's impossible to form an idea of the shape the world of the future will assume. But there's one thing I can predict to eaters of meat, that the world of the future will be vegetarian!' (*Hitler's Table Talk*, p. 125). He could almost have been quoting Ford.
14 Saunders, vol. 2, 371.

CITY BURLESQUE:
THE PLEASURES OF PARANOIA IN FORD'S
MISTER BOSPHORUS AND THE MUSES[1]

Colin Edwards

Christopher Tietjens takes his opportunities to play at being God when on active service in the trenches. In *No More Parades*, he had already shown an uncanny ability to spot the detail of things – supplies, food, tents, or else the individual needs of the men with their 'unliterary hands' presenting their 'slow, ungainly' bodies, with their papers, for inspection.[2] It is when the *strafe* begins, in *A Man Could Stand Up –,* that he is seen to take on a more active role, as Saviour.

If Christopher's superhuman traits are apt to annoy more people than his wife, Sylvia, Christopher's own self-image is infected – blessedly – with a sense of comic detachment, and this ironic, distancing quality may redeem him for many readers. For example, this passage is taken from just before the *strafe*:

> He reclined, on his right shoulder, feeling like some immense and absurd statue: a collection of meal-sacks done in mud, with grotesque shorts revealing his muddy knees. . . . The figure on one of Michael Angelo's Medici tombs. (*PE* 636)

Very soon, however, his role in the collapsed trenches is to bring Lance-Corporal Duckett out of an early grave (his 'face […] black, but asleep…. As if Valentine Wannop had been reposing in an ash-bin'; *PE* 642). This is only one of several premonitions for the reader that Valentine and he will meet again. Tietjens is unable to stop himself 'willing her to submit to his will' (*PE* 636).

The experience of the war is one both of paranoia and of a kind of *Amor Fati* in Tietjens: both of these emotions are discovered from a world of responsibilities in which he feels deeply, physically immersed. One slip of his pen can be an immense mischance for a certain Private 197394, Thomas Johnson (*PE* 332). Or, indeed, for Tietjens himself.

But on the whole, Christopher doesn't leave too much to chance. Until Sylvia arrives in person, France may be said to help him to build up in his mind the kind of 'parallel universe' that has recently been diagnosed by David Trotter, inside the minds of a number of Ford and his contemporaries' heroes – only some of whom use this device so as to be godlike! Essentially, these are fictional universes of escape, or ways of coping by means of a new form of 'paranoid modernism': 'In this parallel universe, neither wealth, nor status, nor nationality, nor gender has any meaning *in itself*. Instead, paranoid symmetry adjusts the degree of fantasized grandeur to the degree of fantasized persecution'.[3]

Certainly, there is a highly theatrical construction of grandeur and professional esteem in the relationships of Captain Tietjens and the 'Other Ranks', as they await 'the *strafe* that Brigade reported to be coming in.... Twenty-seven minutes, by now!' (*PE* 565). Although 'completely mysterious' to each other in the mass, they will, however, give a 'glimpse of a passionate desire' now and then (*PE* 570). Depersonalisation and uncanny intimacy are both part of the paranoid universe of the trenches: '. . . you knew that they watched you eternally and knew the minutest gestures of your sleep – you got some sort of indication as to how they regarded you: "You are a law unto yourself!"' (*PE* 570).

If, as David Trotter argues, our sense of the inner worth of professionalism is occasionally confirmed by our coming into proximity with the slovenliness of its very opposite (one thinks of the role played by the shell-shocked McKechnie, gazing 'into Tietjens' eyes like a forlorn mistress fit to do a murder, with a sort of wistful incredulity of despair'; *PE* 574), there is – as I shall hope to demonstrate – an allied but quite contrary coexistence of paranoia with pleasure itself, in Ford's writing of the 1920s.[4]

The flip-side, as it were, to paranoia and disgust arrives, in *Parade's End*, in the form of another set of theatrical gestures: cockney gestures which are near to city comedy, but which I will here call 'City Burlesque'.

When Tietjens grants his men a future holiday – promising to 'give every man of you a ticket for Drury Lane next Boxing Day' – the *camaraderie* and the dramatic resonance of that personal gesture are felt through to the end of *A Man Could Stand Up* –; especially through Valentine's eyes during the tumultuous *finale* at Lincoln's Inn, the celebration of Armistice (*PE* 572). Ford choreographs the sequence without losing Valentine's sense of its grotesque ingredients (she even thinks that Aranjuez's eyes are 'soft, like a deer's' before she notices that one of them is missing; *PE* 671). For all that, this is a moment where Valentine's barriers against public participation, including her awareness of being seen as 'Tietjens' mistress' and 'Friend of friend Hun's', are overcome: 'All around them the world was roaring' (*PE* 672). It is highly significant that the two lovers are treated as, in some sense, being public property, to the point of having almost pantomime roles assigned to them, and that their reunion is made a part of a quite vulgarly unceremonious celebration:

> No one like Fat Man Tietjens. He lounged at the door; easy; benevolent. In uniform now. That was better. An officer, yelling like an enraged Redskin, dealt him an immense blow behind the shoulder blades. He staggered, smiling into the centre of the room. An officer gently pushed her into the centre of the room. She was against him. Khaki encircled them. They began to yell and to prance, most joining hands. Others waved the bottles and smashed underfoot the glasses. (*PE* 673)

Ford was, later, to write that the time of his departure from England (a home-leaving that was to become permanent) and arrival in post-War France in late 1922 was the moment in which his thoughts of writing about the War – 'on an immense scale' – really germinated.[5] Written in both countries, between October 1922 and June 1923, *Mister Bosphorus and the Muses* might be viewed as a text which looks backwards: Ford's 'Last of England', rather than a text opening new perspectives. I want to argue that the atmosphere of City spaces, and songs, which dominate both early and late sections of its text, allows Ford to exhibit the Janus-face which Max Saunders has diagnosed throughout Ford's writing, within the medium of some bold and extraordinary theatrical devices.[6] Ford adopts an unusually public set of idioms in which to ventilate his more private anxieties. At nearly all points, *Mister Bosphorus* embraces an historical set of perspectives: the modernism of the 'Cinematograph Effects, and Many Other Novelties' in its sub-title is clearly offset by its quainter description as a 'Variety Entertainment'. In several respects, *Mister Bosphorus* is both of, and about, the City culture that its writer's paranoid imposture wishes to dramatise. Yet, partly by its very theatricality, Ford puts the distance between himself and that culture into a spin. It is a giddying vortex of pleasure and distaste that is to be produced: one in which the 'City' mindset is renounced, whilst simultaneously being claimed, as his own.

The series of dissolving – at times overlapping – scenarios which Bosphorus, the dreamer at the centre of this long stage-poem, constructs, offers suggestive parallels with Tietjens' 'Rag-Time Army' and the comic-paranoid entanglements and escapes which beset him, particularly in the trenches (*PE* 571). Centrally, it is the demotic language of the City, the world of London's popular entertainment – specifically, its use of the songs and repartee of the Music Halls – that I shall be focusing on: moreover, it is the common ground of spoken utterance – impromptu, unliterary, slang – held between the dreamer and 'his' worlds, which allows the hero both to be 'of' those worlds, and also – uncannily – bigger than them.

Certainly, *Mister Bosphorus* presents scenes in which everything except for our eponymous hero himself regularly changes shape. Whereas he will change only his clothes – slipping from the 'workhouse uniform' (used for the Utopia of Act the Third, for example), into an unlikely 'bedraggled white-satin costume as of a Watteau shepherd' for Act the Fourth – his fellow actors actually effect bold shifts in their stage *personae* (*MrB* 71, 95). His Southern and Northern Muses only belatedly identify themselves as such in Act the Third, having posed as aristocratic sponsors and rivals for Bosphorus's affections. Northern Muse ('Duchess' or 'Lady Claris de Beevil') figures as the dark, and colder, side of a warmer, more promiscuous, Southern Muse (Clarissa), but this does not stop them, at this mid-point in the 'variety entertainment', from quarrelling:

> DUCHESS: [...] poets are a fickle race, indiscriminating in their amours [. . . .] No, it is not unusual, that poets should turn from the great to the apparently inattractive.
> CLARISSA: A ... h ... em!
> DUCHESS: As the dog to his vomit, my dear Clarissa!
> CLARISSA: *Touchée, Madame.* (*MrB* 78)

Bosphorus seems to figure as passive instigator and object of other characters' personal and aesthetic differences, and is rarely given much of a chance to assert himself in the present moment. Ordered, in Act the Third, to lecture to the Orthodox Intelligentsia, by the Keeper of the Utopian State, he is immediately relegated to the back of the stage. He is always defiant, but – alas! – barely heard: 'LABOUR MASTER: ... whilst the State exists, I, its servant, am its loyal servant. I therefore do my best to have all lecturers – and in particular this 34241 – interrupted to the point of inaudibility' (*MrB* 79). Clad in his 'workhouse uniform' and reduced to the label 'voice 34241' for this ironic-Utopian portion of his odyssey, it is not as if

Bosphorus is lacking in good reasons to be paranoid. The Labour Master even goes so far as to order his troops of Orthodox-Intelligentsia-Censors to 'seize and bind' their lecturer, for he is to be 'shot at dawn'! (*MrB* 82). Bosphorus, however, is immune to the 'little experiment' of this militant age of prose (*MrB* 82). He will give his lecture (and so Act the Third begins) in his sleep, if necessary: – it is as if he is oblivious to the jump/cut of his transposition out of Act the Second, where he had acted in a more exalted role as Odyssean poet-sage.

Still, if it is the lot of the poet to fall upon hard times in this lapsed age of prose, he appears to be aware that he is the carrier of symbolic capital.[7] Poetry may have taken 'refuge in prose' (and indeed he recognises that the 'punishment of all poets is death') and yet Bosphorus's vision is stoical and insists on the survival of values deeper than those borne by the shape-changing Muses who quarrel over him upon the Forestage (*MrB* 86). His lecture isn't to be completely drowned out, and indeed it is clearly the audience which is being addressed when Bosphorus speaks with the passion of poet-legislator:

> VOICE of 34241:   Ugly, sordid, little, of imbecile and discreditable ambitions and aims! Who amongst you has a thought he would not blush to own! But yet, humanity! And the distillation of you – as the distillation from a mash of crushed grapes is wine – the distillation of you is poetry. (*MrB* 86)

The stage device of a 'cinematograph curtain', used to represent certain institutional or authority-structures from which Bosphorus himself is excluded, is made somewhat clearer to the reader by the beautiful woodcut designs of Paul Nash which accompany the text (*MrB* 39). In Act II, Scene 1, it had been the square edifice (the 'packing case'; *MrB* 24) of the British Museum which loomed over Bosphorus, as if to demarcate the zone of High Culture from which the indigent Bosphorus (sitting on a workhouse bench) was, as it were, cast out.[8] And although, in II.2, a naked Female Chorus ('impersonations of Athis') at first seemed to offer Bosphorus the sort of homecoming that any wayfaring poet might dream about, the first half of the poem is decidedly about loss (*MrB* 54). As the Act III stage directions indicate, the sign on the arbour through which he is to make his next 'escape' makes clear that Bosphorus isn't nearly home yet: the place belongs to 'Master and Officials only … Beware of Dog!'

(*MrB* 53). Even Cerberus (the dog) understands its limitations in this respect.

Poignantly, the position of the dreaming Bosphorus is to 'own' the territory – and the actors in it – but without actually being recognized as Godlike. In Act II, Hercules himself may be impressed by Bosphorus's prowess with the ninefold chorus, but he still can't help it that 'Poor, great Bosphorus ... [has] ... fallen on evil days' (*MrB* 63). It would appear that the 'classic modes' of II.2 represent only a portion of the great march of Bosphorus, inexorably downhill towards the Prose Age.

The longer trajectory of the four-act piece is – avowedly – to attempt to restore Bosphorus to his Southern Muse. However, the first phase of the action runs distinctly on the theme of losses and pains. All too briefly, and to the annoyance of the (ninefold) Male Chorus, Bosphorus allows himself to linger upon the different physical manifestations of his teeming (and 'Classic') Muse. Yet the wistful subtext which pursues Bosphorus's megalomaniac dance across literary culture, in Act II, is that he and his muses are both subject to mortality:

> BOSPHORUS: From Athis' lips my vagrant Muse disporting
> Led me to Glaucis. Then from Glaucis' lips
> I sipped the nectar; marvelled at her hips;
> Her wheat-hued hair; her chiton's snowy hues;
> And Glaucis had the tribute of my Muse! (*MrB* 58)

Along with sexual desire, pain, loss and mortality are indeed prominent *motifs* in the discussions between Bosphorus and his seductive Southern Muse. By the time these two lovers do make their final dream-flight to the golden sands of the timeless Mediterranean, Bosphorus has not only been through spectacular stage-rites of ageing (in a white night-gown, he is to become the *commedia dell'arte* figure of absurdity and second-childhood, Pantaloon) but also has to 'participate' in the solemn rites of his own interment in Westminster Abbey, having been 'stage-flattened' by a Rolls Royce! His night-garments now become a shroud. Amongst his mourners, we find: '*Publican, Pawnbroker, Seedy Individuals; Errand-boys, Prostitutes from Leicester Square attracted by minute gun-fire; Members of Middle-class ...*' (*MrB* 117).

With his use of an 'Harlequinade' and 'Transformation' scene in Act IV, it is as if Ford's artistic *antennae* are picking up some of the very newest ingredients of modernist dance-styles, to put alongside his use of 'variety entertainment'. 1920s Paris is grafted upon the stage/cinematographic backdrop, representing the 'London Fog Humour'. Some of this newness is arguably nearer to 1916 (nearer to the 'Ballet Réaliste' of Jean Cocteau, Diaghilev and Stravinsky) but there is, possibly, a foreshadowing of the sort of cinematic delirium shortly to be offered by René Clair, and others in the post-War group of *Surréalistes.*[9]

But what underscores all of this experimental engagement with the New, from Act I to the final stages of the piece, is the language and the stage iconography of the City of London itself: specifically, popular Variety entertainment and the Music Hall tradition. Here is the 'City Burlesque': forms of art that are apt to inspire shuddering embarrassment as well as uncanny recognition and desire. None of these emotions is to be disdained by the would-be (or has-been) hero, Bosphorus. Rather, 'City Burlesque' becomes the natural concomitant of his 'godlike' quest.

From his 'workhouse bench', in Act II, the poet-dreamer Bosphorus identifies himself with the culture of popular entertainment. The image of the British Museum on the back 'cinematograph curtain' is soon replaced by an erratic silent-screen inscription from a proletarian hand:

> How
> Poets Live
> FEAT
> Uring Mr. BOSPHORUS and
> MUSA POORE
> (Rotten Films Ltd.) (*MrB* 40)

Our hero is not abashed by this: neither is he shocked by the New, nor even cross with the 'preliminary stutterings' of the screen image (*MrB* 43). He is, indeed, seated with his back to the audience, so that, looking (as it were) over his shoulder, we realise that we are 'seeing' projections from his unconscious mind. The seated Bosphorus will shortly, however, enter into his screened dream, a kind of cradle-to-grave mock-epic of his own life. The stage directions for the film *scenario* are as follows:

> A London street in an obviously poor quarter. Old, small houses. Shops beneath. Two shops shown, preternaturally large. One is a pawnbroker's, the three golden balls protruding; the other an undertaker's, coffin-lids standing

outside. The film shifts; pawnbroking establishment vanishing, the undertaker's seems to jump, rather unsteadily, at the spectator. (*MrB* 42)

The companion, or stooge, who sits with Bosphorus is '*An aged pauper – Bulfin by name [who] hobbles to sit beside Mr. Bosphorus*' (*MrB* 40). Bulfin is sceptical about the quality of their entertainment, until the two of them are drawn nearer to the screen world.

Bosphorus urges Bulfin to play along with his screen-devices, one of which is to turn Bulfin, very shortly, into the figure of a critic. In short order, poor Bulfin becomes 'split' into the nine-fold chorus of critics. Bosphorus is sanguine about the outcome, and prepares to sing:

> B[OSPHORUS]:   Verses all heard before
> Make up our great tradition of to-day!
> Pew-opener you! To the piano I!
> P. BULFIN:
> 'Ere wats-all-this! I've got a nuniform!
> A goleliced cap n little flashing lantern!
> Wheredyor armonium come from?
> B.:   The poet's mind
> In a fine frenzy rolled....
> P. BULFIN: It's not so bad!
> A job I've often wanted! Showin gents
> N cuddly females into empty seats.
> Gord bless ther luvvin wies. (*MrB* 44)

Whilst the two prepare for their initiation into cockney screen-stardom, the *mise-en-scène* becomes a little less misty:

> Hurried passengers with improbable gift of speed. A policeman's back; improbably white-gloved hands folded behind him. An eminently, even improbably respectable Widow, crêpe bonnet, white apron, passes alone across picture. She has on her arm a large basket; basket is filled with paper scrolls. From foreground starts forward Picture-Bosphorus towards Widow. There intervene a number of Young Men: they wear black morning coats, lightish, improbably elegant trousers and light grey Trilby hats; they twirl incipient moustaches and regard Picture-Bosphorus agitatedly. (*MrB* 43-4)

After this choreographed action, '*The screen* exhibits legend: A HARD PURCHASER. WIDOW TRIES TO SAVE HOME BY PARTING WITH VALUED TREASURES (*MrB* 45).' The 'valued treasures' come from the 'basket ... filled with paper scrolls': they are, of course, Bosphorus' writings, his artist's literal and symbolic capital, and we are about to witness the scene of his humiliation, when they don't sell....

Using the kind of *tableau* so central to the art of the Victorian stage, it would seem that Ford is playing with – even celebrating – the idea of a stylistic hybridity. More than this, he constructs a world without a settled register of class consensus, in use of language and manners. Arguably, he allows a combination of stage gesture and stuttering film-sequence to drain away from the piece the idea of there being either a settled context to, or a settled audience participating in, Bosphorus's dream-universe. It's as if the artist – in forgetting to use the professional rules – is using his Widow-Muse so as to achieve a sort of enjoyably tawdry pathos. Bosphorus is allowed to bask in a misty atmosphere of stunned pleasure, tantalised by the fake grandeur of his own screen-humiliation: '*Legend again:* HIS AUTOGRAPH POEM SCORNED' (*MrB* 46). Meanwhile, from his workhouse bench, Bosphorus's film-commentary has shuttled, unevenly, sonorously, between the idioms of Tennyson and Patmore, and 'the seamier sides of spacious times':

> My cradle came from the pawnshop; my obsequies
> Perforce will be inexpensive; public-houses
> I never entered much; at times; at times!
> My mother used to get my pre-natal Stout
> From that establishment, which lends it interest. (*MrB* 43)

Along with the drip-drip effect of mild, and heavy, bathos, the text is punctuated with little gestures (particularly via the stage directions) in the stolid manner of professional incompetence and forgetfulness: '(*The screen* performs another Close-up or whatever is the technical term. ...)' (*MrB* 44) – even as Bosphorus attempts to smooth over any deficiencies by his 'vamping' at the piano and the 'throaty' accompaniment of his singing:

> Poets who cannot sell their manuscripts
>   Must Hope! Hope! Hope!
> Poisons are costly and to hang yourself
>   Needs rope! Expensive rope!
> Summer's flow'rs are coming and for rhyme they give
>   much scope!
> So! If there's no money in sham Tennyson
>   Try Pope! Pope! Pope! (*MrB* 46)

(The above is, of course, to be delivered with immaculate 'throatiness', to the staccato strains of 'Pack up your troubles'!)

What, then, is the real purpose of all this *burlesque* extravagance? And with what deeper purpose, and artistic intent, is it that Ford – as Max Saunders has argued – turns 'his near-paranoid anxiety about an orchestrated obliteration of his reputation into a celebratory fantasy of escape and regeneration' (Saunders, vol. 2, 124)...? No-one can miss the touches of autobiography: Bosphorus's ill-fortune at the pawnbroker's is surely a rueful, comic re-casting of the rejection of Ford's *The Marsden Case* – by Knopf, Brentano's, Holt, Scribner's, and Dodd Mead – before Duckworth took it, as Ford and his family left for France, in November, 1922 (Saunders, vol. 2, 124). We might, indeed, start to ask whether the figure of Bosphorus can be taken as an incarnation of the 'joker' in Ford himself. Such a figure is, I believe, to be met with, occasionally, in Ford's own letters.

There is, for example, the delightful teasing of the celebrated agent Pinker, to whom Ford once failed to sell the literal (and no doubt symbolic) capital of his own country Utopia, his smallholding:

> My famous pedigree pigs ANNA and ANITA, 344702 and 344704 in the herd book of the Large Black Pig Society cost a deuce of a lot to keep; but when, as they certainly will, they take prizes at the Lincoln Show I will stand you a champagne dinner. I could supply you with February hatched ducks at 96/- the dozen. You never seem to reply with any enthusiasm to my offers of farm produce. Why is this?[10]

Similarly – from 1921 – we can see a shadow of Bosphorus in the way in which Ford writes to a friend (Flint) about his costume-changes for dining at Coopers Cottage, in Sussex: 'Bring an old dinner jacket with you if it's not too much of a bore. I go about in filth all day & put on a cricket shirt & very old dress things at night – not for swank but because I have only one other respectable suit...'.[11]

And yet, I believe there is a *gravitas* held within the various costume-changes and stage-impersonations of our Mister Bosphorus, which make him quite other than simply a mouthpiece for some of Ford's real-life views and attitudes. We can't assume that *Mister Bosphorus* was written specifically, and only, in order to register Ford's personal musings about leaving England, even if the work did come to be influenced by Ford's plans to travel, with Stella Bowen and daughter Julie, to a climate less inhospitable. Retrospect makes it all too tempting, thus, to see Ford's life's events alone as dictating the victory of the Southern Muse over the colder Northern-Muse-Duchess. It can't be that simple.

Rather, there is a more interesting, internal dream-logic to be discovered in the way in which sluggish, lecherous Bosphorus is allowed to dictate the course of the poem's events. His slumberous inattention, or at least his air of *désinvolture* in the face of the pantomime-like escalation of events, is in fact too suggestive of the mannerisms adopted by Tietjens during the interval before and during bombardment in the trenches, for the coincidence not to become noticeable:

> He did not know what to do, what he ought to do by the book. He knew what he would do. He would stroll about along those deep trenches. Stroll. With his hands in his pockets [. . . .] He would say contemplative things as the time dragged on.... A rather abominable sort of Time, really. . . . But that would introduce into the Battalion a spirit of calm [. . . .] (*PE* 576)

It is a manner of unperturbed aloofness which Tietjens has had time to practise, in the company of Sylvia. A slumberousness of this sort can be a successful antidote to paranoia, as David Trotter has finely argued.[12] Tietjens acts, like Bosphorus, as if he owns the territory, but his 'Other Ranks' are convinced by the act, and do find him Godlike. In *Mister Bosphorus*, the condition is exploited with a similarly calculated air of duality, as if the dreaming protagonist is both participant and outsider in the chain of events transforming the London of Act II into the condition of carnival (which it achieves in Act IV). Both Tietjens and Bosphorus risk imminent death of a sort, and indeed both of them inhabit an atmosphere of rapt romanticism and absolute prosaicness. Similar to the contemplative Tietjens who feels like 'some immense and absurd statue', Bosphorus can't easily stop looking back at his complicated sentimental self, and the vivid, particular city-scape in which his Northern Muse has dwelled:

> *Dimly-illuminant shop-windows show through fog; motor head-lights in extreme confusion; sounds of horse-hoofs on granite setts; Ford horns; whistles; fog-signals; ex-servicemen's cornets; London fog – humour; the constant exclamation: MOVE ON THERE; WHERE YER SHUVVIN'; a lugubrious and ancient barrel-organ plays [. . . .]*

VOICE OF BOSPHORUS:
   This, this is what they offer us
   To versify.
VOICE OF SOUTHERN MUSE: My Bosphorus,

> From the dull confines of this drooping North
> Now we go forth. (*MrB* 101)

Let us be clear: taken away from its immediately theatrical context, this is no 'Unreal city'. The noises, sights and voices of this London are registered with a specific order of poetry, one that is quite unlike the contemporaneous achievement of T. S. Eliot in *The Waste Land*.[13] As Hugh Kenner once pointed out, in an article on 'The Poetics of Speech', Ford can be enlisted amongst the poets who write inside a 'documentary tradition'.[14] The deeper motives inspiring Ford's use of a cockney 'Rehelisum' in this strange *Fantasia* should be related to the critical attitudes he had developed before the War: to his insights into a growing loss of proximity between the literary world and the parallel realities of the city street (*MrB* 17). And there is a sense in which *Mister Bosphorus* is written to protest against that loss.

When Bosphorus says: 'This, this is what they offer us to versify', he does not then proceed to refuse the task (*MrB* 101). He does not put distance – poetically – between himself and his fellow Londoners. More precisely: he manages the trick of speaking from within that city world as well as holding himself apart from it, the bearer (as it were) of a 'critical attitude':

> But how is it possible that men hold dear,
> In these lugubrious places,
> This dreary land; the clod-like, inglorious races,
> The befogged, gin-sodden faces;
> The lewd, grim prudery; for-ever-protracted chases
> After concealëd lechery; hog-like dull embraces
> Under a grey-flannel sky…. (*MrB* 103)

As Kenner suggested, Ford is emphatically not using his Londoners as the poetic vehicle for a 'profound revelation'.[15] His attempt is, rather, to catch the distinctive and unsung music – the 'unspectacular idiom' – of a more documentary approach: a 'reality' which requires the tuning of the ear to spoken resonances: to an echo of a more real London.[16]

Ford's use of both literary culture and music hall slang makes for a complex effect: the opposing registers of social class seem to draw attention to, rather than dissolving into, each other. This, avowedly, is not Ford's most 'seamless' piece of writing: indeed, he calls it his 'Dunciad'.[17] Verbal ungainliness and hybridity are, however, the source of coarser, and yet sophisticated, pleasures.

But it is not a case, I think, of Ford baptising himself in the humour of the London working classes, so as to claim 'solidarity' with them. Rather, he is trying to take a look at metropolitan culture – including the sexual *mores* of the English – without either high-mindedness or the use of terms from a more professional discourse. There is little sense of class evasiveness, or 'politeness' in the verse quotation given (above).

Indeed, it is as if Ford is trying to open imaginative conduits, here, for the expression of a broader sensibility: his critical attitude is designed so as to leave his writing open to the insights both of the 'scientific historian' and the 'hack writer who assembles salacious details'.[18] Ford is as good, here, as the words he pronounced before the war: 'The artist is, as it were, the eternal mental prostitute who stands in the market-place....' (*CA* 64).

Perhaps the spoken qualities of an anecdote from Douglas Goldring – about Ford's editing practices – may make the point a little clearer. And perhaps it may also help to give us the flavour of the mind of a Christopher Tietjens (a 'mind' which can muse on George Herbert or Shakespeare ... 'Or Pericles! Or Augustus!' (*PE* 566) only seconds before he will be offering his men free tickets to the pantomime at Drury Lane or the Shoreditch Empire):

> ... it was Ford's singular practice to attend the 'second house' at the local musichall. At least once a week my first task, on arriving at Holland Park Avenue, was to secure a box or two stalls at the Shepherd's Bush Empire. After dinner I went out and stopped a hansom and editor and 'sub' drove down to Shepherd's Bush with the MSS which had accumulated during the day. During the performance, or rather during the duller turns, Ford made his decisions and I duly recorded them. But when someone really worth listening to – the late Victoria Monks for example, or 'Little Tich' or Vesta Victoria – appeared on the stage, the cares of editorship were for the moment laid aside. After the show, we went back to the flat and worked on, sometimes until two in the morning. There must have been a good deal to be said for the Shepherd's Bush Empire, from Ford's standpoint. The atmosphere was conducive, there was no one to worry him and he could think undisturbed.[19]

The relaxed posture of the literary editor (making his 'Godlike' decisions) inside this theatrical context is suggestive in itself. It is as if the demands of professionalism were to be improbably fulfilled in a universe of shared illusion; where, as if by a kind of contagion, one were to acquire, and even lend, Tietjens's ability to stroll: to step outside of the universe of regulation and discipline.

*

Like Tietjens's ordeals (particularly, his near-death experiences in the trenches, and his riotous celebrations during Armistice day) Mister Bosphorus's ultimate escape to the 'warm sand' and the 'yielding breast' of the Southern Muse is only to be achieved after a series of explosive stage shocks (*MrB* 125). At times – as, when 'Arlequin' is made to turn the handle of a barrel organ – it is as if Ford is trying to dissolve into each other the stage traditions of North and South:

> (ARLEQUIN *turns handle of barrel-organ. It wheezes:*
> *Tike me beck, beck, beck to meyome agen,*
> *Nile th carpet to th flore!*
> *Theyole broke carch jus stend dahn there*
> *Jus ware it stood be-fore.*
> *N. Nah! Mister Lanlord, if I owesyer any rent*
> *Ile pie yer: don't yer shaht....)*

> *ARLEQUIN pirouettes up-stage, striking boards with his sword, which, gracefully bending, he allows to remain on ground. The Rolls-Royce hoots and advances until front wheels touch sword. Loud explosion of front tyres. LABOUR MASTER is pitched over front-screen in somersault. Alighting on his feet, he is seen to be POLICEMAN* [. . . .] (*MrB* 104)

Indeed the idea of merging his two Muses into one is arguably the unattainable desire towards which *Mister Bosphorus* would wish to move itself: beyond the paranoid condition of making impossible choices, and beyond the idea of needing to 'escape' indeed. *Mister Bosphorus* has much more of this spirit of accommodation and reconciliation about it, finally, than of an idea of 'settling scores'.

In this respect – and importantly – the action plotted for Bulfin the Pauper-Critic is not, finally, to act as Bosphorus's nemesis (or, specifically, the reason his manuscripts won't sell). Rather, he is to be restored to his side, still in the form of 'Nine Young Gentlemen', as if Criticism had become Bosphorus's *doppelgänger*, or at least the travelling companion, of the two refugee lovers. He is given the final lines of the drama, and declares himself: 'content! / We're very well content!' before the curtain falls (*MrB* 126).

And yet, Joseph Conrad's written response to this *burlesque* of the City (having been sent a copy of *Bosphorus*) is a sure, and a precise, response too: ' ... I had no idea that your versatile genius could master so well the comic spirit / both so grim and so ferociously gay'.[20] The note of 'ferocity' is to be detected as much in the stage action, including its violent stage magic, perhaps, as in the verse. Bulfin the Pauper-Critic – notably – is made to 'grovel' after a 'snowstorm' of 'thousand dollar notes' (*MrB* 113). This is one of several climactic *tableaux*, when the London Pawnbroker meta-morphoses into the figure of Uncle Sam. It is American money that will 'rescue' Bosphorus's reputation:

> PAWNBROKER, *indicating ecstasy, enters shop by door; emerges headlong through window. He now wears red-white-and-blue-striped trousers; a blue tail-coat embroidered with white stars; white high hat, and white goatee. He bears strapped across him a bookmaker's money wallet of enormous proportions. It is lettered P. MORGAN.*
>
> CHAR-LADY, *the* NINE [critics], POLICEMAN, PUBLICAN, *and* CROWD *of seedy individuals and errand-boys all kneel.*
> *Barrel-organ wheezes:*
>> *My country 'tis of Thee,*
>> *Sweet Land of Liberty,*
>> *To thee we sing!* (*MrB* 112)

It is as if Ford is making his City theatrically 'unreal' in order to escape the intensity of its imaginative hold upon his life. But the hybrid stage style in which he achieves this is (as Bosphorus's name might suggest, indeed) about making bridges and connections, not about artistic megalomania. Ford uses this dreaming Bosphorus so as to forge links between two phases of a life; between the two Muses (Northern and Southern); and also between London's two linguistic communities. In this last of his 'bridges', Bosphorus is connecting the world of English Literature, and its *Reviews*, with the parallel universe of popular entertainment. As in the case of Tietjens's experience, this link with 'Other Ranks' was to be an immense resource in Ford's writing. And it was gained, I contend, by allowing himself to respond with pleasure to a wider writing community than the one he found in London's post-War literary circles. Using the idioms and stage devices of that older culture – notably the songs and humour of the rougher and more 'levelling' muse, that Ford had found as Editor, in the City – Ford was also starting to open up new artistic possibilities for himself. 'City Burlesque' – with its abrupt, theatrical, improbable transitions – offered him ways of accommodating the theatre of the professional mind (including its scales of grandeur and abjection) to the more earthy, companionable and shared time-scales that were to be found at pavement-level.

NOTES

1   *Mister Bosphorus and the Muses, or a Short History of Poetry in Britain, Variety Entertainment in Four Acts, Words by Ford Madox Ford, Music by Several Popular Composers, With Harlequinade, Transformation Scene, Cinematograph Effects, and Many Other Novelties, as Well as Old and Tried Favourites. Decorated with Designs Engraved on Wood by Paul Nash*, London: Duckworth, 1923 – henceforth *MrB*.

2   *Parade's End*, Harmondsworth, Middlesex: Penguin, 1982 – henceforth *PE*; pp. 319, 318.

3   David Trotter, *Paranoid Modernism: Literary Experiment, Psychosis, and the Professionalization of Society*, Oxford: Oxford University Press, 2001, p. 210 ('Good Soldiering', pp. 210-19).

4   *Ibid.*, ('Good Soldiering'), p. 213: 'Disgust is the only feeling creatures like Bagshawe arouse, and disgust becomes henceforth the source of Dowell's identity [...]'.

5   Ford, *It Was the Nightingale*, London: Heinemann, 1934, p. 180.

6   Max Saunders, *Ford Madox Ford: A Dual Life*, 2 vols, Oxford: Oxford University Press, 1996 – henceforth 'Saunders'; vol. 2, p. 124: 'Though he was about to leave England, the Ford who had written *A House* and was soon to write *Parade's End* knew how it was that a man could hold England dear'.

7   Trotter, *op.cit.*, draws upon Pierre Bourdieu's notion of 'symbolic capital' in his account of Daniel Paul Schreber, 'the most exhaustively documented and debated of all psychotics' (*Paranoid Modernism*, p. 52). The difference between commodities which, for Bourdieu, are 'designated by their rarity as distinguished, those of the fractions richest in both economic and cultural capital', and, on the other hand, those which are 'socially identified as vulgar because they are both easy and common', is poignantly revealed in the *burlesque* stage action surrounding the fate of Bosphorus's manuscripts (Bourdieu, *Distinction: A Social Critique of Taste*, tr. R. Nice, London: Routledge, 1984, p. 176).

8   Nash's woodcut (p. 38) represents a square, and rather ungainly, figure of Bosphorus tipping his bowler hat to the elegant figure of one of his muses. On the cinematograph curtain, the 'B.M.' is a combination of a Cecil B. DeMille Hollywood stage set and Bosphorus's own description of it as a 'packing case'.

9   This argument about Modernist stage, and film, action, is partly derived from Francis Steegmuller, *Cocteau, A Biography,* London: Constable, 1986, p. 162: 'Each performance of *Parade* was to last no more than twenty minutes, but [Cocteau] felt it a privilege to be devoting himself to the details of the then novel "realistic" sights and sounds of which it is composed' (it is subtitled 'Ballet Réaliste'). *Parade* and *MrB* both combined the use of Music Hall and Circus into their scenarios, and both make notable use of typewriters (and, in the case of *MrB*, telegraph keyboards) on stage.

10 Ford to Pinker, 17 May 1921: *Letters of Ford Madox Ford,* ed. Richard Ludwig, Princeton: Princeton University Press, 1965 – henceforth *LF*; p. 132.

11 Ford to F. S. Flint, 12 May 1921: *LF* 131.

12 Trotter, *op.cit.* ('Ford Madox Ford and the Quality of Entanglements'), pp. 331-7.

13 The argument over Ford's possible debt to Eliot's poem is still an unsettled one. See Saunders, vol. 2, 124: 'Ford's love of music hall [...] his use of peasant speech in his early verse, all point towards his having been able to arrive at the techniques of the poem on his own'.

14 *Ford Madox Ford: Modern Judgements,* ed. Richard Cassell, London: Macmillan, 1972, p. 177.

15 *Ibid.,* p. 177.

16 *Ibid.,* p. 177.

17 Ford to Conrad, 8 November, 1923; *LF* 157.

18 Ford, *The Critical Attitude*, London: Duckworth, 1911 – henceforth *CA.*

19 Goldring, *South Lodge,* London: Constable, 1943, p. 32.

20 Conrad to Ford, 20 November, 1923. In Saunders, vol. 2, 124.

FORD'S PRE-WAR POETRY AND THE 'ROTTING CITY'

Ashley Chantler

> In the first place what I am always striving to get at is:
> The ultimate reasons of the futile earth
> And crawling swarms of men . . .[1]

Ford visited the city throughout his poetic life,[2] sometimes for pleasure, to write of the joys of love and belonging,[3] but often to critique the 'rotten age'[4] of religious, moral, social and political decay, of 'dead faiths' and 'dead loves',[5] of selfishness, blindness, alienation, and uncertainty. For some reason, though, Ford's poems are often marginalized by scholars interested in late nineteenth- and early twentieth-century literature, and even Ford specialists usually pass over the early poems.[6] A reason for the latter is perhaps because of a tendency to be drawn to significant names and events and guiding statements. Conrad Aiken said that *Antwerp* 'is one of the three or four brilliant poems inspired by the war'[7] and T. S. Eliot praised it as being 'the only good poem I have met with on the subject of the war'.[8] In an article in the *Egoist*, Richard Aldington, after mentioning work by W. B. Yeats, F. S. Flint and Ezra Pound, suggests that Ford's 'On Heaven' is 'the best poem of any of them';[9] Harold Monro's *Chapbook* devoted an issue to *A House* (March 1921), which won the 1921 *Poetry* magazine prize (conferred in previous years on H. D., John Gould Fletcher and Robert Frost); Pound wrote that Ford's modernist poems were 'significant and revolutionary'.[10] Perhaps Ford is associated too closely with modernism. Perhaps the early poems, which on first reading do not seem to have connections with the modernist Ford, are overlooked because of this. But origins, as Ford often demonstrates in his work, are important, and to help understand his modernism and the developing role of the city in his poetic oeuvre, it is useful to turn to Ford's pre-war city poems. Critical engagement with them also contributes to a deeper understanding of late nineteenth- and early twentieth-century literary meditations on the discordant self, politics, morality, religion, and knowledge. This essay

will, therefore, look at two long poems from Ford's first poetry
collection, *The Questions at the Well* (1893), and then consider several
poems from *The Face of the Night* (1904) and *High Germany* (1912).

Ford's first city poem is 'The Story of Simon Pierreauford',[11]
from *The Questions at the Well*.[12] It opens:

> DOWN there near the Gare du Nord,
> At the corner of the street,
> Where the double tram-lines meet,
> *Bonhomme*[13] Simon Pierreauford
> And his nagging wife Lisette
> Kept their Café, he and she.
> He lets life slip carelessly,
> She a sleepless martinet. (*QW* 13)

Set in Paris in the late nineteenth century,[14] the poem is a forerunner
of the later *fin de siècle* London poems of John Davidson, Ernest
Dowson, W. E. Henley, Lionel Johnson and Arthur Symons. These
poets saw in the city material for a poetry of urban life. As G. Robert
Stange has written: 'It was only in the nineties that, for poets, painters
and novelists, London ceased to be regarded as a noxious drain or
force of devastation'.[15] Ford's city contains murder and mud, and is
one where people are tired by the toil of urban life: 'So the city panted
on, / And men ate and drank and slept / And died' (*QW* 22). There is a
possible echo here of Tennyson's 'Ulysses' (1842) – 'a savage race, /
That hoard, and sleep, and feed'[16] – which reinforces the poem's
concern with degeneration: the city and its inhabitants have become
animal-like, reduced to a basic existence, the 'And died' suggesting the
futility of the struggle. Ford returns to this idea in *Ancient Lights* (1911)
when discussing the 'struggle for existence' in contemporary London: 'It
is a quaint thought, but a perfectly sound one, to say that we are nearer to
habits of barbarism, that we could more easily revert to days of savagery
than we could pick up again the tone of thought, of mind and habit, of the
men of thirty years ago'.[17]

'Hearing from a customer / Of a new-caught murderer' (*QW*
15), Simon goes for a walk; purchasing 'an evening sheet / Wherein
all the details stood', he sits on a bench and 'the traffic's rhythmic
roar, / Like surf-thunder on the shore, / Lulled him till he fell asleep'
(*QW* 16). The slumbering and the nature simile describing the traffic
show Ford here illustrating that temporary solace can be found within
the urban environment and that poetry has the ability to render the
complexity and contradictions of city life perhaps not merely as

depressing but also as vital. But the simile reminds the reader of the artificiality of the 'roar' and might imply that a less transitory solace can only be found outside the city, beyond the man-made and the simulated.

Less transitory, not permanent, because whether in the city or the country, death cannot be escaped. Lisette dies unexpectedly of 'a fit, / And without the Church's grace' (*QW* 18): she dies without her last rites being administered, unshriven. It is possible, therefore, that she will go to hell. Simon withdraws from public life desiring 'to lie at rest / Freed from dread uncertainties' (*QW* 20). His desire relates to his understandable uncertainty about when 'Death would fell him with his flail' (*QW* 20) but it also relates to the poem's interest in whether a person will be saved or damned, or if there is even an afterlife.

Although he converted to Catholicism when he was nineteen, Ford's writing throughout his life returns to questions of truth and epistemological uncertainty. In her entry for 25 March 1892, Olive Garnett wrote in her diary:

> I was [...] very much shocked when Ford admitted that as a relief from the gospel of perfect indifference to everything, he sought refuge in bigoted pietism in the Brompton Oratory, not that he thought Catholicism was rational [...]; he balanced the two parts of his nature one against the other. Atheistic indifference on the one hand, bigoted pietism on the other.
>
> I was as much surprised when Ford also declared that the only thing really interesting & unfathomable was love, not the higher kind, but the lower kind. 'Helen of Troy the everlasting symbol.' Men to become beasts etc.[18]

Many of the tensions in the poem (and in the poems discussed below) come from its concern with the city as a place of schisms, but where a balance is denied between atheism and Catholicism, indifference and concern, and the irrational and rational. It is also concerned with the 'lower kind' of love: love that is inseparable from, and confused by, sexual desire, and has the dual potential of integration or destruction; after Lisette's death, Simon shuts himself away in his 'shaky bed':

> 'It must serve me for the time,'
> Thought he, through his weariness.
>
> But one night he waked alone
> As a new year drew a-nigh,
> And the earth was white with rime.
> 'Year and bed will last my time,'
> Mused he, gazing at the sky,

Where the new moon, crescent, shone. (*QW* 22-3)

It seems strange to state here that 'one night' Simon 'waked alone', since as an hermetic widower it is already assumed that he sleeps by himself. It is possible, of course, that 'alone' was added for the sake of the half-rhyme with 'shone'. However, the poem earlier states that Simon's niece 'now kept his house for him, / Humouring his every whim' and complains that 'it is so far to climb / To your wretched little room' (*QW* 21). In her domestic role and her nagging, the niece has replaced Lisette, thus Simon waking 'alone' provokes the suggestion that he and his niece are having a sexual relationship. Incest is referred to in passing in a later poem, 'Süssmund's Address to an Unknown God' (see below), hinted at in later novels, notably in *The Good Soldier* and *Parade's End*, and is made explicit in *A Little Less Than Gods* (1928). It is often coupled in the novels with guilt, thoughts of suicide, and an internal struggle with religious dogma.[19] In 'Simon Pierreauford', there are no such anxieties, reinforcing the poem's concern with degeneration, revealing the emerging loss of humanity through the disintegration of conscience that can occur when individuals live in a city that fosters isolation and disaffection.

The following two poems in *The Questions at the Well*, 'Faith' and 'Hope', listed in its contents page as 'Faith and Hope – Part of a Trilogy',[20] meditate on similar themes. Each poem is split into two parts: 'Faith in the Park' and 'Faith in the Parlour'; 'Hope in the Park' and 'Hope in the Parlour'. In the park is a starving man 'Shivering upon a seat' and praying for 'food' (*QW* 32). The speaker thus suggests that the reader should:

> Rouse him with a gentle hand,
> Under your umbrella stand,
> And, with accents mildly bland,
> Tell him of the Promised Land,
> Of Him that died, the Crucified,
> Who died, who died, who died, died, died,
> To save the wicked far and wide.
>
> String off the platitudes,
> Say that no worldly goods
> Equal God's beatitudes. (*QW* 33)

'[W]ith accents mildly bland' and 'String off the platitudes' prevents any ambiguity about the speaker's (and presumably Ford's) view of a religious belief that avoids engagement with the realities of the world.

This point is reinforced in 'Faith in the Parlour' where a family and a vicar are gathered in the fire-warmed room:

> When the dinner-time arrives
>   All the talk is of the Churches.
> How the wicked Low Church strives
>   To shake the High Ones from their perches –
> For the Vicar's very 'High.'
> But the talk drifts by and by
>   (Mixed with carving)
> Till it rests on poverty
>   And the starving.
>
> 'We have all our woes to bear,
>   Either physical or mental,
> We must find relief in prayer,
>   Present pain's but incidental.
> We must bear the Will Divine –
>   Really this is very fine –[21]
>   Such body!
> A most extremely grateful wine,
>   No shoddy!' (*QW* 36-7)

The vicar seems unintentionally to echo the words of Christ at the Last Supper: 'this is my body' (Mark 14. 22), when Christ was, however, referring to the bread, not (as here) to the wine.[22] This fatuous High-Churchman seems impervious to the irony of his exclamation, and his enjoyment of the wine, ironically subverting his advocacy of Christian stoicism, further stresses his ignorance. The roast meat and expensive wine emphasize the family's financial comfort to further the contrast between them and the man in the park, and thus point up the hypocrisy of this complacent Christianity.

The satire here is not necessarily related to the city, implying that it alone breeds such bigotry, but the opening of 'Faith in the Parlour' seems to suggest that a connection be made between context and religious belief:

> From the Church they've travelled,
> And the maze of fog-filled streets
>   Safely they unravelled.
> 'It was like a pilgrimage
> In a mediæval age,'
>   Laughs one maiden. (*QW* 34)

The girl's simile is weak: there is a marked contrast between an unrooted pilgrim, who has foregone materiality and luxury, and the privileged whose lifestyle, ignorance and insincere faith seem to be born of living in the city.

In response to the suggested 'platitudes', the man in the park:

> Answers hot: 'Me, God forgot,
> It is my lot, my God, my lot
> To lie for ever and to rot.
>
> 'Yes, that is blasphemy,
> I am damned eternally,
> What else *could* you have from me?
> In this throbbing panting sea
> Many such as I go down,
> And we drown, we drown, we drown,
> That a weary while I've known.
>
> 'How can I think of Him
> Who hearkens but to Cherubim?
> Hunger is too grey and grim,
> And my aching eyeballs swim.
> My love is fled from Him who bled,
> I pray for bread, for bread, for bread.
> Could one fare worse though damned and dead?' (*QW* 33-4)

The speech suggests Calvinist despair (and thus contrasts with the High-Church dogma of the family and vicar) and recalls William Cowper's 'Lines Written During a Period of Insanity' (1774):

> Damned below Judas: more abhorr'd than he was,
> Who for a few pence sold his holy master.
> Twice betrayed Jesus me, the last delinquent,
>   Deems the profanest.
>
> Man disavows, and Deity disowns me:
> Hell might afford my miseries a shelter;
> Therefore hell keeps her ever hungry mouths all
>   Bolted against me.

And 'The Castaway' (1799):

> No voice divine the storm allay'd,
>   No light propitious shone;
> When, snatch'd from all effectual aid,
>   We perish'd, each alone:
> But I beneath a rougher sea,

And whelm'd in deeper gulphs than he.[23]

The man in the park's reference to the 'throbbing panting sea' is ambiguous. It might refer, as 'The Castaway' does, to the 'gulphs' of the despondent self cut off from God 'who hearkens but to Cherubim'. ('Cherubim' might be a reference to one of the types of angels in the Bible, often used by God as sentinels (Genesis 3. 24 and 37. 7-9) or to act out His will (Ezekiel 10. 7); it might, however, be a metaphor for the angelic on earth to whom God listens because they, unlike the 'damned' man, are of the elect.) But 'panting' recalls 'So the city panted on' in 'The Story of Simon Pierreauford'. Perhaps, therefore, the man and 'Many such as' he are drowning in the city, in a place, the poem suggests, that ironically brings people together to divide them.

This echoes (perhaps unintentionally) Swift's 'Description of a City Shower' (1710) – 'Now in contiguous drops the flood comes down, / Threatening with deluge this devoted town' – where he uses the rain to pool 'various kinds, by various fortunes led'[24] and expose the divisiveness and inhumanity in London. 'Faith' also foreshadows Ford's most famous investigation into the schisms between people and religious beliefs, *The Good Soldier*: when looking at the Protestant's 'Protest', Florence 'laid one finger upon Captain Ashburnham's wrist': 'Don't you see,' [Leonora] said, […] 'Don't you see that that's the cause of the whole miserable affair; of the whole sorrow of the world? And the eternal damnation of you and me and them. . . .'; 'don't you know that I'm an Irish Catholic?'.[25]

'Hope' reinforces the themes of 'Faith'. 'Hope in the Park' returns to the man, but now he seems to have drowned himself in the canal:

> But hush! here floats a sleep-fraught face.
> […]
> The World was grey and pitiless,
> It wrested all he had from him –
> His food, his faith, his happiness –
> He fought throughout in silence grim.
>
> It threw him though he strove his best,
> It grizzled grey his hair – once black –
> It broke the firm arch of his chest,
> It bowed his head and bent his back. (*QW* 40, 41)

The 'pitiless' 'World' oppressed him until, rather ironically, he looked like a country labourer: he 'bowed his head and bent his back'. The reader might question the man in the park for not going on, but 'They drove him from the dripping Park' (*QW* 40): the man could not live a stoic, solitary life because he was not allowed to. The poem suggests that the individual in the city can only survive if he or she becomes a part of the crowd, and thus loses independence.

In *The Soul of London* (1905), Ford describes a woman whose speed at making 'matchboxes at 2¾d the 144':

> was like watching all the time some feat of desperate and breathless skill. It made one hold one's own breath.
>
> In face of it any idea of 'problems', of solutions, of raising the submerged, or of the glorious destinies of humanity, vanished. The mode of life became, as it were, august and settled. You could not pity her because she was so obviously and wonderfully equipped for her particular struggle: you could not wish to 'raise' her, for what could she do in any other light, in any other air? Here at least she was strong, heroic, settled and beyond any condemnation.[26]

The woman has accepted her part in the city and the capitalist machine, thus the city and the machine have accepted her.

In 'Hope in the Parlour', the family 'sit and wait':

> Till the guests arrive,
> They are drest in state
>   All with hope alive.
> What does each one hope
>   Deep down in the breast?
> Very wide's the scope
>   Of joys they hope to wrest
> From life;
>   And each will do his best
> To conquer in the strife. (*QW* 43)

Their ostentatious public display hides their private desires: the father hopes his 'cuffs show off' his 'links' and that his 'wife won't hear / Of where I was last night' (*QW* 43); the son hopes his 'parting suits' his hair and that he can acquire the money he owes (*QW* 44); the daughter 'sits and schemes / To gain the drawing prize' (*QW* 44); and the mother looks at the daughter:

> And notes, with happy smile,
>   Her child's good looks increase.
> And much must be the gold
>   Such beauty rare to buy.
> For she herself was sold,
>   Whilst yet her hopes ran high,

And now,
>The hour is drawn a-nigh,
>That sees her child on show. (*QW* 45)

The ideas here, of appearances, concealed and selfish desires, and the individual isolated from others, parallel those in Arnold's 'The Buried Life' (1852). But Arnold suggests that an understanding of oneself and another, and a joining of selfless people, can occur:

>When a beloved hand is laid in ours,
>When, jaded with the rush and glare
>Of the interminable hours,
>Our eyes can in another's eyes read clear,
>When our world-deafen'd ear
>Is by the tones of a love'd voice caress'd –
>A bolt is shot back somewhere in our breast,
>And a lost pulse of feeling stirs again.
>The eye sinks inward, and the heart lies plain,
>And what we mean, we say, and what we would, we know.[27]

Love can transform; the body and voice of a beloved can convert. 'Hope in the Parlour', however, ends:

>Their hopes all soar above,
>>Such paltry things as food,
>Conjugal faith – or love –
>>Fishers of men[28] they brood,
>And wait,
>>And their own flesh and blood,
>Is their heroic bait. (*QW* 46)

The family's 'flesh and blood' do not join them communally, like the partakers of the bread and the 'cup' at the Last Supper (1 Corinthians 16-17), but separates them from each other and from the poor (such as the suicidal man in the park). The poem's conclusion again emphasizes familial and social divisions and the lack of that faith, charity and community represented by the Last Supper.[29]

Coleridge's 'Faith, Hope, and Charity' (1815) ends:

>And whoso loves no earthly song,
>But does for heavenly music long,
>Faith, Hope, and Charity for him,
>Shall sing like wingéd Cherubim.[30]

Ford's 'Faith' and 'Hope' revise such a view, suggesting that a longing for 'heavenly music' (a longing for death) might be caused by the lack of charity in the city. 'Faith, Hope, and Charity' are not a harmonious triumvirate upon which the individual can rely.

It seems that Ford originally intended to have a complete trilogy of 'Faith', 'Hope' and 'Charity'. An early collection of autograph manuscripts at Cornell is titled 'Faith, Hope and Charity' and there are fragments of what seem to be 'Charity in the Parlour'. There are no extant manuscripts of 'Charity in the Park'. It is only possible to speculate on Ford's reasons for not including 'Charity' in the printed versions. The drafts of 'Charity in the Parlour' seem to reveal dissatisfaction with what he was writing: based on perhaps the realization that the monologue, with its overt swipes at socialists, 'Reformers' and social injustice, was at odds with the style and tone set by 'Faith' and 'Hope'.[31] The fact that Ford titled the poem in the contents page of *The Questions at the Well*, 'Faith and Hope – Part of a Trilogy', perhaps suggests that he also realized that the lack of 'Charity' might be more resonant than a poem about the lack of charity: the reader is provoked into pondering its absence.

Ford returned to overt swipes at various city-dwellers in *High Germany* (1912). In 'Süssmund's Address to an Unknown God', 'Mr Hueffer has impartially and eloquently cursed this age and all the earnest and officious persons who would make it unbearable, if they could.'[32] Purporting to be 'a quite free adaptation' of a poem by 'Carl Eugen Freiherr von Süssmund, b. 1872, d. 1910' (*HG* xxvi),[33] 'Süssmund's Address' is a witty tirade against a 'rotten age' (*HG* xxx):

> MY God, they say I have no bitterness!
> Dear Unknown God, I gasp, I fade, I pine!
> No bitterness! Have firs no turpentine?
> If so, it's true.
>
> Because I do not go wandering round Piccadilly
> Like an emasculated lily
> In a low-necked flannel shirt beneath the rain.
> (Is that what you'd do,
> Oh God Unknown,
> If you came down
> To Piccadilly
> And worried over London town?)
> Wailing round Covent Gardens [*sic*] what I should do
> Declaiming to the beefy market porters
> Dramatic propaganda about social wrongs [...] (*HG* xxvi)

The satire here is first directed at the Aesthetes and their followers:

> Æstheticism, which originated with Burne-Jones and Morris, was a movement that concerned itself with idealizing anything that was mediæval. It may be symbolized by the words, 'long necks and pomegranates.' Wilde carried this ideal one stage further. He desired to live upon the smell of a lily. I do not know that he ever did, but I know that he was in the habit of sending to young ladies whom he admired a single lily flower, carefully packed in cotton-wool. And the cry from the austere realism of my grandfather's picture of *Work*, or Holman Hunt's *Saviour in the Temple*, was so far that I may well be pardoned for not recognizing Wilde at all under the mantle of a *soi-disant* Pre-Raphaelite. (*AL* 153)

Gilbert and Sullivan's *Patience* (1881), their satire on the Aesthetic movement, contains the following lyric: 'Though the Philistines may jostle, you will rank as an apostle in the high aesthetic band, / If you walk down Piccadilly with a poppy or a lily in your medieval hand'.[34] But those who declaim 'Dramatic propaganda about social wrongs' are more politically active than the Aesthetes whose attention was on art or self-image. Ford is probably here extending the satire to include the later, politically-active Morris. In *Ancient Lights*, Ford says that 'Morris dragged across the way of Æstheticism the red herring of socialism' (*AL* 148): Morris's *A Dream of John Ball* (1888) and *News from Nowhere* (1891), for example, are both socialist fantasies. The Garnetts, Ford's Rossetti cousins (Mary, Helen, Arthur and Olive), and the many socialists, Marxists, anarchists and miscellaneous radicals he met through them, were probably also behind the declaimers.[35] In *Henry James* (1914), Ford reasserts the sentiments of the poem, suggesting that the 'profound moral purpose of the 90's' was: 'a curious thing made up of socialism, free thought, the profession of free love going hand in hand with an intense sexual continence that to all intents and purposes ended in emasculation'.[36]

The poem goes on to criticize all 'Reformers', including, among many others, 'Anti-Vivisectionists and Friends of Peace', 'Neo-Psychics, Platonists', Whigs, Tories (*HG* xxviii), and 'a Jail Reform / And Pure Milk Rotter' (*HG* xxix). The problem Ford had with such people seems not necessarily to be because he outrightly disagreed with their views[37] but because they are so 'earnest': 'earnest, cold-in-the-heart and practised preachers' (*HG* xxix). They are dogmatic and narrow-minded; in their unswerving missions they ignore (or are perhaps blind to) the complexity, paradoxes and ambiguities of humanity. The speaker thus responds with an image of heaven that is deliberately provocative:

> Where there's no feeling of the moral pulse,
> I think I'd find some peace – with treachery
> Of the sword and dagger kind to keep it sweet –
> – Adultery, foul murder, pleasant things,
> A touch of incest, theft, but no Reformers. (*HG* xxxi)

Provocative, perhaps merely to outrage or irritate the reformers, but perhaps to encourage their reformation by confusing, and thus hopefully getting them to consider, their definitions of what is 'pleasant' and unpleasant, 'moral' and immoral.

The city poet can only bear so much. In 'To All the Dead' (*High Germany*), the poet escapes to 'An endless trackless, heather forest' on the outskirts of Trêves:

> When my mind's all reeling with Modern Movements
> And my eyes are weary, my head at its sorest
> And the best of beer has lost its zest,
> I go up there to get a rest
> And think of the dead. . . .
>
> For it's nothing but dead and dead and dying
> Dead faiths, dead loves, lost friends and the flying,
> Fleet minutes that change and ruin our shows,
> And the dead leaves flitter and autumn goes,
> And the dead leaves flitter down thick to the ground,
> And pomps go down and queens go down
> And time flows on, and flows and flows. (*HG* xlvii)

E. Buxton Shanks, in his review of the 1913 *Collected Poems*, accused 'To All the Dead' of being 'tedious': 'it gives me an impression of Mr Hueffer writing and writing because he was too tired to stop'.[38] This is rather reductive. The speaker is repetitive, digressive, circuitous, indecisive, questioning, forgetful, mundane, impressionist, to illustrate the sense of inundation felt by the individual in the city and the limited control he or she has:

> For the life of to-day is more and more becoming a life of little things. We are losing more and more the sense of a whole, the feeling of a grand design, of the co-ordination of all Nature in one great architectonic scheme. We have no longer any time to look out for the ultimate design. We have to face such an infinite number of little things that we cannot stay to arrange them in our minds, or to consider them as anything but as accidents, happenings, the mere

events of the day. And if in outside things we can perceive no design but only the fortuitous materialism of a bewildering world, we are thrown more and more in upon ourselves for comprehension of that which is not understandable and for analysis of things of the spirit. (*AL* 62)

This and 'To All the Dead' revise the argument of an earlier poem, 'Grey Matter', from *The Face of the Night* (1904), which suggests that it is the 'little things' that can give the individual a sense of purpose and place in the Godless, city-driven, modern world. In it, a woman asks her partner:

> [...] Where shall I,
> The woman, where shall you take part,
> My poet? Where has either of us scope
> In this dead-dawning century that lacks all faith,
> All hope, all aim, and all the mystery
> That comforteth [. . . .] (*FN* 31)

Her question is provoked by her reading the work of:

> A crabbèd, ancient, dried biologist,
> Somewhere very far from the sea, closed up from the sky,
> Shut in from the leaves [...] (*FN* 30)

The scientist's 'Erster Heft' ('First Volume'), his empirical study of consciousness, destroys the imagination and the transcendental. There are connections here to Romantic thought (see, for example, Keats's 'Lamia', ll. 229-30: 'Do not all charms fly / At the mere touch of cold philosophy?'[39]) and to post-Darwinian Victorian angst. The poet calls such science a 'mist', which inverts the traditional idea of its enlightenment: 'Nature and Nature's Laws lay hid in Night. / GOD said, *Let Newton be!* and all was Light'.[40] Faith, hopes, dreams and 'the mystery / That comforteth' (superstition and any non-empirical thought) are also mists, arbitrary constructions that are created to provide answers, or at least analogies, in a 'bewildering world'. The difference between them and empiricism is that they 'comforteth', they prevent solipsism.

The poet comforts his partner by reminding her that what matters is that they, 'in the lush, far meads', 'Poet and woman, past the city walls':

> Believe what we believe, feel what we feel,
> Like what we list of what they cry within
>   Cathedral or laborat'ry

[...]
The right, true, joyful word, the sweet, true phrase,
The calling of our children from the woods these gardens days
Remain.– These drops of rain have laid the dust
And in our soft brown seed-beds formed the crust
We needed for our sowings. [...] (*FN* 32)

Away from the city, the couple have freedom of thought, but the 'little things', such as children's voices, rain and earth, keep them centred and, like Marlow's 'rivets' that 'stop the hole',[41] they stop them falling 'in upon' themselves.

For how long the couple's freedom will last is unknown. In the same volume as 'Grey Matter', '"The Mother": A Song-Drama'[42] suggests that the city might eventually encroach upon the country. Four personifications animate the argument: 'The Spirit of the Age'; 'The Mother' (Nature); 'The Little Blades of Grass' and 'The Little Grains of Sand and of Dust' (brothers, sons of the Mother).

> Scene.—*Just outside a great city. Battalions of staring, dun-coloured, brick houses, newly finished, with vacant windows, bluish slate roofs and yellow chimney pots, march on the fields which are blackened and shrouded with fog. Innumerable lines of railway disappear among them, gleaming in parallel curves. Fog signals sound and three trains pass on different levels; the lights in their windows an orange blur. A continuous hooting of railway engines.* THE SPIRIT OF THE AGE, *leaning on the brick parapet of the upper embankment, speaks towards* THE MOTHER, *who is unseen in the fog above the fields.* (*FN* 43)

The ominous, monotypic houses and excessive amounts of railway track[43] are products of the Spirit of the Age (urbanisation, new techno-logy, democratisation, capitalism, materialism), who says in his opening speech to the Mother, echoing Blake's *Jerusalem* (1804-20):

> IT'S I have conquered you.
> It is over and done with your green and
> over and done with your blue.
> Conquered you. Where is your sky?
> Where is the green that your gown had
> of late? (*FN* 43-4)

The country is being engulfed, overwhelmed, raped, by the 'rotting City' (*FN* 49) and its allies. It is the same city that Dickens, in *Dombey and Son* (1847-8) and *Little Dorrit* (1855-7), and Hardy, in *The Woodlanders* (1887), see impinging upon the country, and the same consumerist spirit that Oliver Goldsmith in *The Deserted Village*

(1770) says is monopolising rural areas. Like those writers (but perhaps not conscious of the connections between their work and his), Ford sets up a polarity between the past and the present – 'Strike down the old; cry onwards the new' (*FN* 53) – and the country and the city: the oppositions are used to show the dangers of unquestioned 'progress':

> *The Mother* (*very softly*).
> Where is Troy?
>
> *The Spirit of the Age.*
> What's Troy compared to me?
>
> *The Mother.*
> Where Carthage, Nineve,
> Where Greece, where Egypt, where are all
>   that host
> Whose very names are lost?
>
> *The Little Blades of Grass* (*whispering*).
> When we crave them,
> Then we have them.
>
> *The Little Grains of Sand and of Dust.*
> When the wind blows we o'er-ride them,
> And we hide them
>   Silently. (*FN* 50)

'The Mother' ends implying that England's '*great city*' will disappear. Ford's later poetry suggests nothing so bleak, but his critique of the city and the 'Spirit of the Age' continued, sometimes with despair, sometimes with hope.

NOTES

1   Ford to Galsworthy, 'October, 1900': *Letters of Ford Madox Ford*, ed. Richard M. Ludwig, Princeton NJ: Princeton University Press, 1965, p. 11.
2   Ford published eight individual poetry volumes (the abbreviations used to refer to them in this essay are given here): *The Questions at the Well* (*QW*; 1893), *Poems for Pictures* (*PP*; 1900), *The Face of the Night* (*FN*; 1904), *From Inland* (1907), *Songs from London* (1910), *High Germany* (*HG*; 1912), *On Heaven* (1918), *New Poems* (1927); two *Collected Poems* (*CP1*; 1913; and *CP2*; 1936) and a one-

hundred-and-twenty-six-page dramatic poem illustrated by Paul Nash, *Mister Bosphorus and the Muses* (1923). He also published a pamphlet of *Antwerp* (1915), illustrated by Wyndham Lewis.

3   See Joseph Wiesenfarth's essay in this volume.

4   'Süssmund's Address to an Unknown God', *High Germany*, London: Duckworth, 1912 – hereafter cited as *HG*; p. xxx.

5   'To All the Dead': *HG* xlvii.

6   A notable Ford scholar, Robert Hampson, dismisses *The Questions at the Well* as being 'very much juvenilia' (p. 94), but does acknowledge favourably the following two volumes – *Poems for Pictures* and *The Face of the Night* – and writes sensitively about several of their poems; see '"Experiments in Modernity": Ford and Pound', *Pound in Multiple Perspective: A Collection of Critical Essays*, ed. Andrew Gibson, Basingstoke: Macmillan, 1993. Since the publication of Ford's *Selected Poems*, ed. Max Saunders, Manchester: Carcanet, 1997, there has been a relative boom in critical engagement with Ford's middle and late poems: see Paul Skinner, 'Poor Dan Robin: Ford Madox Ford's Poetry', in *Ford Madox Ford: A Reappraisal*, ed. Robert Hampson and Tony Davenport, Amsterdam: Rodopi, 2002, pp. 79-103, and Sara Haslam on 'On Heaven' in her *Fragmenting Modernism: Ford Madox Ford, the Novel and the Great War*, Manchester: Manchester University Press, 2002, pp. 167-78. There is a short discussion by Pamela Bickley of 'Ford's Pre-Raphaelite Poetry' in *Ford Madox Ford: A Reappraisal*, pp. 59-78.

7   Conrad Aiken, 'The Function of Rhythm: Ford Madox Hueffer', *Skepticisms: Notes on Contemporary Poetry* (first published 1919), New York, Books for Libraries Press, 1970, p. 82; reprint of a review of *On Heaven* in *Dial*, 65 (16 Nov. 1918), 417-8.

8   'T. S. E.', 'Reflections on Contemporary Poetry', *Egoist*, 4:10 (Nov. 1917), 151.

9   Richard Aldington, 'Modern Poetry and the Imagists', *Egoist*, 1:11 (1 Jun. 1914), 201.

10 Ezra Pound, 'Mr. Hueffer and the Prose Tradition in Verse', *Poetry*, 4:3 (Jun. 1914), 120; reprinted as 'The Prose Tradition in Verse' in Brita Lindberg-Seyersted ed., *Pound/Ford: the Story of a Literary Friendship: the Correspondence Between Ezra Pound and Ford Madox Ford and Their Writings About Each Other*, London, Faber & Faber, 1982.

11 'Simon Pierreauford' has several possible meanings. 'Pierreauford' might be an ephemeral joke if translated as 'Pier water ford'. However, 'Simon Pierreauford' can be translated as 'Simon Peter Ford', Ford replacing Paul (who also changed his name, from Saul) in the biblical triumvirate that mixes the saintly (Peter and Paul) with the sinful (Simon). The name might also be an early example of Ford's interest in the blurring of the biographical and the fictional, the real and the imaginary: 'Simon Pierre' is perhaps a pun on 'Simon Pure', which when used as an attribution means 'real, genuine, authentic' (*SOED*): 'Simon Pierreauford' might therefore suggest that the man in the poem is the 'real' Ford. 'Pierreauford', however, is perhaps also a compound of Pierrot and Ford. Pierrot was a typical character in French pantomime and *QW* 22 states that Simon 'talked by pantomime'. Simon is perhaps, therefore, half Ford and half fictional, half real and half imaginary. But perhaps by associating himself with Pierrot, Ford offers a hint of self-parody. On Pierrot in Dowson, Symons and Beardsley, see R. K. R.

Thornton, *The Decadent Dilemma*, London: Edward Arnold, 1983, pp. 99-101, 186-7.

12   London: Digby, Long, 1893 – hereafter cited as *QW*. Ll. 1-16 appeared, with minor variants, in *Living Age*, 190 (11 Nov. 1893), 322. The poem was not reprinted in *CP1* or *CP2*.

13   '*Bonhomme*' can mean simply 'fellow' or 'peasant' but it was also a name given to the Albigenses, the members of a heretic sect in twelfth- and thirteenth-century Southern France. Regarding Ford's stay in Paris in 1892 and his being received into the Church on 7 November, Arthur Mizener notes: 'The kind of Catholicism that appealed most strongly to his imagination was the Albigensian variety that had flourished in Provence in the Middle Ages, and from the time of his poem, "On Heaven," written in 1913, to his final books about the Great Trade Route, he wrote enthusiastically about the Albigenses', *The Saddest Story: A Biography of Ford Madox Ford*, New York: Harper & Row, 1971 – hereafter cited as Mizener; p. 20.

14   Ford seems to have visited Paris at least twice in the early 1890s. See Ford, *A History of Our Own Times*, ed. Solon Beinfeld and Sondra J. Stang, Manchester, Carcanet, 1988, pp. 182-3; Ford, *Return to Yesterday*, London: Victor Gollancz, 1931 – hereafter cited as *RY*, pp.112, 103-6; Mizener 528 n. 21; Max Saunders, *Ford Madox Ford: A Dual Life*, Oxford: Oxford University Press – hereafter cited as Saunders; vol. 1, pp. 53-4.

15   G. Robert Stange, 'The Frightened Poets', *The Victorian City: Images and Reality*, ed. H. J. Dyos and Michael Wolff, vol. 2, London: Routledge and Kegan Paul, 1973, p. 489.

16   Alfred Tennyson, *In Memoriam, Maud and Other Poems*, ed. John D. Jump, London: Everyman, 1995, p. 44.

17   *Ancient Lights and Certain New Reflections*, London: Chapman and Hall, 1911 – hereafter cited as *AL*; p. 269.

18   Olive Garnett, *Tea and Anarchy!: The Bloomsbury Diary of Olive Garnett, 1890-1893*, ed. Barry C. Johnson, London: Bartletts Press, 1989, p. 70.

19   For further details, see Saunders, vol. 1, 623, and vol. 2, 684.

20   The poems were not reprinted in *CP1* or *CP2*.

21   For typographical consistency, the line should not be indented; the error also appears in the proofs of *QW* at Cornell University Library.

22   On Ford's implicit use of 'This is my body' in *The Good Soldier*, see Carol Jacobs, *Telling Time*, Baltimore: Johns Hopkins University Press, 1992, pp. 75-94; part of this chapter is reprinted as 'The Passion for Talk' in Martin Stannard's edition of the novel: New York and London, W. W. Norton & Company, 1995, pp. 337-44.

23   William Cowper, *Selected Poems*, ed. Nick Rhodes, Manchester: Carcanet, 1988, pp. 37, 78.

24   Jonathan Swift, *Selected Poems*, ed. Michael Bruce, London: Everyman, 1998, p. 19.

25   *The Good Soldier*, ed. Martin Stannard, New York and London: Norton, 1995, pp. 37, 38.

26   Ford Madox Ford, *The Soul of London*, ed. Alan G. Hill, London: Everyman, 1995, p. 60.

27 *The Works of Matthew Arnold*, ed. Martin Corner, London: Wordsworth Editions, 1995, pp. 170-1.

28 Ford provides a reference for this phrase: '*See* St Luke v. 10.' This is incorrect; Luke 5. 10 reads: 'And so *was* also James, and John, son of Zebedee, which were partners with Simon. And Jesus said unto Simon, Fear not; from henceforth thou shalt catch men.' 'Fishers of men' occurs twice in the Bible, in Matthew 4. 19 and Mark 1. 17.

29 See Christopher Rowland, 'Eucharist as Liberation from the Present', in *The Sense of the Sacramental: Movement and Measure in Art and Music, Place and Time*, ed. David Brown and Ann Loades, London: SPCK, 1995, pp. 200-15.

30 Samuel Taylor Coleridge, *Poems*, ed. John Beer, London: Everyman, 1993, p. 430.

31 For details of the manuscripts and Ford's revisions, see Ashley Chantler, 'A Critical Edition of Ford Madox Ford's *The Questions at the Well* (1893)', diss., University of Leicester, 1993, pp. 184-9.

32 E. Buxton Shanks, 'COLLECTED POEMS. By Ford Madox Hueffer', *Poetry and Drama*, 1 (Dec. 1913), 493; reprinted in *Ford Madox Ford: The Critical Heritage*, ed. Frank McShane, London: Routledge and Kegan Paul, 1972, pp. 59-61.

33 Saunders notes that 'Süssmund' is 'a fictional baronial alter-ego (with "Süssmund" perhaps echoing the Middle High German poet Süsskind von Trimberg, but translating ironically as "sweet-mouth")', *Selected Poems*, xi.

34 In *The March of Literature* (New York, Dial Press, 1938), Ford writes: 'The writer [...] begs the reader not to consider that we pre-Raphaelites were the depressed beings that Gilbert and Sullivan ridiculed, or that Mr. Oscar Wilde, dining on the smell of a lily, represented us, *les jeunes* of the movement. Not a bit of it' (p. 704). And in *AL* 148: 'When poor Oscar Wilde wandered down Bond Street in parti-coloured velvet hose, holding a single red flower in his hand, he was doing what in those days was called "touching the Philistine on the raw"'.

35 See *RY* 96-111 and Saunders, vol. 1, 44-6.

36 Ford, *Henry James*, London: Martin Secker, [1914], p. 45.

37 In *AL*, Ford writes: 'I must, personally, have had three separate sets of political opinions. To irritate my relatives, who advocated advanced thought, I dimly remember that I professed myself a Tory. Amongst the bourgeoisie whom it was my inherited duty to *épater* I passed for a dangerous anarchist. In general speech, manner and appearance, I must have resembled a socialist of the Morris group. I don't know what I was: I don't know what I am' (pp. 120-1). 'Ford's satire on "Reformers" continues with different degrees of bitterness until after the war (when his advocacy of the small producer and self-sufficiency begins to turn him into his own reformer). *An English Girl* (1907) was originally going to be called "The Reformers"; the title would have done well for *The Simple Life Limited, The Panel*, or *The New Humpty-Dumpty*' (Saunders, vol. 1, 416).

38 Shanks, 'COLLECTED POEMS', 493.

39 John Keats, *The Complete Poems*, ed. John Barnard, Harmondsworth: Penguin, 1988, p. 431.

40 Alexander Pope, 'Epitaph Intended for Sir Isaac Newton', in *Alexander Pope*, ed. Pat Rogers, Oxford: Oxford University Press, 1993, p. 242.

41 Joseph Conrad, *Heart of Darkness*, ed. Robert Kimbrough, third edition, New York: Norton, 1988, p. 30.

42 First published in the *Fortnightly Review*, 69 (Apr. 1901), 741-6.
43 In *The Soul of London*, London: Everyman, 1995, Ford writes: 'Nowadays we
     have discovered, as if in the night, a new secret of rapid communication: with that,
     as with every previous modification of the kind, the face of London bids fair to
     change unrecognisably. Whilst the pen is actually on my paper London is
     spreading itself from Kew towards Hounslow, towards Richmond, and towards
     Kingston, and on its other bounds towards how many other outlying places? The
     electric tram is doing all this' (pp. 27-8).

CODA TO THE CITY

Joseph Wiesenfarth

Ford placed 'On Heaven' at the head of his *Collected Poems* in 1936. This, his best-known poem, however, is not his best poem altogether. That honor belongs to 'Coda', which he placed at the end of *Collected Poems*. Ford's two best separate volumes of poetry – *On Heaven and Poems Written on Active Service* (1918)[1] and *Buckshee* (1931/1936, 1966)[2] – also, respectively, find themselves introduced by 'On Heaven' and concluded with 'Coda'.

Ezra Pound pronounced Ford's 1913 version of 'On Heaven' to be both 'the most important poem in the modern manner. The most important single poem that is' and also the 'best poem yet written in the "twentieth-century fashion"'.[3] That made it carry more freight than Ford intended. It is, nonetheless, inescapably Ford's attempt to topple the Blessed Damozel over the golden bar of heaven – warm from her breasts and wet from her tears – and drop her into a 'long red English racing car' pulling into a Provençal town like Tarascon, just outside the Alpilles, where God has cannily enough purchased his earthly mansion.[4] There she and her lover meet God for a drink at a sun-baked café instead of having her cry her eyes out in some remote galaxy because she's in heaven without her man. Ford had said that Rossetti gave 'the art of writing in English' the 'numbing blow of a sandbag' when he published 'The Blessed Damozel'[5] because he 'expresses the thoughts of Dante in the language of Shakespeare'.[6] Ford responded with 'On Heaven', written in the idiom of his day, in order to make the language of poetry once again immediately accessible to ordinary readers. Or to use C. H. Sisson's fine phrase, Ford 'found English literature poetical and left it spare'.[7]

That the poet's lover meets him in a Provençal town is important because Ford established the significance of cities to a civilized way of life in 'The Old Houses of Flanders', which was published in the same volume as 'On Heaven':

> The old houses of Flanders,
> They watch by the high cathedrals;

> They overtop the high town-halls;
> They have eyes, mournful, tolerant and sardonic, for the ways of men
> In the high, white, tiled gables.

Struck by exploding shells, the houses and churches and town-halls are utterly destroyed and family life, religious life, and civic life are destroyed with them. Ford personifies the old houses as sinking into death at this ghastly moment:

> And those old eyes,
> Very old eyes that have watched the ways of men for generations,
> Close for ever.
> The high, white shoulders of the gables
> Slouch together for a consultation,
> Slant drunkenly over in the lea of the flaming cathedrals.
>
> They are no more, the old houses of Flanders.

The destruction of centers of civilization is something that Ford revisits in 'Coda' where he imagines the willful destruction of Paris by a soulless army that hates and fears those who think and create:

> Sure, if there be a place where frugal thought,
> The love of the Arts, knowledge and temperate learning,
> Some sort of just appreciation of life's values
> And pity and moderation naturally grow
> Like pellitory of the wall on crumbling stones.
>
> Then, let its fame spread a little about the earth,
> And you will find all mankind in hordes without ruth,
> Bankers and tailors, poor men, pimps and sailors, rich men and tinkers
> Grasping axes and arrows
> And torches and powder and rifles and gas-shells and bombs
> All mankind flying together in planes towards that detested focus
> All men crying together from planes: 'Bedammned to their hocus-pocus'.
> Razing the buildings, cutting the throats of the thinkers,
> Rifling the tombs,
> Driving great steam-ploughs to level the ground,
> With great harrows
> Harrowing in salt by the ton,
> Wiping their brows and crying: 'That's well done.
> There shall never again grow the herb called Thought
> On this land of oblivion'.

This awful moment of destruction, which Ford envisions before the Second World War begins, condenses in 'Coda' all the destruction that is amplified in the *Poems Written on Active Service*. It depicts a return to that barbarous instinct that seeks to destroy civilization itself.

'On Heaven' presents an afterlife modeled on a perfect vacation taken with God's blessing in the shadow of his very castle in the Alpilles. First written before the war, it served the cause of the war:

> That poem was, during the War, published under the auspices of the Ministry of Information – as government propaganda! It might encourage young men who were about to die if they thought they would go to a nice heaven.[8]

The poem gave soldiers who fought on the Western Front a glimpse of their likely reward should they die opposing the forces of barbarism that Ford describes in his war poems and in 'Coda'. 'I think', Ford wrote in his Preface to *On Heaven and Poems Written on Active Service* 'that, in these days and years, we have got to believe in a Heaven – and we shall be all the happier if it is a materialist's Heaven' (*OH* 7). My own copy of this volume, for instance, was once owned by the Quartermaster's Office of the 3rd Cheshire Regiment and suggests the popularity these poems had among the troops. In contrast, the first eight poems of the *Buckshee* volume treat a love-story not unlike that told in 'On Heaven'. But 'Coda' then allows the lovers to live as long as they continue to create – as long as they advance the arts that lead the struggle of civilization against chaos. They suggest the welcome truth that it is not necessary to die to be happy. At the same time *Buckshee* shows that love itself demands struggle.

'Coda' tells the story of lovers in Paris: a writer and a painter. He is nameless; she is Haïtchka. Biographers tell us Ford is writing about himself and Janice Biala and that the poem as a whole celebrates their life together.[9] He is working on a book; she on a canvas:

> Slowly across the blackness of the wall
> Glimmer a square and a scroll.
> Just there. . . You see? . . . A scroll.
> That's not poetic imagery, those
> Illuminated by a taxi, crawling below
> Are all my past and all your promise, they
> Being my roll of proofs like Michelangelo's
> Scroll of the Fates on a Cumaean lap.
> And the pale square's your *Spring in the Luxemburg*,
> Like his table of your Law on Moses' knee.

If in 'The Old Houses of Flanders' the monuments of the human soul in its civilizing activities are destroyed, in 'Coda' the human soul endures through its artifacts. The barbaric soul, mindless and destructive, attacks it with axes and arrows, gas-shells and bombs but cannot prevail if Time allows the creative soul to think and work. The principal obstacles to thinking and creating in the *Buckshee* volume in general are the problems of two artists in love. Apocalyptic moments are remembered, as we have seen; but emotional problems are dramatized as the stuff of everyday life. 'Coda' shows Ford and Haïtchka standing up to their differences in age and temperament; to their differences in friends and fame; to their different preferences for a Parisian lifestyle; and to the threat of Time to their creative lives altogether. So it is about a man and a woman, troubled but in love, in a specific place at a specific time – Paris in the 30s – trying to make a life for themselves and a place for their art in spite of a deteriorating political situation that threatens apocalypse. In short, Paris is the stage for them to live out the creative life in all its complications, small as well as great, individual as well as political.

In writing 'Coda' Ford reprises two other poems, 'A Night Piece' and 'To All the Dead'. 'A Night Piece' has him lying abed next to his sleeping lover and thinking about their lives in Time. And 'To All the Dead' shows him unable to think at all in Paris by day because of the unremitting noise of the city. 'Coda' presents a silent Paris in the dead of night with only a clock striking to remind Ford, awake at two in the morning, of Time's unremitting passing. He takes advantage of the quiet and the dark to meditate on his life with Haïtchka, which the *Buckshee* poems dramatize in moments of conflict and celebration. If they follow in the footsteps of Michelangelo, they do so haltingly as frail people whose situation makes them more truly and representatively human as artist and writer.

'Buckshee', the title poem of the volume, celebrates Haïtchka as an unexpected gift, but not an unproblematical one, given her many contradictions. Nevertheless, Ford having been away from her, 'Compagnie Transatlantique', poem II, shows him longing to return to her because his life without her has been dull, even dead; as his ship nears the port and Haïtchka, he becomes excited and lively again. But in Paris in 'Fleuve Profond', poem III, Haïtchka's friend criticizes Ford and his fiction, hating Tietjens and loving the gorgeously vicious Sylvia of *Parade's End*. Having been lionized in the States, Ford finds himself stalked by a lion hunter in Paris. Even worse, in 'Chez Nos

Amis', poem IV, Ford finds Haïtchka herself heartless. But he is not cowed. The poem imitates Blake's 'The Tiger', suggesting that a poet who can measure up to Blake has something of the lion in him still.

Ford then shows in 'At the Caveau Rouge', poem V, that he can also be as good a poet as the Yeats of 'When You Are Old'. Translating the song of a chansonnier for Haïtchka – Ronsard's 'Quand vous serez bien vieille' – he thinks her heart should break on hearing it, but decides she hasn't got a heart at all. He reiterates this in 'Champêtre', poem VI, the bitterest one in the volume and the one in which *Buckshee* touches emotional bottom. 'Ripostes', poem VII, finds Ford persisting. Haïtchka's preoccupation with other men makes him jealous and ever more attracted to her. So it is more a poem of wanting than one of blaming. 'L'Oubli –, Temps de Secheresse', poem VIII, finds them in Provence in a physical and emotional drought; but just as the one will end, so will the other because, as he says to Haïtchka, 'Yes, you have a heart'. And that is what he celebrates. Ford ended the collection on this upward trajectory toward an emotional peak when he published the poems in 1931. But he later returned to the volume and added 'Coda' to it in 1936 – 'Coda', which when first published bore the title 'Latin Quarter'.[10]

By the time we come to 'Coda', then, we have lived through an emotional cycle of ups and downs finally to arrive at reconciliation. Ford and Haïtchka are back in their Paris apartment when the bell tolls for them:

> Two harsh, suspended, iron tocsin notes
> Reverberate panic from that clock of Richelieu's.

Ford hereby recalls Shakespeare as well as François Villon. He puts us in mind of 'the midnight bell' that

> Did, with his iron tongue and brazen throat
> Sound on into the drowsy ear of night

in *King John*[11] as well as of the 'iron voice of the tocsin calling to arms in the night', which Ford celebrates in his discussion of Villon's poetry in *The March of Literature*.[12] These references are appropriate overtones of the bell which awakens the drowsing poet and calls him to take arms against 'Chronos, old Time that will not stay'. He awakens to assess his situation and Haïtchka's, their having made it back to the Latin Quarter together from the drought in Provence. Time and place now become the subject of his thoughts.

Ford, with Haïtchka quietly sleeping beside him in their Paris flat, meditates on how time and space relate to artists and writers – artists and writers, often lovers, who have lived and died in Paris, but are nonetheless still triumphantly alive:

> Yet it is not merely that Dante
> With his as yet unmerited aura,
> Pondered in these streets or that Heloïse
> Here confronted the summer breeze. . . .
> (And don't forget, here sang Heine, with his Mouche,
> Shaking all Almaigne
> With the scorn born here in his brain
> On unending midnight mattresses of pain.)

Ford and Haïtchka aren't alone, then, but they are in the midst of a vast array of thinkers, lovers, and artists who are present now as they were in times past:

> We must
> Have Names and Affairs and Past Passions by which to adjust
> The mind and get some sort of perspective
> Into this era of plumbing and planes,
> And the maniacal passion of invective,
> The gigantic monotone,
> Of execration passing between nation and nation.

Ford passes on to Haïtchka the gift of his wisdom to help her through the trying times to come, just as artists, lovers, and thinkers have lived through trying times in Paris from time immemorial. He thereby completes their reconciliation begun in 'L'Oubli' by giving the best of himself – the wisdom of his imagination expressed in poetry – to Haïtchka. Their like-mindedness is then seen in each taking up the task of their respective arts as the poem ends.

Paris in this poem becomes the axis of the earth – 'place is a haven / And we have found a haven in this place' – where time puts on immortality because Paris is the center of thought and love and art. The tocsin warns of trouble, of destruction of the life of the spirit – destruction of the kind that Paris has seen before and is likely to see again. But in the perspective of Immortality –

> For you cannot measure time or thought by the clock.
> It can't be done.

– destructive moments are sterile moments that cannot obliterate
what is fertile in the mind, heart, and imagination.

> Imagine honeycomb
> > Boxed as you see it on your market stalls,
>
> A hundred boxes, row on row over row
> In a parallelogram? Your eye selects
> Box Two, Row Four. Then that's alive for you.
> > But, should your glance
>
> Pass to Box Nine, Row Ten, Box Two won't die
> Though you don't see it. . . Immortality
> Is no more strange than that!

Box Two remains even though it is not the thought of the moment. It
remains because it contains genuine honey – the honey of creation –
that is incorruptible: 'Life transmuted into rustless gold'. Thus when
night passes into day the lovers who are artist and writer must arise
and return to work like 'Bee-Man Time' to fill the honeycomb with
gold.

> > And old Time
>
> Dons incorruptibility and Life's
> Immortal. Untimely, the sun shines in
> And you must drop your brush, Praxiteles
> Having grown jealous.

Jealous of what? Jealous of what artists and writers have made happen
for centuries behind

> > the pellitory of the wall that grows
>
> Over the mouldering stones

in the City of Light.

NOTES

1   Ford Madox Ford, *On Heaven and Poems Written on Active Service*, London:
     John Lane, 1918 – hereafter cited as *OH*.
2   The *Buckshee* poems, without 'Coda', were first published in *New English Poems: A
     Miscellany of Contemporary Verse Never Before Published*, ed. Lascelles
     Abercrombie, London: Gollancz, 1931, pp. 172-92. That anticipated their publication
     in *Poetry: A Magazine of Verse* XXXIX, 5 (February 1932), 233-45, and XXXIX, 6

(March 1932), 317-23, much to the disappointment of Harriet Monroe, the editor of *Poetry*. They were first published with 'Coda' – 'Coda', with minor changes, having seen initial publication as 'Latin Quarter' (*London Mercury* 34 [1936], 391-96) – in Ford Madox Ford, *Collected Poems*, intro. William Rose Benét, New York: Oxford University Press, 1936, pp. 291-319. *Buckshee* appeared as a separate volume in 1966 as Ford Madox Ford, *Buckshee*, intro. Robert Lowell and Kenneth Rexroth, Cambridge, Mass: Pym-Randall Press, 1966.

3 Ezra Pound, 'The Prose Tradition in Verse', rpt. Brita Lindberg-Seyersted, *Pound/Ford: The Story of a Literary Friendship*, New York: New Directions, 1982, pp. 16, 17. I emphasize the year 1913 because 'On Heaven' underwent revisions in its reprintings.

4 Of the geography of his poem, Ford writes in *Return to Yesterday*, New York: Liveright, 1932, that 'I had written a long poem about Heaven which I placed in the Alpilles, tiny grey mountains just outside the town of Tartarin' (p. 401).

5 *Memories and Impressions: A Study in Atmospheres*, New York: Harper, 1911, p. 59.

6 'Literary Life: A Lecture Delivered by Ford Madox Ford,' ed. Joseph Wiesenfarth, *Contemporary Literature* 30.2 (1989), 176.

7 For a detailed discussion of Ford's critical attitude toward Rossetti and of 'On Heaven' as his attempt to supersede 'The Blessed Damozel', see Joseph Wiesenfarth, 'Ford Madox Ford and the Pre-Raphaelites or How Dante Gabriel Rossetti Started the First World War', *REAL*, 9, ed. Herbert Grabes, Winfried Fluck, and Jürgen Schlaeger, (1993), 109-48. For C. H. Sisson's remark, see his *English Poetry 1900-1950: An Assessment*, New York: St. Martin's Press, 1971, p. 52.

8 Ford Madox Ford, *Return to Yesterday,* New York: Liveright, 1932, p. 402.

9 See Arthur Mizener, *The Saddest Story: A Biography of Ford Madox Ford*, New York: World, 1971, pp. 402-04; and Max Saunders, *Ford Madox Ford: A Dual Life*, Vol. 2, Oxford: Oxford University Press, 1996, p. 373.

10 'Latin Quarter' was first published in the *London Mercury* 36 (September 1936), 391-96.

11 This is Ford's rendering of the lines in *The March of Literature*, New York: Dial, 1938 – hereafter cited as *ML*, p. 458. The Folger Library edition reads as follows: 'If the midnight bell / Did, with his iron tongue and brazen mouth, / Sound on into the drowsy race of night' (III.iii.43-45). *The Life and Death of King John*, The Folger Library General Reader's Shakespeare, ed. Louis B. Wright and Virginia A. LaMar, New York: Washington Square Press, 1967, p. 49.

12 *ML* 438. Ford discusses *King John* in *ML*, pp. 458-9.

REAL CITIES AND VIRTUAL COMMUNITIES: FORD AND THE INTERNATIONAL REPUBLIC OF LETTERS[1]

Elena Lamberti

> For the Art of Writing is an affair as International as are all the other Arts – as International, as Co-operative and as mutually uniting.
>
> Ford Madox Ford, *The English Novel*

Historical Contingency and Forlorn Hopes

Some people pursue the same dream throughout their lives with a perseverance that makes it difficult to decipher whether to achieve that dream is the goal of their existence, or whether their life is shaped by that very dream, in a more or less conscious way. Ford Madox Ford (1873-1939) spent his entire life dreaming of, pursuing and living in an (imaginary) 'International Republic of Letters', something that he seemed to have inherited through his hybrid 'genealogy'. To the critic, he has left biographical and literary traces which seem to have been skilfully conceived intentionally to muddle up his dreams and the facts of his life;[2] they are, in fact, always 'double traces', which at once puzzle and seduce the reader, who is forced to investigate them more through personal and literary suggestions, than through rigorous and precise evidence.

The idea of an 'International Republic of Letters' (the 'forlorn hope' discussed here), that Ford often recalls in his critical essays (and especially in his editorials[3]), would certainly have appealed also to the Italian director Pietro Germi, who was emblematically born in 1914, at the outbreak of World War I. 'Frontiers do not exist, they are man's construction' – Germi used to repeat – 'And where there are frontiers, there are also men wearing uniforms'. Ford's dream was precisely that of contributing, through the creation of literary works, to a world without frontiers, a new league of nations united in the name of the Arts and of Letters; a new world (a new Europe) no longer ruled by materialistic, commercial or political logic, but interested only in establishing peace and in achieving nobler standards of life for each

individual; a world in which the idea of nationality would be entirely
reconsidered:

> I never had much sense of nationality. Wherever there were creative thinkers
> was my country. A country without artists in words, in colours, in stone, in
> instrumental sounds – such a country would be forever an Enemy Nation. On
> the other hand every artist of whatever race was my fellow countryman – and
> the compatriot of every other artist.[4]

Although the historical moment was making it look more like an
anachronistic mirage than a truly achievable goal, Ford defended his
dream tenaciously. With the same force and perseverance which often
distinguish Don Quixotes and dreamers from any period, he opposed
his Republic to all those imperialistic politics which, in a short span of
time, led to two World Wars and to the definition of new geographical
borders that men wearing different uniforms insisted on defending for
many years to come (the inescapable 'historical contingency'). In
1924, a few years after World War I, when new and terrible
nationalistic movements which led to devastating racial and xeno-
phobic claims began to spread, Ford confirmed his hopes for a trans-
national and open community, and tried to turn it into reality by
founding a new literary review. In Ford's view, his *transatlantic
review*, published at the same time in Paris, London and New York,
was an ideal bridge linking various literary, artistic and cultural
settings; a bridge which would unify nations in spite of all
geographical borders and uniforms:

> *the transatlantic review*, the first number of which will appear on January 7,
> 1924, will have two only purposes, the major one, the purely literary,
> conducing to the minor, the disinterestedly social [. . . .] The first is that of
> widening the field in which the younger writers of the day can find
> publication, the second that of introducing into international politics a note
> more genial than that which almost universally prevails. The first conduces to
> the second in that the best ambassadors, the only nonsecret diplomatists
> between nations are the books and the arts of nations. There is no British
> Literature, there is no American Literature: there is English Literature which
> embraces alike Mark Twain and Thomas Hardy, with the figure of Mr. Henry
> James to bracket them [. . . .] The aim of the Review is to help bringing about
> a state of things in which it will be considered that there are no English, no
> French – for the matter of that, no Russian, Italian, Asiatic or Teutonic –
> Literatures: there will be only Literature, as today there are Music and the
> Plastic Arts each having Schools, Russian, Persian, 16th century German, as
> the case may be. When that day arrives, we shall have a league of nations no
> diplomatists shall destroy, for into its comity no representatives of
> commercial interests or delimitators of frontiers can break.[5]

This league of nations, united in the name of the arts and for the good of the arts, pervades Ford's idea of an 'International Republic of Letters': it is a league that exists only in Ford's vision, and not in the real world, and seems to be the ideal projection of his dream; using today's terminology, it is possible to refer to it as to a sort of (proto) 'virtual community'. And yet, Ford tries to locate a 'real' capital city for this 'virtual' Republic, a real city that Ford, pursuing his dream, idealizes: the city of Paris. In post-war Europe, in fact, Ford opposes Paris to London, presenting the latter as a lost city: after the great expectations of pre-war years, when the artists of the Great Vortex had forged their artistic dreams against a lively setting, Ford describes post-war London as the capital-city of a new-forming and 'real' community that he dislikes, because it is ruled by lost diplomatists and delimitators of frontiers.[6] In his editorials, London becomes the symbol of all that Ford stands against: the old imperialistic logic, which encourages the creation of barriers and borders, and the new capitalistic world, which subordinates frontiers to the market and to the needs of a new cast of powerful businessmen now ruling upon all politics. In contrast, Paris becomes the embodiment of a dream, a mythical (and idealized) place which offers a possible 'objective correlative', a sort of urban and architectonic model which gives hope to the making of Ford's Republic. Therefore, Ford's idea of the 'International Republic of Letters' seems to shift between two different, yet contiguous, levels, one real and one virtual. Real cities are turned into symbols of virtual communities giving shape to a peculiar, imaginary geography, anticipating some situations typical of the world today, as virtual communities become an increasingly tangible component of our own 'reality'. A reality which forces us to rethink some long-established sociological and anthropological paradigms.

Real Cities and Virtual Communities
It is, in fact, common to associate the term 'city' with that of 'city-planning': generally speaking, we want to know where a city is located, we want to know something about the architecture, we enquire about the related topography. Therefore, we tend to situate a city, or a town, to map it, to visually translate it into a physical reality. To fix a 'visual' correlative for a town is so important that we tend to work out models and schemes also for many of those 'ideal cities' conceived, in time, by various imaginative thinkers. Needless to say, the best examples are those offered by the perfect cities that Utopian writers have so carefully described, either through language or the

drawing of articulated maps, in so doing giving a shape to their ideal architectures. Yet, today the traditional idea of the 'city' appears to be a concept 'in progress': new technological environments tend, in fact, to encourage what could be perceived as a sort of 'semantic shift' of the original idea. In the electronic and digital world, the idea of a 'city' is less associated with that of city-planning, as traditionally understood, and more with that of a 'virtual community', a concept distantly related to the original implications of the Greek concept of POLIS. In the new 'web-geography', virtual communities group individuals across trans-national spaces whose architecture is extremely difficult to fix, to locate, and to map. The image of the NET, now used to define the World Wide Web, is, by its very nature, ethereal and shifting, a combination of fluctuating, electric intersections which reconfigure constantly. Therefore, the net presents itself as a virtual space, as a new electric city-plan, along which individuals move and (re)group on the basis of common interests, goals, and values. This is what enables a comparison between these newly-established ideas of community, cities, and Ford's vision of the 'International Republic of Letters'.

His vision questions exactly the geography established by Western Powers on the basis of materialistic logic, and aims at bringing people from different nations together by encouraging a reconciliation built upon respect for all cultural and artistic differences. Ford intends to create a 'network' of trans-national correspondences which move around the values of the Arts and Literature, values that he sees as universal and unbiased. He intends to encourage a widespread 'virtual' community of individuals sharing the same ethical and aesthetic project, no matter where they live. Needless to say, to the critic of today this may well appear to be an anachronistic, though fascinating, dream, or even a more forlorn hope: just while Ford is pursuing this vision, Europe is moving steadily in the opposite direction, both in terms of reinforcement of various barriers (geographical, commercial, political), and in its definition of new nationalistic politics. Yet today it remains a topical dream, as it seems to anticipate situations and needs which both Europe and the rest of the world have started to pursue only in the second half of the twentieth century.

It is therefore interesting to retrieve the unusual geography of Ford's 'Republic': as in the case of the new 'web communities', Ford's 'International Republic of Letters' is characterised by a sort of 'virtual geography', which superimposes itself on the real one and which includes intersections and crossroads shifting in time and in space. In fact, Ford located various real spaces onto which he mapped the territory of his 'Republic'; each of them became, in turn, the vital core, the 'capital-city' around which the community moved and grouped: pre-war London, that is the London of the Great Vortex illusion; post-war Paris, the fabulous melting-pot of various cultural and artistic experience; New York and Chicago in the 1930s. (This provided confirmation of the fact that, from that moment, North America became the new dominating culture.) At the beginning of the twentieth century, the best medium that Ford had at his disposal to spread his dream and to encourage the making of the 'International Republic of Letters' was still the literary review. From the end of the 1920s, and especially in the 1930s, when he was writer in residence at Olivet College, Michigan, Ford made use also of radio broadcasting, radio being one of the first electric media able to address (and therefore to bring together) people across nations and, significantly, do so simultaneously.

Therefore, Ford's idea of a 'Republic of Letters', as expressed in his editorials at the time of *The English Review*, and embodied as pre-war London (1908-1910), and defended also in those published in *the transatlantic review*, and embodied as post-war Paris, recalls and somehow anticipates the idea of 'virtual communities'. Ford envisages a community of artists and thinkers who do not share a limited common, geographical space, but, instead, share a common set of values, experiences, hopes, and move across nations in order to find each other. More importantly, they share a common goal, the establishment of a higher form of civilization through the assessment and maintenance of new trans-national artistic standards: in Ford's view, to be part of this ideal communal land, individuals must believe in the arts and literature as 'civilizing agencies', and, if writers, they must possess 'clarity of diction and earnestness of purpose',[7] in contrast with all those literary and moral commonplaces which had characterized most late-Victorian and Edwardian productions.

Unfortunately, unlike many utopian writers, Ford never explicitly designed for his readers a visual model of such a community; he never overtly worked out its possible 'architecture' or 'structure': it remaina a dream-Republic, without tangible shape. Yet, for a while, as I have suggested, he persuaded himself he had found this impossible Eldorado here on Earth: after having been deceived by post-war

London, in the early Twenties, Ford moved to continental Europe, and looked to France as a possible 'common land' for all imaginative thinkers and artists, and to Paris as its natural capital. Ford came to make use of a 'true' geographical reality to give shape to his dream and to implicitly suggest a model for his Republic; he chose France because of '*toutes les gloires de la France*', something that he presented as a communal, European heritage.

'The Second Country'

> Finally as to affairs inter-tribal! There was a United States naval officer who once said: 'My country right or wrong!' France being the second fatherland of every human being [...] the Review will have but one motto: Our Second Country right; Our Second Country wrong; but right or wrong our Second Country. This because of toutes les gloires de la France [. . . .] It is only in France that you will find the Art of Peace esteemed above science and warfare'.[8]

In order immediately to signify the importance of Paris in the development of his idea of a new 'inter-tribal', that is trans-national, culture, Ford chose the coat of arms of the city of Paris as a logo for *the transatlantic review* – a ship upon waves – and explained his choice to his readers:

> What about Paris? 'Fluctuatur nec mergitur'. You read that device below her coat of arms. Her emblem being a ship upon waves. 'She has her vicissitudes, but does not sink'. So the transatlantic review takes for her motto the word 'Fluctuatur'. She has – she will have – her vicissitudes. May she one day add: 'Nec Mergitur'. That is your affair.[9]

Ford uses that emblem to challenge his readers; in turn, post-war Paris became the perfect setting encouraging new forms of civilization. In Ford's imagination, Paris became the 'sun' capable of enlightening all other 'satellites, the sun triggering a true understanding among nations':

> It was not merely Paris that was alive to the Arts: it was the whole world [....]
> So communication should be established between that Sun, Paris, and the furthest satellites, and between them and Paris. St. Louis, Mo., must be told what Picasso was doing and Picasso and Mr. Joyce must be enlightened as to the activities of Greenwich Village. And Lenin reading of these deeds in his palace in Petrograd would be moved to give the Arts a higher place in his body public. It was a fine idea. (*IWN* 282-3)

And, yes, indeed, it was a fine idea. But, unfortunately, it too was no more than an idea, a dream, a 'Fordian vision'. Representatives of the Lost Generation have left several accounts of Paris in the 1920s, and, apart from the great communal excitement following the end of World War I, and the will to retrieve some enthusiasm for life in all its possible 'manifestations', the sense that one gets when reading those memoirs is that of a deep trauma, of a barely hidden 'malaise' for which Paris offers a convenient setting.[10] Certainly, expatriates in Paris made the city 'alive to the Arts' and turned it into a sort of impromptu trans-national community; but, it is important to recall that it was precisely in Versailles, a few kilometres South of Paris, that the new Europe was born on June 18, 1919. A new Europe where national frontiers mattered more than ever before.

Ford's idea of an International Republic of Letters, of a community of virgin minds united for the good of nations, is something that one should try to hold in mind when dealing with his work, as it forms the basis of his poetic, and constitutes a subtle leitmotif which affects all his discussions on life, art, literature and politics. And this is because, in Ford's view, there was a precise link between the cultural and the political crisis of his time. It is this kind of thinking that renders Ford more a European than a British writer or, at least, a writer whose poetic encourages a European communal vision, well ahead of his time.

Ford's 'Republic'

The idea of an 'International Republic of Letters' is first suggested in the editorials published in the *English Review*; it is in these editorials that readers find some interesting clues pertaining to Ford's Republic. Trickily enough, however, they are all 'indirect clues', because, as previously suggested, Ford never describes the Republic in a direct way, he never presents it as a well defined cultural project based on an artistic 'manifesto' or a given 'architecture'; instead, he implicitly forces his readers to imagine his ideal community by means of oppositions, by means of contrasts, that is by 'indirect means'. That's why he makes use of two different paradigms and, implicitly, invites his readers to use them as complementary touchstones in order finally to give some shape to this imaginary Republic. By pointing at what this Republic is not, he ends by providing a clue of what it could possibly be; this is a strategy which is somehow typical of Ford, who was in favour of 'suggestions' and against 'dictates',[11] who wished to encourage a 'critical attitude' in his readers and who more than once admitted that education and knowledge are better achieved through indirect means.

The two touchstones, or paradigms, for our consideration are respectively the city of London, that Ford uses metonymically as a symbol for a wider, philistine and materialistic Anglosaxondom (something that, in Ford's view, opposes his idea of an International Republic of Letters), and Plato's 'Republic', a classic, philosophical model that Ford sees as one of the major causes leading to contemporary materialism, and, therefore, to 'materialistic London'.

Ford's *English Review* editorials are meaningfully grouped under two different titles: 'On the Functions of the Arts in the Republic' (Dec. 1908-March 1909), and 'The Critical Attitude' (until Feb. 1910). I say 'meaningfully' because these two titles complement each other: in fact, according to Ford, the major function of the Arts in the Republic is precisely that of inducing people to adopt a critical attitude, something that he considers to be a fundamental antidote to a growing materialism. Indeed, the virtual minds that inhabit Ford's Republic should first of all possess a critical attitude. In this respect, Ford's Republic perfectly opposes Edwardian England, at least as this latter is presented by Ford himself: 'Anglosaxondom' is seen by Ford as the land of 'accepted ideas', a nation ruled by 'unfortunate opportunists, who whether they like it or not, are at the mercy of innumerable daily godlets'. These poor rulers take a firm hand in manipulating a practically illiterate 'man of the street' through new media and, therefore, in homogenising, to their favour, the multitude: '. . . we are coming nearer and nearer to government by panic. The governing class appeals more and more to sensationalism in order to obtain its end'.[12] Ford perceives the newly reforming mass-society as a by-product of its cultural attitude, and as the result of a much broader crisis, both of which are linked to the loss of ancient values and to the acquisition of a new, appealing style of life fomented by new forms of communication which turn original thinking into subliminally controlled commonplaces. London, and by extension Anglosaxondom, is presented as a dying land, as a place in which freethinking is perceived as the greatest of crimes; London is a grotesque theatre where small groups of philistine rulers control a growing mass of passive puppets; puppets that can be directed and fomented by what Ford calls 'fugitive organs', or also 'the half-penny press'. What, some years afterwards, T. S. Eliot will describe in *The*

Waste Land as the living-dead flowing over London Bridge, Ford somehow anticipates in his editorials when he writes:

> The fact is that what humanity desires, passionately and almost before all other things, is a creed. It craves for accepted ideas; it longs more for a mind at rest [....] All questions have become so exceedingly complicated, there is so little opening for moral fervour that the tendency of the great public is more and more to leave all public matters in the hands of a comparatively few specialists.[13]

The situation that Ford had already reported in the *English Review* editorials becomes more serious in the post-war period: 'A social system had crumbled. Recklessness had taken the place of insouciance. In the old days we had esteemed that we had ourselves well in hand. Now we were drifting towards a weir' (*IWN* 63). Furthermore, 'after the war Authority itself became an offence to the Realm [...] Life became a perpetual round of petty annoyances and the once faithful servants of the public a horde of petty spies in the hands of contemptible dictators (*IWN* 69).

After World War I, Ford felt that he no longer belonged to England: he denounced the way in which his home country was becoming an increasingly closed system, isolated from the rest of the 'civilized' world, favouring illusory and corporate myths, and celebrating a sterile nationalism which tended to deny all forms of cultural interaction to the advantage of cultural standardization. Ford tried to fight this deleterious spiral with the only weapons that he could use: critical attitude, literature and the arts, and the new literary review that he founded in Paris and used to launch his cry for a new trans-national culture. After the war, in fact, to return to the old imperialistic logic would mean to run the same risk twice:

> We fought to preserve a land fit, not for heroes, but for imaginative writers. Having done it most of us set to work to extirpate them. We seek to extirpate them for being more decent than ourselves; more frugal; more educated – but that is the national, the racial, the Anglo-Saxon 'we'. The We of the transatlantic review exists, as a just man in Sodom, if possible to redress the balance.[14]

The 'we' Ford employs stands for a trans-national 'we', not a 'national', 'racial' 'we' in the sense politicians tended to imply; in fact, according to Ford's analysis, the latter is a false 'we', an instrumentally corporate idea which fosters separation and boundaries, and is based on established and blind forms of individualism. Ford's 'we' is about starting from one's own culture and moving always to embrace new ones: it is only through a mutual sharing and understanding that progress (cultural, social and political) can be achieved. Therefore, Ford's 'we' does not deny differences, but, on the contrary, takes them as a resource to process, through comparison, new knowledge in any culture. In particular, Ford seems to blame the individualism of the English men of letters for the lack of progress on that side of the Channel, as this is something which reinforces the segregation of society itself and accelerates cultural and political decay. Ford is quite explicit in his analysis and writes:

> There is an inherent individualism in the English man of letters; there is an inherent shame in him which makes him desire to be regarded as anything but a man of letters. His aspiration is to be always a social figure, a philanthropist, a preacher, a fisherman, or a 'man of action'. The actual practice of his craft thus loses its cohesive force, so that it is almost impossible to find in England what is found in almost every other European capital – a society of men eagerly discussing their Art, sinking personal jealousies in the thirst for mutual sharpening of the wits, in the divine curiosity to discover how things are done. The English man of letters of any distinction lives apart, dotted over the face of the country, each one isolated, as it were, upon a little hill.[15]

By contrast, Ford's Republic should be seen as a community formed by a brotherhood of artists and imaginative thinkers joyfully co-operating for the good of the nation by the communal development of their arts and craft. More a brotherhood than an elite of artists segregated in a closed *Academe*, because in Ford's view, as in T. S. Eliot's: 'no poet, no artist of any art, has his complete meaning alone'.[16] Ford's ideal artists and imaginative thinkers should not live isolated on little hills, nor should they pretend to possess the truth and therefore impose their moral biases on the community; instead, they should sit 'in the corner of bars and places, and . . . listen; they don't take the centre of the stage; they are Private Persons'.[17] These virtual minds humbly serve the Republic, act more as apprentices in open art-shops, live their time in full and try to put their fellow-citizens into contact with the true spirit of their time. They try to encourage a critical attitude in their community: they are, at once, artists and social historians.

The second paradigm Ford implicitly refers to comes to mind, once again by contrast, when reading the title he gave to some of his editorials: 'On the Functions of the Arts in the Republic'. The use of the very term 'Republic' in this context, and the fact that Ford points explicitly to 'the functions of the arts' in such a Republic, polemically subverts the canon as established by the Greek philosopher, Plato. In later years, Ford distinguished Plato the Poet from Plato the Philosopher, a difference clearly stated, for instance, in *The March of Literature*, a book which serves to bring into focus Ford's formation of the Republic of Letters.[18] If Ford tends to support Plato the Poet because of his clear and simple prose (which appears to be in tune with Ford's impressionist tenets), he dramatically condemns Plato the Philosopher for the exclusion of all poets and artists from his Republic. Plato's 'Res-Publica' is, in fact, a carefully conceived state structured upon different classes (the workers, the warriors, the philosophers), but ruled by an aristocracy of philosophers – aristocracy meaning here the 'dominance of the best ones'. Plato sees the philosopher as someone who possesses true knowledge, as someone who has managed to come out of the dark cave and must now show others the right way. On the contrary, in his essays, Ford assigns this very role to the artist who, alone, can show his fellow men and women where they stand. It is evident that Plato and Ford give a different meaning to the concept of 'art': for the Greek philosopher, art is simply an imitation of the sensible world which, in turn, is an imitation of the world of ideas, that is of truth; therefore, art imitates something which is itself an imitation of something else. Instead, for Ford, who speaks to a 1920s audience, art is the only 'civilising agency which is at work today',[19] and it is also impossible to have 'a business community of any honesty unless you have a literature to set a high standard'.[20] Arts and letters are perceived as the only possible antidote to present day materialism, to the loss of a necessary critical attitude. In his essays, Ford's opposes 'imaginative writers' to 'Intelligentsia', the latter being a corporate caste of intellectuals supporting the Establishment and thereby fomenting an uncritical attitude.

In Ford's view, as he formulates it in *The March of Literature*, it was Plato who started it all, precisely by banishing arts from the Republic, therefore opening the path to a sterile way of thinking that cannot but bring men back to the cave:

> As sentimentalists, realists and Empiricists, our hatred and suspicion of Plato the philosopher may be boundless. We may well see in him the root of all evil [. . . .] Having no basis at all, his philosophy abounds in completely self-destructive contradictions. He will banish poets from his ideal republic and yet he will say that his ideal republic begins to go to pieces when education consists of the dry study of law, rather than the consumption of the sweet

fruits of the muses [. . . .] In short, in the long arguments as to whether a
creative artist can ever be a man of intelligence, those who oppose that theory
may well acclaim Plato as their greatest instance.[21]

Among Plato's champions, it is interesting to note that Ford includes
Professor Jowett of Balliol College, Oxford, a man who, in Ford's
words, 'was reported to have exclaimed: "Here I stand, my name is
Jowett / What there is to know I know it. / I'm the master of this
college / What I know not is not knowledge"' (*ML* 153). Professor
Jowett provides a perfect example of that Intelligentsia that Ford
attacks in his editorials, both in the *English Review* and the
transatlantic review, an Intelligentsia that, following what Ford
perceives as Plato's sterile philosophy, can exist 'with perfect
equanimity in a vacuum':

> the difference between the arts and these pseudo-intellectual movements lies
> precisely in this, that the arts draw their being from humanity and can never
> be perfectly unaffected by the vicissitudes of surrounding mankind, whereas
> the other side battens solely on scraps of paper and could exist with perfect
> equanimity in a vacuum.[22]

In his editorials, Ford insists on the difference between the
'Intelligentsia' and imaginative writers, and asserts that the latter
possess a social honesty that the former deny:

> The ambition of the writer is to cast light; to make clear. His purpose is to
> make man, above all, clear to his fellow men; the purpose of the Intelligentsia
> is to suppress all such illuminations as they do not conduce to rendering more
> attractive their own special class [. . . .] Literature exists for the Reader, and
> by the Reader [. . . .] The quite natural tendency of the Intelligentsia is to
> make of literature as unconsumable a thing as may be, so that, acting as its
> High Priest, they may make mediocre living and cement over an unlettered
> world. It is an ambition like any other, but more harmful than most.[23]

In particular, Ford points out the dangerous effects which accompany
the co-operation between this caste of 'pseudo-intellectuals' and the
Establishment: it is precisely this caste, enslaved to power, that
foments an uncritical attitude among readers; it is this caste that makes
use of the new 'half-penny press' to control, through sensationalism,
the masses, therefore encouraging a false idea of nationalism which
denies a true understanding among nations and plays into the hands of
those governments which sustain Intelligentsia itself. In this regard,
Ford mentions the case of the historian Mommsen in pre-war

Germany: in Ford's analysis, Mommsen used both his prestige and his studies of the Roman Empire to encourage a war-mongering spirit which contributed to the outbreak of World War I.[24] Similarly, in England, men of the Establishment like Professor Jowett have been instructing those doomed to wear the new uniform of the British Empire:

> Fortified, no doubt, with the maxims of Plato, Jowett turned out from Balliol College, Oxford, so many consuls, pro-consuls, governors-general, and viceroys for the British dominion overseas that the British Empire has been called Jowett-land. (*ML* 153)

It is against this logic that Ford fought all his life; given these premises, the 'International Republic of Letters' becomes the symbol of his personal war, as an artist and as a man, against the new world in progress.

Anglosaxondom, Jowett-land, the country of accepted ideas: these are all synonyms in turn used by Ford to represent the England of his time, a perfect example of what his Republic should not be. More than anything, it is the isolationism of England that Ford opposes, the rigidity of a given paradigm which combines the lowering of cultural standards and narrow-centred policies, and which leads to what Ford often defines as a 'hopeless standard of life'. By contrast, Ford's Republic appears as an ideal and wide-spread community, which dwarfs cities, overlaps geographical boundaries and groups individuals across nations.

NOTES

1   A version of this paper appeared first in *Interpreting/Translating European Modernism: A Comparative Approach*, ed. Elena Lamberti, Bologna: COTEPRA, 2001, pp. 43-60.

2   The title of Max Saunders's biography, *Ford Madox Ford: A Dual Life*, Oxford: Oxford University Press, 2 vols, 1996, clearly defines the strong interrelation which exists between 'fact' and 'imagination' (impressions) in Ford's life, something which, inevitably, conditions and pervades many critical works on and investigations of Ford.

3   Ford was the founding editor of two literary reviews: *The English Review*, published in London from December 1908 to February 1910 under his editorship; and *the transatlantic review*, published in Paris from January to December 1924.

4   Ford, *It Was the Nightingale* (1933), New York: The Ecco Press, 1984 – henceforth referred to as *IWN*; p. 74.

5   B. J. Poli, *Ford Madox Ford and 'the transatlantic review'*, Syracuse, NY: Syracuse University Press, 1967, pp. 37-39.

6   See Brian Groth's essay in this volume for further discussion of Ford's changing view of London.

7   See Ford's announcement of *The English Review*, quoted in N. Tomlinson, *Ford Madox Ford and 'The English Review'*, MA dissertation, Hatfield Polytechnic, January 1986.

8   B. J. Poli, *Ford Madox Ford and 'the transatlantic review'*, p. 40.

9   Ford, *transatlantic review*, 1:1, January 1924, 77-78.

10 See Caroline Patey's essay in this volume for further discussion of Paris as the setting for *the transatlantic review*.

11 See Ford, *The English Novel: from the earliest days to the death of Joseph Conrad* (1930), Manchester: Carcanet, 1983, p. 24.

12 Ford, 'The Critical Attitude', *English Review*, 2, April 1909, 139.

13 Ford, 'The Critical Attitude', *English Review*, 4, December 1909, 102.

14 Ford, *transatlantic review*, 1:4, April 1924, 200.

15 Ford, *English Review*, 1, March 1909, 797.

16 T. S. Eliot, 'Tradition and the Individual Talent', *The Sacred Wood*, London: University Paperbooks, 1920, p. 49.

17 J. Wiesenfarth, 'The Ash-Bucket at Dawn: Ford's Art of Poetry', *Contemporary Literature*, 30:3, Fall 1989, 247.

18 Ford, *The March of Literature: from Confucius to Modern Times*, London: Allen and Unwin, 1939.

19 Ford, *transatlantic review*, 1:4, April 1924, 169.

20 Ford, *Henry James. A Critical Study* (1914), excerpted in *The Ford Madox Ford Reader*, ed. Sondra J. Stang, London: Paladin, 1987, p. 189.

21 Ford, *The March of Literature*, New York: Dial Press, 1938 – hereafter cited as *ML*, pp. 146-7.

22 Ford, *transatlantic review*, 1:6, June, 1924, 451.

23 Ford, *transatlantic review*, 1:4, April 1924, 169.

24 Ford, 'Stocktaking: towards a Re-valuation of English Literature – VI. Pirata Nesquissimus', *transatlantic review*, 1:5, May 1924, 442-52.

RIGHT BANK, LEFT BANK AND AN ISLAND: FORD'S FRAGMENTED *VILLE LUMIERE*

Caroline Patey

Unlike that of other modernists, Ford Madox Ford's Paris hardly offers a unified image of the French metropolis, nor, conversely, does it point to a clear-cut status of the British writer in the moving waters and geographies of the capital's cultural life. Around Ford, none of the hero worship that surrounds the august stones of Rue de Fleurus where Gertrude Stein held court to the worthies of international art and letters; precious little, as well, of the comfortable mid-western ease shown by Hemingway and of his athletic enjoyment of the urban space; no trace either, indeed, of the priest-like dedication to the word practised in Adrienne Monnier's and Sylvia Beach's saintly establishment, Rue de l'Odéon. As is often the case, Ford's impressions and renderings are complex and defy simplification. Like Stein, he has many friends who do not however form a *cénacle*; there is a breathlessness in the instability of his domestic and sentimental conditions which, though he, also, was on the move from one love to the other, Hemingway ruthlessly appears to have little sympathy for:

> he was breathing heavily through a heavy, stained mustache and holding himself as upright as an ambulatory, well-clothed, up-ended hogshead [. . . .] I was trying to remember what Ezra Pound had told me about Ford, that I must never be rude to him, that I must remember that he only lied when he was very tired, that he was really a good writer and that he had been through very bad domestic troubles. I tried hard to think of these things, but the heavy, wheezing, ignoble presence of Ford himself, only touching-distance away, made it difficult.[1]

As to his passion for art and literature, while alive and kicking in Paris as elsewhere, it never achieved the almost mythical iconicity attached to *Shakespeare and co*. It is true that reminiscences of a Parisian Ford, his own and others', are many, but they do not fall into a neat portrait and too easily tend to facile caricature. If Stein semi-fondly recalls enjoying 'his stories of Mistral and Tarascon', the irony of comparing Ford to a French royalist 'on account of his resemblance to a Bourbon claimant'[2] is more biting; and while James Joyce did show gratitude in dubbing Ford the godfather of *Work in Progress*, he had no qualms about lampooning him for his many wives – eight or eighteen, ponders the monogamous Irishman?:

> O Father O'Ford, you've a masterful way with you,
> Maid, wife and widow are wild to make hay with you,
> Blonde and brunette turn-about run away with you,
> You've such a way with you, Father O'Ford.[3]

Ford himself adds to the multiple images: not so much through the inevitable inaccuracies in his records and the sheer pleasure of tale-telling that sometimes alters factual truth; but rather through the perceptiveness of his vision that scans the capital of France in its historical depth as well as in its contemporary languages and even in the future of its cultural status. Paris, thus, is ineluctable, resounding with the humming of multiple voices, illuminated by famous faces and dramatic encounters, witness to and cradle of another review and endless literary activity; yet, in Ford and to Ford, the city remains somehow mysterious and multilayered, exploded in various modes of writing, told in fragments and dissonant visions, in tune indeed with the aesthetics of modernity that it was hosting and promoting. Life throbs in between the multiple frames of Fordian reminiscences, narratives and literary expertise, and it does so in the complex and creative way unique to their author. Paris, therefore, is a specific urban and cultural reality, but it is also the city you write about *from* somewhere else, or alternatively, the space where one lives thinking of other places: "'That, you see, is *l'art moderne*", he explained years later: "you paint New York from Provence and the shores of the Mediterranean from New York... Indeed, this is the way I write.'"[4]

A City with a Past
Such a lingering sense of displacement has to do with Ford's age, slightly anachronistic in the post-war Paris of nascent talents and youthful effervescence:

> I remember very well the impression I had of Hemingway that first afternoon.
> He was an extraordinarily good-looking young man, twenty-three years old. It
> was not long after that that everybody was twenty-six. It became the period of
> being twenty-six. During the next two or three years all the young men were
> twenty-six years old. It was the right age apparently for that time and place.
> (*Toklas* 229)

The weight of Ford's fifties had little to do with biology and more with memories enfolding the image of the other, earlier and different Paris that had shaped his childhood visions: a capital city on the morrow of the Franco-Prussian war and of the *Commune*, active, noisy, and not untouched, in Henry James's records, by the vulgarities of the third republic:

> The numerous Americans who have been spending the summer in Europe congregate doubly during September and October upon the classic region, about a square mile in extent, which is bounded on the south by the Rue de Rivoli and on the north by the Rue Scribe, and of which the most sacred spot is the corner of the Boulevard des Capucines, which basks in the smile of the Grand Hotel. The ladies, week after week, are treading the devious ways of the great shops – the Bon Marché, the Louvre, the Compagnie Lyonnaise; the gentlemen are treading other ways, sometimes also, doubtless, a trifle devious… Paris seems more than ever, superficially, a vast fancy bazaar, a huge city of shop fronts.[5]

This is the city of arcades and of department stores that offer women socially acceptable spaces, the newly Haussmann-designed metropolis; it is Walter Benjamin's capital of the nineteenth century. More crucially, to Ford, this Paris is home to some of the new literary giants who entered his life very early:

> […] George Sand's apartment in Paris roared and rocked with the laughter of Flaubert, Turgenev, the Goncourts, Zola, Daudet and Pauline Viardot when the depressed Sainte-Beuve on a Sunday would turn himself into a whitened sepulchre in the attempt with his lips to pick a wedding-ring off a pyramid of flour.[6]

However humorous, the anecdote reveals Ford's long-lasting and deeply felt affection for the French pantheon and its modes. Led by Flaubert and Maupassant as guides on the road to the new narrative idiom, a road strewn with idealized cameos of smoky literary discussions and epic aesthetic debates, Ford, a devotee of 'Félicité', 'La Nuit', *Une Vie*, encounters vicariously his first Paris, through Flaubert's *cénacle*: a city whose heart pulses – with money, art and commodities – on the right bank of the river and whose literary life gravitates around the famed abode of Rue du Faubourg Saint Honoré. No Montparnasse and no left bank were in sight when Ford's role models met on the Sunday afternoons of the mid-seventies. This number included, of course, the Russian Turgenev – whenever he was

given leave by the daunting Pauline – and, closer yet to Ford, Henry
James who:

> expressed intense dislike for Flaubert who 'opened his own door in his
> dressing gown' and he related, not infrequently, unrepeatable stories of the
> ménages of Maupassant – but he much preferred Maupassant to 'poor old
> Flaubert'... He preferred Maupassant to Flaubert because Maupassant was
> *homme du monde* – or at any rate had *femmes du monde* for his mistresses.[7]

The tales about the meeting of Flaubert and James are notoriously full
of discrepancies; hateful as he may have been, the French novelist
managed all the same to strike James as 'an excellent old fellow,
simple, naïf and *convaincu*, in his own line, and extremely kind and
friendly, not to say affectionate'![8]

James's emotional oscillations do not alter the fact that Paris
was then Flaubert's Paris, offering the revolution of the novel its
urban context, a lesson James himself learned, elaborated and passed
on to others. And Ford well knew that *The Good Soldier* was
somehow generated in Rue du Faubourg St. Honoré. There is a direct
thread from Emma Bovary to Florence,[9] who are sisters in their social
and erotic aspirations and ultimately joined in a similarly poisonous
death – procured by prussic acid or arsenic. More important still, the
visual style of *Madame Bovary* and the constant metamorphosis of
ordinariness into stylistic adventure – *l'aventure du style* – are part
and parcel of the poetics of Ford's novel, which is deeply rooted in an
intensely pictorial and visual experience:

> French Realist novelists of the latter part of the nineteenth century became of
> necessity virtuosi of literary description. Their ambition to be historians of the
> present [...] obliged them to experiment with literary stratagems whereby
> texts seemed to present to the reader the actual spectacle of modernity. The
> notion of the novel as 'une tranche de vie', as a slice of life, became a familiar
> convention, a common-place. Romantic plots and peripeteia became the
> enemy of the essential task of showing life 'à l'état normal'. Description, and
> especially visual description, assumed unprecedented status in narratives. The
> aesthetic of the realist novel became increasingly visual.[10]

In such a visually charged context, the seemingly random
allusion to the Académie Julian – where lugubrious, silent and morose
Jimmy studied even though 'he had no talent as a painter'[11] – opens
yet another window on Ford's Paris. Tucked in the Passage des
Panoramas, a most Benjaminian urban site, Rodolphe Julian's art
school offered an alternative education to the many young talents who

were not accepted at Alexandre Cabanel's class on the other side of the river, at the official Ecole des Beaux Arts. In the seventies, Julian numbered George Moore among its students, an experience he remembers in *Confessions of a Young Man* (1888) with great fondness, though it led to no artistic achievement. As Moore also recalls, the school in the Passage des Panoramas welcomed girls, a liberality not practised at Cabanel's that lured many American and English would-be female artists to the backdrop of Boulevard Montmartre, offering them the slightly transgressive opportunity to concentrate on male models posing in the nude. The trail of the Académie Julian evokes other figures known to Ford: among them Bob Stevenson, an early admirer of Impressionist painting, Fanny Osborne's daughter and Marie Bashkirtseff, who actually depicted the studio of fully dressed women focusing their attention on a semi-naked boy.[12] To the narrative and visual city of the seventies and eighties, another feature should perhaps be added. By the Seine, modernist autobiography was being shaped, precisely in George Moore's *Confessions* in which 'realistic' truth entails flights into subjectivity and a highly personal treatment of time and sequence: modes of self portraiture destined to leave a deep imprint on Ford's future circumnavigation of his own days and ways. As Ford himself has it, even though George Moore's part in the renewal of the novel is always forgotten (*RY* 282), the Irish writer was still a fellow worker towards a similar scope:

> I have suggested that we were more alone in our search for the New Form, than, very likely, we actually were. Mr Bennett, at least, at that date, was engaged in acquiring the immense knowledge of French tricks and devices that his work afterwards displayed. And there was always Mr. George Moore. (*RY* 159)

In years to come, Ford's attention would be captured by the other bank: 'To-day for me civilization consists in the Left Bank, Asia, Africa';[13] but, nonetheless, there is some geographical justice in the coincidences that cluster around the Rue Notre Dame des Champs, where Stella and Ford rented a studio many years later. There, before it moved to Passage des Panoramas, was the seat of the Académie Julian; there, of course, James McNeill Whistler used to have a studio that would fleetingly become an impossible object of desire to Stella in 1927, as if indeed the Paris of the 1870s and 1880s kept haunting the streets and memories of *les jeunes*.

Liminal Spaces

The choice of Quai d'Anjou as home to the *transatlantic review*, or
rather the chance offered by William Bird, has in itself a sort of
metaphorical truth. Not only does the island location echo the *fluctuat*
logo of the review and the stream of consciousness of many texts to be
published in it – as of course the first instalment of Joyce's fluvial
Work in Progress – but it is also the point of intersection of the
different souls of Paris: the Quai d'Anjou faces the *rive droite*, but the
Ile St. Louis is truly where the two banks meet and marry. A properly
in-between place therefore for a literary enterprise wishing to 'bridge
the gap between the prewar and the postwar generations', between the
English Review and international Paris, between the sentence of Henry
James and the first 'words of many, many young giants as yet
unprinted'.[14] The island also resists the alternative cultural
polarizations of the city, whose fulcrum, during the nineteenth and
early twentieth century, kept crossing the Seine and moving from
North to South, from the Baudelairean *boulevards* to the
Montparnasse *ateliers* and back again to the right bank, near the opera
and the arcades, where the Surrealists chose to repair in the Twenties,
'par haine de Montparnasse, par goût aussi de l'équivoque et des
passages'.[15]

    Thus, both location and vocation of the review contributed to its
destiny as go-between; it was, after all, conceived to bring about a
'state of things in which it will be considered that there are no English,
no French – for the matter of that, no Russian, Italian, Asiatic, or
Teutonic – Literatures: there will be only Literature' (Poli 37); no little
scope after the general slaughter provoked by nations at war! The
dialogues launched on the pages of the *transatlantic* cover many areas,
starting with literary genres: long and short coexist, as indeed do verse
and prose, in a continued disruption of consolidated barriers between
forms and linguistic registers. Just as the two banks are joined by the
Pont de Sully, the Dadaist Tristan Tzara, a nihilist destroyer of
Western bourgeois values, shakes hand with Gertrude Stein who is
working on the creation of a new language together with those she
calls the 'virginal' Americans. As they interact in the pages of the
transatlantic, the end of old Europe meets the dawn of another
literature being born to the English language and stemming out of
American culture; 'America having begun the creation of the
twentieth century in the sixties of the nineteenth century', and

because, of course, as Stein wrote, 'there is for me only one language and that is English' (*Toklas* 87, 77).

The dialogue taking place between Europe and America is also the encounter of different spaces, with largely urban extensions on one hand and the Wild West on the other:

> On Sunday, disappointed tea-drinkers hammered all day on the locked doors. They were all would-be contributors, all American and nearly all Middle Westerners [. . . .] Mr. Hemingway had, I think, been a cowboy before he became a tauromachic expert; Mr Robert McAlmon the printer-author certainly had; so poor Dunning, the gentle poet; even Mr. Bird had been a rancher in his day and Mr. Pound had come over to Europe as a cattle-hand![16]

This is why some pages of the *transatlantic* lead their readers to the shores of a northern Michigan lake in the company of Indians hired to cut logs, and investigate the tensions between untrammelled nature and the strictures of marriage; while other stories linger on Parisian landscapes and the exhausted emotions of the cosmopolitan world, like Djuna Barnes's 'The Passion': 'He called only once after that, and only once or twice was she seen riding in the Bois, limned in pink, a mist behind a tight drawn veil, for shortly after that she did not live anymore'.[17] In its conversations with the visual arts too, the *transatlantic* juxtaposes safe values and newly-discovered talents. Printing on the same page a famous *Nature morte* by Georges Braque and the very lively *Drawing* of a young girl by Gwen John undoubtedly provokes a sort of creative shock and somehow enhances the quality of both artists, revealing the geometric and abstract qualities of the latter and the fleshiness and rotundity, as it were, of the former. And not to forget the *Tête de Femme* with flowing hair and naked breasts, by Braque, followed by a fruit, and then a musical, *Nature morte*. These announce yet another striking 1903 nude by Picasso, and Brancusi's single line flexed silhouette, a series concluded by the *Dessin* of, possibly, the sculptor's *atelier*: bodies, fruit, the shape of a guitar and the gesture of the sculptor stage a manifesto of synaesthesia and express a deeply felt belief in the unrestricted conversation between forms and languages.[18]

But there are dissonances, not surprisingly in a review that pioneers the forms of atonality and the questioning of harmony practised by its musical contributors Erik Satie and George Antheil. Somehow the alchemy of the dialogue between idioms and forms – the magic union embodied in the confluence of the merging arms of the Seine – does not take place: variety and jocosity do not hide divergences and barriers in mutual comprehension. First, and most important, among these, perhaps, is the Frenchness of the French, however inclined to Anglo-Saxon experiments. The voice of Paris in Philippe Soupault's *Lettres*, in particular, is hardly in tune with the general mood. His walks in the city cover territories little connected to the left bank, starting from the Eiffel tower, as it happens in his first contribution to the *review*, crossing the river and up to the dreamy Rue Berton, where Balzac's house still stands, private and hidden, full of nineteenth century memories:

> De la terrasse du petit jardin, je puis apercevoir dans les salons, sur les trottoirs, les fantômes élégants de Lucien de Rubempré, de Rastignac ou d'Arthez. Ils portent tous d'autre noms, mais leurs ambitions sont restées les mêmes.[19]

It is true that the poet's steps then take him to Montparnasse, and the bars where rags are played while everyone dances and alcohol flows freely, but there is a strange detachment in the final evocation of the '"ambassadeurs" dont James a fait le portrait', a group Soupault describes with some gentle condescension: 'On parle beaucoup et sans méchanceté. Tout est tempéré, simple, correct... Il y a un grand effort doublé d'une très bonne volonté pour se comprendre et se conseiller'.[20]

The second letter is an autumnal celebration of the French poets Mallarmé and Apollinaire, the latter remembered as he walked '... dans les jardins du Champ de Mars, à l'ombre de la Tour Eiffel', while the living future has the face of Jean Giraudoux, rather than Ezra Pound or James Joyce! Even more significant are the first textual signs of the surrealistic imagery that would soon become Soupault's literary home: 'Les grands moutons d'or se groupent dans le ciel pour brouter l'immense prairie du clair de lune'.[21] Affiliated to different geographical areas, true to heterogeneous memories, Frenchness and Anglo-Saxondom meet, drink together, but do not marry. Ford himself would have conceded this, not without a shade of melancholy:

> It is in that that to me the Montparnasse district is profoundly disappointing. Before the war Paris was a truly international centre, artists of all shades and nations meeting and interchanging ideas very freely [. . . .] The Montparnasse district is a bran-new [*sic*] phenomenon as an artists' quarter, but it is a phenomenon purely foreign where artists of every nationality except the French simply dislike the one the other amidst an atmosphere a great deal too

much impregnated with alcohol [. . . .] The foreigners come seeking a fabulous cheapness, or a fabulous laxness in sexual morality, that have no existence beneath the measly sumach trees with which the Boulevard is planted. (*MF* 107, 108)

In the shadow of the creative *rive gauche* that emanates from the *transatlantic review* down there at the Quai d'Anjou, a more disquieting city is enfolded, a divided urban space, dotted with hints of alienation and perhaps even death. It is a picture that finds confirmation in the preface to Jean Rhys's *The Left Bank*, in which Ford concludes that something mythically mournful attaches to almost all uses of the left.[22] Beyond the bad augur, however, there is, more crucially, an awareness that the winds of culture and novelty were moving west and that perhaps artistic and literary Paris was in the process of being eclipsed by New York, a perception typical of Ford's many prophetic intuitions:

> Except that there is a strong current away from what it is convenient to call eighteenth-centuryism, there is no strong current amongst the French young of to-day and, were I to have to put a name to any French movement that at all predominated amongst the Jeunes of the Latin Quarter, I just could not, though for a long period I have been receiving most of the books and periodicals published by those very Jeunes. But I can perceive no general direction in it all. (*MF* 97)

Subtly, and without rhetorical flourish, Ford was capturing the spirit of the time and following the business of art about to cross the ocean.

Vivent les Femmes
'We exist as twin civilizations a little removed above the stage of brutes – because France exists. France exists because her women treat the handling of domestic life as if it were an art' (*MF* 200). While it is true that Ford's dedication to French womanhood, in the seventh chapter of *A Mirror to France,* concentrates primarily on the culture and intelligence of food, the mind does not run here to kitchens and ovens, but to another way of handling domestic and gastronomic life as an art: painting it, as did Stella Bowen in the almost Holbeinesque picture of the owners and staff of the restaurant Au Nègre de Toulouse, or recollecting the warmth and conviviality attached to the *bistros*, like the 'Mariniers' where the Seine fishermen used to eat on the Quai d'Orléans, or the:

Maison Paul in the Place Dauphine on the Cité...It was a nice, steamy little
place with sawdust on the floor and a zinc bar and a pot of flowers between
the spotted lace curtains and Mr. Paul, when on his mettle, was a marvellous
cook. He was kept pretty closely in the kitchen by madame, but after cooking
us a special *plat*, he would creep out and hang around the doorway, shyly
twisting his apron in his hand until somebody spotted him, when he would
come forward to receive our congratulations.[23]

There is more than a little poignancy in the laughing images of chatty
restaurant tables, flowing wine, *bals musette* and arty parties, common
in both Bowen and Ford. For, while certainly conveying the exhilarat-
ion to be experienced in Paris, they cannot mask the underlying
anxiety of homelessness. Bowen's home-hunting anecdotes are of
course the documents of practical difficulties, but their obsessive
reiteration and the despair they trigger unveil something more similar
to an existential condition: 'The story of my life during the next three
years is of a long, unequal struggle to get together another permanent
home. It overshadowed everything' (Bowen 114). Stella's Paris is
similar to a huge and hostile *agence de location*, full of crooks, so
immense that it requires endless 'trampings in the rain' and 'hopeless
journeys in suburban trains' (Bowen 114). Such a city is uncannily
close to that of Marya, Rhys's character, lost in her 'wanderings in
sordid streets'. 'She spent the foggy day in endless, aimless walking',
Rhys writes, 'for it seemed to her that if she moved quickly enough
she would escape the fear that hunted her'.[24] True, Rhys's Paris in
Quartet is more bleak than Bowen's; either unlimited, as in the Rue de
Vaugirard, a street so long it may never be walked to the end, or
labyrinthine and sure to hide a monstrous Minotaur at its centre – as in
the Palais de Justice where Marya is informed of Stephan's sentence.
Or, worse still, it proves similar to a prison in which one is confined,
as in the inappropriately named la *Santé*; urban space affords no
security, let alone homeliness! And if Stella does not endure the
combined pathologies of claustrophobia and agoraphobia that plague
Marya, their versions of Paris differ only in degree and intensity of
unheimlichkeit.

Such displacements and dislocations tell more than the mere
story of national estrangement or psychological alienation; they are,
also, and perhaps primarily, the signs of a female condition
undergoing profound and uneasy transformations, a process owing
much to its taking place, precisely, in Paris. As Bowen writes:

The feminine role is so much better understood and honoured there than in England, and there is much less offensive masculine patronage to resent. Women have so much real and actual power that the political shoe pinches less hard than it does in a country where wives have to account to their husbands for their expenditure, instead of vice versa, and where billiard-rooms and smoking-rooms and clubs are filled with able-bodied males, schoolboys in all but years, who simply don't like women very much, except when feeling amorous; and even then, they don't acknowledge their debt with very much grace. (Bowen 157)

Thus, to so many women of the two banks, Paris, a city with fewer censors and less censorship than elsewhere, was both challenging social, sexual and cultural roles and teaching lessons in freedom and the conquest of identity. And it did so in many ways. One, for instance, was light and frivolous, the way of fashion and clothes. From Stein to Bowen, to Djuna Barnes and even unhappy Jean Rhys, the feminine path to identity has something to do with the sensual pleasure of touch and sight procured by a dress or a beautiful hat:

We talked hats. Fernande had two subjects, hats and perfumes... Later on once in Montmartre she and I were walking together. She had on a large yellow hat and I had on a much smaller blue one. As we were walking along a workman stopped and called out, there go the sun and the moon shining together. Ah, said Fernande to me with a radiant smile, you see our hats are a success. (*Toklas* 19)

Stella Bowen is less flamboyant than the first Mrs Picasso, but she does linger with satisfaction on party dresses and a Golden Blouse and going to the sales with Olga Rudge.[25]

However, there is more to frocks and hats than the caress of soft fabrics. Dresses, millinery and feminine fineries, for one, are in constant conversation with art: Fernande's passion for her hats is thus entangled in Matisse's *La femme au chapeau*, a picture bought in 1905 by Stein and central to her memoir as a hymn to chromatic freedom. Dressing the character, then, or indeed cross-dressing her or him, was also part of a deeper reflection on roles, appearances and the body, leading to the apprehension of the potentially subversive function of clothes and fashion, as androgynous Stein knew, as indeed did everyone in the lively Sapphic circle gravitating around Nathalie Barney.[26] Because, yes, the life and attributions of women were changing, as if the Seine were infecting them with a new spirit. There is something extraordinarily cheerful and energetic attached to Stella Bowen's words, in spite of the dark thoughts of homelessness recorded above, when she is seen to explore the new territories of feminine solidarity and expression that Paris was then offering women. Many are the friends that cross Stella's path and occupy her affections: Jenny Bradley, who did much 'to civilize me and at the same time exploded the remains of those Adelaide prejudices which still fogged the corners of my mind' (Bowen 126); there is the closeness to Hadley Hemingway, engaged in the painful process of divorcing Ernest; there are the girlish pleasures of going to the movies together, or enjoying the concerts with Olga Rudge or discussing domestic matters and Julie's ballet dress with Gertrude Stein. Page after page, detail after name, worry after joy, a new woman takes shape in Stella's letters and autobiography, yearning for independence, economic and sentimental, as well as for professional recognition; discovering new modes of being and striving to bypass conventions and achieve self-knowledge and joy. However subdued the modes of her gentle vision, Bowen conveys the turbulence of the twenties and the combined excitement and complications of changing roles and altering relations:

> Do you remember those two dismal Englishwomen introduced to us by Lett and Cedric...Well they wrote and said they'd got a studio, and would I go to tea, and they had something to show me which 'would amuse me considerably'. So I went...and [they] produced a fine boy of seven weeks... Apparently, a man friend 'lent his services'... (Stang and Cochran 279, 332, 333, 344)

But the pangs of such an empowerment were related, more importantly still, to art and to the community of women artists that had eventually evolved out of the Académie Julian. They were following the routes established by French artists such as Berthe Morisot, and American artists too, like Mary Cassatt. Once again, Ford was at the heart of the matter, ready to promote, encourage, congratulate, help and of course publish, whenever possible, members of this group, starting of course with the women of his Parisian life, Bowen and Rhys. Indeed, the *transatlantic review* was quick to capture the feminine vibration in the artistic air:

> And if you do not agree with Schopenhauer in regard to women, there are possibilities for you in the name of some of the women painters of France: Marie Laurençin, Irène Lagut, Hélène Perdriat. And there is that shy Englishwoman, Gwen John, sister of Augustus John, who paints in a high grey house at the end of a street that winds up to the wall of an old Terasse in a suburb of Paris.[27]

Often, the destinies of these women artists have proved to be paved with complications, struggles or singularities. Gwen John's apprenticeship with Rodin, and doomed love for him, followed by years of loneliness and reclusion, are a telling example.[28] As for Marie Laurençin, Jeanne Forster remembers vividly her witch-like eyes, and the striking explorations of female bodies, 'young girls with their pets, doves, and slim deer and strange dogs'. In Laurençin's portrait of Coco Chanel (1923), the motive of fashion encounters, once again, the urgency of creativity, offering a kind of female icon of Paris in the Twenties. So, in her more sedate way, does Stella Bowen, steadfastly striving to find her own idiom, to overcome self-doubt, to work in a studio of her own, to be born, as an artist, in Paris. Whatever the hardships often inflicted on a generation of women in search of their own voice and their own image, Paris had given them a medium, tools and its feminine aura; the rudiments, in a word, of new artistic idioms. As a spokesman, artificer and witness of such memorable achievement, Ford is at the heart of this process.

Ford's vision encompasses the many souls of Paris. It sheds light on the nineteenth-century metropolis whose crowds flow on newly-opened boulevards – Ford hated them – or disappear in obscure arcades: the city of his masters and mentors, Gustave Flaubert and Henry James. But Ford also captures the spirit of the city marked by the war, as he discovers it on the day of his 1922 arrival, and in the universal mourning of Marcel Proust, 'the Unknown Soldier of the literature' of the last decade (*IWN* 198). His is a vision that shares, naturally, in the feast of the Twenties and is quick to perceive its deep motivation, its healing function and its revolutionary meaning:

> Paris gyrated, seethed, clamoured, roared with the Arts [....] It was the real reaction from the war, the artist making his claim for glory as against the glory of the warrior. Mars was to be disgruntled. (*IWN* 282)

Many *villes lumière* thus intersect their images and destinies in Ford's writings and literary activities; so much so, indeed, that in his keen knowledge of the urban palimpsest – layer upon layer, historical moment upon historical moment – Ford even had the perception that Paris would have to surrender, soon enough, its role as an intellectual leader, possibly to another city of further complexities, New York. But whatever the distance of time and space, Paris would have remained to him 'the Northern extremity of the civilized world', for, in the symbolic and literary geography of Ford Madox Ford, 'France begins

with the bookstalls of Quai Malaquais and ends with Marseilles' (*MF*
92, 86).

NOTES

1   Ernest Hemingway, *A Moveable Feast*, New York: Simon and Schuster, 1996
    (1960), pp. 83, 86.
2   Gertrude Stein, *The Autobiography of Alice B. Toklas*, Harmondsworth: Penguin,
    1966 (1933) – hereafter cited as *Toklas*, p. 232.
3   Richard Ellmann, *James Joyce*, Oxford: Oxford University Press, 1966 (1959),
    pp. 575, 649.
4   Max Saunders, *Ford Madox Ford: A Dual Life*, 2 vols, Oxford: Oxford University
    Press, 1996 – hereafter cited as 'Saunders', vol. 1, p. 353. Letter to Julie Ford, 11
    Sept. 1935.
5   Henry James, *Parisian Sketches. Letters to the New York Tribune, 1875-1876*, eds
    Leon Edel and Ilse Dusoir Lind, London: Rupert Hart-Davis, 1958, p. 6.
6   Ford Madox Ford, *Mightier than the Sword*, London: Allen & Unwin, 1938, p.
    200.
7   Ford Madox Ford, *Return to Yesterday* (1931), ed. Bill Hutchings, Manchester:
    Carcanet, 1999 – hereafter cited as *RY*, p. 161.
8   James, letter to his mother, 11 January 1876: quoted in *Henry James: A Life in
    Letters*, edited by Philip Horne, London: Penguin Books, 2000 (1999), p. 63.
9   See Saunders, vol. 1, 428: '*The Good Soldier* owes much to Madame Bovary
    too... Edward is a male Emma Bovary, naively romanticising himself to self-
    destruction'. As I try to explain above, I tend to differ on that point.
10 Richard Hobbs, 'Visual display in the Realist novel: "l'aventure du style"',
    Impressions of French Modernity: Art and Literature in France 1850-1900, ed.
    Richard Hobbs, Manchester and New York: Manchester University Press, 1998,
    pp. 118-134, p. 118.
11 Ford Madox Ford, *The Good Soldier* (1915), ed. Martin Stannard, New York and
    London: W. W. Norton & Company, 1995, p. 63.
12 Tamar Garb, 'Gender and Representation', *Modernity and Modernism. French
    Painting in the Nineteenth Century*, ed. Francis Frascina *et al*, New Haven &
    London: Yale University Press, 1994 (1993), pp. 219-290. The painting (c. 1880),
    now lost and of unknown dimensions, is reproduced at p. 240. See also John
    Milner, *The Studios of Paris: the Capital of Art in the Late Nineteenth Century*,
    New Haven & London: Yale University Press, 1988.
13 Ford Madox Ford, *A Mirror to France*, London: Duckworth, 1926 – hereafter
    cited as *MF*; p. 59.
14 Bernard J. Poli, *Ford Madox Ford and the transatlantic review*, Syracuse, NY:
    Syracuse University Press, 1967 – hereafter cited as Poli, pp. 41, 40.
15 Louis Aragon, *Le paysan de Paris*, Paris: Gallimard, 1997 (1926), p. 92. Author
    translation: 'due to their hatred of Montparnasse and taste for the equivocal
    arcades'.

16 Ford Madox Ford, *It Was the Nightingale* (1933), New York: Ecco Press, 1984 – henceforth cited as *IWN*; pp. 330, 335-6.

17 Ernest Hemingway's 'The Doctor and the Doctor's Wife' and Djuna Barnes's 'The Passion' were published in the *transatlantic review*, 2:5, May 1924, 497-501 and 490-496.

18 All the drawings mentioned are in the Art Supplement of the *transatlantic review*, 1:4, March 1924 and 1:6, June 1924.

19 Philippe Soupault, 'Lettre de Paris', *transatlantic review*, 1: 2, February 1924, 75-79. Author translation: 'From the terrace of the small garden, my eyes glimpse in the sitting-rooms and on the pavements the elegant ghosts of Lucien de Rubempré, of Rastignac and D'Arthez. The names might be different but their ambitions have not changed.'

20 Philippe Soupault, 'Lettre de Paris', *transatlantic review*, 1:1, January 1924, 86-87. Author translation: ' "...the ambassadors" depicted by James [...] There is a lot of talk, of a harmless kind. All is temperate, simple, proper...One may feel the effort and the wish, both aiming at mutual comprehension and reciprocal advice'.

21 Philippe Soupault, *ibid.:* Author translation: 'The large golden sheep flock in the sky to graze in the immense meadow of the moonlight'.

22 Ford Madox Ford, 'Preface' to Jean Rhys, *The Left Bank and Other Stories*, London: Jonathan Cape, 1927, pp. 7-27 (p. 23).

23 Stella Bowen, *Drawn from Life*, London: Collins Publishers, 1941 – hereafter cited as Bowen, p.128.

24 Jean Rhys, *Quartet*, London: Penguin Books, 1973 (1928), pp. 9, 28.

25 Sondra J. Stang & Karen Cochran, *The Correspondence of Ford Madox Ford and Stella Bowen*, Bloomington and Indianapolis: Indiana University Press, 1994 – hereafter cited as Stang and Cochran, pp. 348, 358, 370.

26 For the culture of women in early XX century Paris, see Shari Benstock, *Women of the Left Bank*, London: Virago, 1987 (1986).

27 Jeanne Forster, 'New York Letter', *transatlantic review*, 1:1, 88-92 (p. 90).

28 See Alicia Foster, *Gwen John*, London: Tate Gallery Publishing, 1999.

NEW YORK IS NOT AMERICA,
BUT THEN WHAT IS?

Robert E. McDonough

Very near the beginning of Chapter I of *New York Is Not America* (1927) Ford Madox Ford declares the content of his book: 'my impressions ... my impressions ... my impressions'.[1] This content seems to imply both a certain tone and a certain method of organization. With Ford's impressions the reader may expect and in fact does here get a conversational tone. The language is informal, relaxed and flowing, full of the wit and vivacity Ford at ease can always command.

In *New York Is Not America*, as generally in Ford's non-fiction, impressions are conveyed through anecdotes. The anecdotes seem at first to be organized by association, one anecdote following another as it is recalled to memory by what precedes it. In fact, the organization of the book is consistent with Ford's theory of Impressionism and enables Ford to communicate a complex realization of New York and America together.

In the article 'On Impressionism', first published in two installments in the magazine *Poetry and Drama* in 1914, Ford follows a chain of reasoning to the conclusion that Impressionist prose requires an appearance of disorganization:

> For the first business of Impressionism is to produce an impression, and the only way in literature to produce an impression is to awaken interest. And, in a sustained argument, you can only keep interest awakened by keeping alive, by whatever means you have at your disposal, the surprise of your reader. You must state your argument; you must illustrate it, and then you must stick in something that appears to have nothing whatever to do with either subject or illustration, so that the reader will exclaim: 'What the devil is the fellow driving at?' And then you must go on in the same way – arguing, illustrating and startling and arguing, startling and illustrating – until at the end your contentions will appear like a ravelled skein. And then, in the last few lines, you will draw towards you the master-string of that seeming confusion, and the whole pattern of the carpet, the whole design of the net-work will be apparent.[2]

The pattern in *this* carpet, as the book's title suggests, includes both
New York and America, with Ford's interest in the city having
priority. It also includes Europe as providing a kind of frame for New
York. Within the seven chapters of the book, Ford's approach allows
him to move back and forth between New York and America as
necessary, though certainly with an emphasis on New York in the first
part of the book changing to an emphasis on America, with occasional
glances at Europe. These seven chapters, 228 of the book's 238 pages
of text, are framed by a six-page 'Author's Advertisement', written
'off Nantucket', and 'L'Envoi', set in Provence after the conclusion of
the trip begun in the advertisement. The complex idea of the book
might   be   phrased   New-York-not-America-and-both-not-Europe.
Moving on from one story to another, Ford shows what New York is
and what America is, making each one more sharply realized as the
negation of the other; he incorporates the condition of change into his
definitions, demonstrating that New York is not what it was and
asserting that America will soon not be what it now is; and he enriches
the reader's understanding of both New York and America by
showing their different relations to Europe. And by the end of the
book Ford's design, his complex impression of New York and
America, is apparent.

Ford's narration by anecdote may be examined in the first five
pages of Chapter I. He begins in story-telling fashion: 'A year or so
ago, when I was coming over here on the *Paris*, there was a great
storm' (*NYNA* 13). Then he tells of the 'lady of a certain age' who
warned him at breakfast, 'You kehn't flirt with Amer'can gels as you
ken with English ones. But if she falls in love with you ... *look aout*'
(*NYNA* 13). From the rendering of the lady's accent, it appears that
she is intended to be perceived as a New Englander, an American as
opposed to a New Yorker, in a chapter that will soon be moving to
anecdotes of New York. That story reminds him of another: 'I was
going somewhat later to somewhere near Danbury on the train'.
Sitting opposite him was a young lady wearing 'leather leggings and
breeches. I looked no higher' (*NYNA* 14). But the train was a very
slow train – he tells a joke about the South-eastern line in England to
illustrate the slowness – and finally his fear of missing his destination
overcame his fear of being thought rude, and he asked the young
woman whether the train had passed Danbury. She said, 'Oh, why
didn't you speak to me before? It would have been so much more
amusing' (*NYNA* 15). Once started she babbled on, even explaining

the purpose of her journey as 'going to Kent County Reservation in Connecticut to catch rattlesnakes for the Bronx Park Zoo' (*NYNA* 15).

At this point, two anecdotes into his book, Ford generalizes so that he can then tell more anecdotes to illustrate his generalization:

> Now, neither of those things would ever happen to you, if you happened to be American and in your own country. But singular oddities have always presented themselves to me whenever I travelled here. I don't mean to say that odd things ever happen to me so long as I bide in New York, between, that is to say, the Battery and, say, Eighty-fifth Street. Nothing odd ever presents itself to me there, and I enjoy relative immunity in Brooklyn or Hoboken; but let me once leave that, as it were, home circle, to go into America .... I will tell you how I went to Coney Island, twenty-odd years ago. (*NYNA* 15-16)

In this passage Ford has begun to make his title's distinction between New York and America and for the first time he delineates the small portion of New York City *he* accepts as New York. (He will do this again, changing his definition of his New York slightly, presumably because his impression is different at different points of the writing.) It is not clear from the passage above whether Ford is aware that Coney Island is a part of Brooklyn. (He may even think it is an island!)

Now the idea that such strange happenings occur only to travelers leads to more examples. On this trip to Coney Island he was thrown off the train by a policeman who insisted he must pay his fare for the third time over. He decided to complete his trip by boat, and on the boat he ran into a barman, who involved him in something like a bad vaudeville routine when Ford attempted to buy cigarettes. ("'What sort of cigarettes do you keep?" He said, "We don't keep 'em. We sell 'em'"; *NYNA* 16-17). Arrived in Coney Island, in a dance hall in which, he had been told, 'the entire population of the United States could dance in comfort', he found in the center of the dance floor only 'a gentleman ... slowly turning round; both his arms were extended and in each hand was a six-shooter which he was discharging' (*NYNA* 17). (The oddness of some of the anecdotes is explained at the end of the chapter. The multiple demands for train fares were due to a fare dispute, the gunman was a madman, 'not a national characteristic', and, because rattlesnakes do not breed in captivity they must be captured in the wild to maintain a supply at the zoo – *NYNA* 31-2).

To proceed by anecdotes and impressions is Ford's method, and in Chapter IV he says that he discovered this for himself in New York. First he runs through the memories he associates with the intersection of Fifth Avenue and Fourteenth Street. 'The other day' on the southeast corner he took leave of 'a very distinguished writer' with whom he had lunched and discussed style, each of them shyly confessing that he liked the other's books (*NYNA* 83; Ford re-tells this anecdote in *It Was the Nightingale*, where he identifies the other writer as Theodore Dreiser). '[T]he corner immediately opposite' (southwest probably, but perhaps northeast) was once the site of a very bad fall (*NYNA* 83). 'The north-western corner and the pavement going from Fourteenth Street to Sixteenth witnessed one of the happiest moods of my life; I remember going along it with almost dancing feet' (*NYNA* 83). And at the tobacconist's store that once stood on the last corner he made many telephone calls when his own telephone was out of order or he wanted to keep the calls private from those with whom he shared his apartment (*NYNA* 83-4).

Ford came upon this literary device only a few blocks north of this corner, on Fifth Avenue 'between Twenty-second and Twenty-third' (*NYNA* 85). At that time, as he recalled a walk of a few days earlier, '[T]here came into my head a sudden half-philosophical, half-literary idea that has ever since formed the chief basis of my technical stock-in-trade and the mainspring of my actions' (*NYNA* 86). He remembered the remark of a friend with whom he had taken this walk past the Flatiron Building:

> And it occurred to me suddenly to think of how the imagination of that figure made the Flatiron live for me, whether as an architectural mass or as a figurative barrier between myself and the sun…. In effect that is why when I wish to give the effect of a city or the exact incidence of a moral apophthegm, I try to do it with an anecdote, essaying the rendering of the turn of a human phrase or the twist of a crooked individual mouth, rather than with any generalisation of a loftier or more academic kind. (*NYNA* 86)

This of course is the method of this book, how he strives to 'give the effect' of both New York and America, and the fact that he associates the method with the city only emphasizes his affection.

In the body of the text within the voyage-to-France frame, Ford follows his title in gradually shifting emphasis from New York to America. Chapter I, 'Travellers' Tales', collects stories, mostly about New York, whose point is the impossibility of generalization. Chapter II, 'My Gotham', discusses the growth and change of New York and suggests there are no native New Yorkers, only people who have moved there from elsewhere. Chapter III, 'Sky-Scrapers', continues to talk about change and identifies New York as the refuge for Anglo-

Saxons. Chapter IV, 'It Is Not So Much the Place', focuses on his earlier discovery of his impressionist method; here too he makes it clear that by 'New York', his New York, he means Manhattan and the Bronx, two of five boroughs (*NYNA* 110; note the slightly different definition of New York from the one given in Chapter I). Chapter V, 'As the People', presents New York not as a social but rather as the artistic center of the U. S., made so by the richness of human contact available there; but this contact also makes it impossible to do steady work, and Ford says he will soon be leaving for his other well-loved place, Provence, in order to write. Chapter VI, 'The Lordly Dish', is devoted to American food. (The 'lordly dish' is the butter provided apparently free of charge in American restaurants.) This is a partial defence of American cookery, maintaining that the food served in the private homes to which he has been invited is far superior to what one gets in restaurants. Chapter VII, 'Regions Caesar Never Knew', reveals that the source of this book was his publisher's request to write a book about America and concludes that it is the Middle West, not New York, which is America, and that while the older generation then in power in the Middle West may be oppressive, the younger generation about to come to power, many of whom Ford has known in Paris, are liberal and artistic.

Ford's essential characterization of New York is as the City of the Good Time, which it has become 'rather by in- than exclusiveness' (*NYNA* 121). New York is 'the city of the good time .... the only place outside Provence where everybody is rich and gay' (*NYNA* 40). But when Ford says so to a lady from Boston (i.e., America), she replies, 'Yes, but to be rich and gay is not the supreme end of life' (*NYNA* 40). Ford disagrees. In Chapter III he envisions New York as the city of refuge for somewhat confusingly defined

> true Anglo-Saxons – the real Hundred per Centers whose names are other than Hunderttausendstrassenheimer or Putz [or Hueffer?] – we are not only Saxon and Norman and Dane, we are Jew and Huguenot and Hussite and Anabaptist and Pilgrim Father and Absconding Bankrupt and Younger Son and Jansenist and Circumnavigator .... We are the Eternal Nuisances of Everywhere who have been kicked out by Everybody, and we have travelled the world around and round and round and round again in search of the City of the Good Time. (*NYNA* 77)

Ford, who considers himself to be 'about as English as they make them' (*NYNA* 122), but whom some America-firsters would not allow into America 'because I cannot be truly Anglo-Saxon, since I am a "subject," not a "citizen," and true Anglo-Saxondom is all the same as true democracy' (*NYNA* 121), treats sarcastically anyone who wants to preserve an imaginary racial and cultural purity for either America or New York:

> It happens to me frequently to be told by gentlemen whose names end in 'berg' or 'felt', or the like, that what America needs is a complete shutting of its boundaries to all Latin and English influences. I am told the same often by other gentlemen whose names begin with Mac or O. New York, they say, must be proudly Nordic, and must become completely self-centred. (*NYNA* 121)

This influx of 'Anglo-Saxons', of which Ford so approves and others disapprove, has meant a change in New York in the time Ford has known it. The actual population has changed. Once, Ford tells us at the beginning of Chapter II, 'It used to be a saying in this city twenty years ago . . . "Little old New York is good enough for me."' And New Yorkers would 'stop and ask you – an obvious foreigner? – "Wal . . . and what are your impressions of New York?"' (*NYNA* 33). At the time he is writing, however, 'whatever the city contains it contains no born New Yorkers. That is one of the phenomena that has here most struck me. I never meet born New Yorkers in the city of their birth' (*NYNA* 34).

Ford sees other changes, too, that are not entirely due to this change in population, but he also feels a continuity of affection. 'She changes so fast that you cannot at any moment say, "This is my New York." And yet your New York it remains' (*NYNA* 89). In the last twenty years it has changed from 'little old New York' to 'a great city' (*NYNA* 33). 'Sky-Scrapers' (the title of Chapter III) have effected much of this change, creating an overcrowding in lower Manhattan that makes moving about the city difficult and slow (*NYNA* 60-3). In addition, within Ford's memory the telephone service has gone from excellent to poor, and the streets have changed from spotless to filthy (*NYNA* 63-6). Nevertheless, Ford loves New York: 'I prefer New York with soiled pavements to other cities set upon floors like those of heaven' (*NYNA* 66).

The new New Yorkers, the 'Eternal Nuisances of Everywhere' who have come 'in search of the City of the Good Time' (*NYNA* 77), make it in Ford's eyes almost a European city. New York is 'the last chance of European civilization. For, say what you like about New York or America, their civilizations are European, like their traditions and their blood, and if New York does not now make a good thing of

it you may write: Fuit Europa et magna gloria ... ' (*NYNA* 98).
(Though Ford here credits America with European civilization, we
shall see below that the country, unlike the city, is not comfortable in
that condition and wants to fight it.)

Ford does give one example of culture in New York not strictly
derived from Europe. He had been invited to a dinner party in order to
meet Edwin Arlington Robinson, and that American poet was two-
and-a-half hours late. Finally Ford and the other literary men there
present began to sing 'Frankie and Johnny', a traditional African-
American ballad, to amuse themselves (*NYNA* 138). (It is not clear
that Ford is aware of the provenance of the song.) 'It is so exactly
what the occupants of Oxford Common Rooms, or members of the
Atheneum, do not do after dinner' (*NYNA* 139). Indeed. And one
would like to believe that it actually happened in New York. (It might
seem that here for once Ford contrasts New York and Europe, but at
this point Ford is probably not thinking of England as European.)

There is only one respect in which New York is not true to its
devotion to the Good Time. It shares with America the fashion for
what doctors – but not Ford – consider to be healthy eating:

> The doctor is like the priest. He tries to kill joy, but along the lines of your
> superstitions and fears. We – you and I Anglo-Saxons – are trying to-day with
> our cookery to condone the sins of our Puritan ancestors. It is the only
> Puritanism that remains in the New York which is not America, and also in
> Great Britain which is not yet America. So we let the physician replace the
> priest to whom we no longer resort, and the doctor, knowing that our
> superstitions trend that way, knowing that we think it sinful to take a delight in
> the palates that the good God has given us for our health and delight – the
> doctor insists that we eat things tasteless, uncondimented, unassoiled, unblest.
> ... (*NYNA* 177-8)

America and New York are therefore places where, though you hate
salads as Ford does ('I guess you are English and hate America, or
you would not say that about American salads', says one of those
ladies from Boston Ford is always meeting on trains – *NYNA* 181),
you will have them forced on you, where your hostess may even
create one in your honour, '*Salade à la Ford*', composed of shrimp
and alligator pears 'with a dreadful – oh, a dreadful – dressing of a
purplish colour . . . a sort of Thousand Island dressing' (*NYNA* 183).
(Of course if Ford *did* like salads, he would do great things with them.
Without naming the Waldorf salad he takes credit for creating it. 'I
invented myself, years ago, a salad of celery, apples and walnuts. I

gave it up after trial. Here it meets one everyday . . .'; *NYNA* 184). The inventor of *Salade à la Ford* is a New Yorker, but she seems to be exhibiting the Puritanism about food Ford finds characteristic of Anglo-Saxondom.

Another lady, this one from America rather than New York, would religiously follow her doctor's order to eat two eggs per day though she hated eggs.

> So it was a question of going through the day to find a meal at which her courage would let her consume those eggs. Sometimes she would eat one at breakfast and one at lunch. Sometimes she would shudder through two at lunch. Sometimes – horribly – she would find herself near bed-time with both uneaten. Then she would have them both, in a crisis of revulsion, beaten up with some milk. (*NYNA* 185-6)

However, Ford insists that it is not absolutely impossible to find good cooking in America. It is true he does not like what he calls 'public meals': 'American public meals are horrible – but so are English public meals, and so for the matter of that are Anglo-Saxonised French, German, Italian and Spanish ones' (*NYNA* 172). Moreover, the determined man can eat well even in restaurants. Ford says he has eaten 'as good food and as well cooked in New York as I habitually do in Paris. That is because, if I may express a he-man's sentiments in soldierly language, I damn well see that I get it' (*NYNA* 174-5). In American restaurants, too, there is always the lordly dish of butter.

'Public meals', however, are not the most important ones. Ford declares the 'Great Truth about cooking' (*NYNA* 170), one that applies in England and France as well, is that 'there is no sense of talking of any national cooking except in terms of meals produced by really skilled professional practitioners in moderately wealthy homes, the meals to be compounded of first-rate materials' (*NYNA* 171-2). And Ford has been well pleased by 'innumerable meals that I have eaten in kindly and hospitable families' (*NYNA* 172).

Except for the matter of Puritanism about food, the distinction between New York and America is sharp. New York loves the Good Time; America fears it. New York itself is very conscious of its greater liberality:

> The West itself and still more the Middle West according to the New York theory is ruled over by tyrants compared with whom Charles I or George III were village policemen, and by tyrannies compared with which that of the

Russian Bureaucracy or the Council of Ten of Venice were village Sunday schools. (*NYNA* 78)

When, towards the end of the book, Ford begins to focus on America, he concentrates on America's repressiveness. In 1927, the distinction is visible most clearly in the issue of Prohibition. Ford does not know how he would decide on Prohibition as an abstract question. He is totally opposed to human beings imposing their version of morality on others. 'I do, indeed, regard that as the greatest sin that one human being can commit against another' (*NYNA* 203). However, because 'the evils caused by drink are so terrible, so profound and so far-reaching [if] a law could be framed that would effectively – absolutely effectively – render all consumption of alcoholic liquor impossible, I should be horribly hard put not to vote for it'; but since the truth is 'that much – that most – of the American drunkenness that I have seen has been the direct effect of Prohibition' (*NYNA* 203), it would seem that the supposititious law can never be absolutely effective, that it is in reality positively harmful, and so Ford's opposition to imposed morality is correct. 'It is obvious that my sympathies are with the Eastern Seaboard rather than with the Middle West as I know it' (*NYNA* 219).

That declaration seems to put him against America, since he has a little earlier said, 'I am going to take the bit between my teeth, amidmost of all this confusion, and boldly to assume that the Middle West *is* America' (*NYNA* 195). And Ford says he has heard many times, if not always in the Middle West always 'outside New York – that if New York and the other Eastern States that have a majority against Prohibition do not submit to the will of the other states, the same measures will be taken against them as were taken sixty years or so ago against other Dissidents' (*NYNA* 212). He refers of course to the American Civil War.

Some Americans have much the same attitude to England. One of the ladies-from-Boston-on-trains, the one who forced herself to eat the two eggs per day, the one who assumed that because Ford is from England he must hate America, with face 'transfused' like that of Joan of Arc announces to Ford that 'in two or three years we shall have forced Prohibition on your own country. That will be the great triumph of America' (*NYNA* 206).

It is this tone in Americans that must have led Gerald Duckworth to request this book. Ford says,

> I was asked to write this book by someone who has a certain right to ask me to write books. No, I do not mean any lady, I mean a publisher. He wanted me to write a book to prove that AMERICA had assumed in the eyes of the outside world the position that Prussia had before the late war. And America undoubtedly has assumed that position – in the eyes of Europe. (*NYNA* 220-21)

Ford concedes, 'Voices do certainly issue from the immense plains that sound remarkably like the voice of the ex-King of Prussia' (*NYNA* 221). He then refers to an article he has read, written 'by, precisely, the President of a Rotary Club of a small town about a hundred miles from Chicago', an unimportant man, in which nevertheless

> One seemed to hear the tread of the iron heel, and to see glimpses of the flashing of the sword. . . . The suggestion undoubtedly was that if Europe continued to talk about the Debt – merely, mark, to talk about it, not to repudiate – United States gunboats running up the Seine would take, for the benefit of Chicago, all the treasures of the Louvre. (*NYNA* 221)

Yet Ford insists that all of this menace in America – not New York – is not permanent. Just as New York has changed so much during the years that he has known it, Ford expects the Middle West that is America to change in the near future. 'Let us, for the sake of argument, grant that the Middle West is the great danger to humanity' (*NYNA* 223). And he will not argue against the claim that 'the dominant generation in Chicago is ignorant, intolerant, corrupt and stupid. Well, the present dominant generation may be all that. I do not know' (*NYNA* 223). However, that generation will soon pass and for the next generation Ford has almost unlimited hope:

> I am quite certain that nowhere in the world – nowhere at any rate in that part of the world that makes the North Atlantic into a lake – is there so great an intellectual curiosity, so great a thirst for knowledge, and so great a determination to put that knowledge in employment. I will not enlarge on what are my particular qualifications to know. (*NYNA* 223)

It seems clear he is pronouncing on the basis of his work with Middle Westerners in Europe, especially on *the transatlantic review* earlier in the decade. After so much said about the difference between city and country in favor of the city, he is nevertheless able to come to the end of his book with something strongly positive to say in favor of America.

    We take leave of Ford not in New York or America but in Toulon. Finally, he loves New York but cannot write there because of the company it provides. In Chapter V he calls New York 'the artistic centre of the Western hemisphere', even 'a World Centre, at least for Anglo-Saxondom' (*NYNA* 117). However, if artists in particular are attracted to New York and make it by their concentration there an artistically stimulating locale, still they must leave in order to do their work:

> The extreme closeness of social relations; the continual indulgence in social gatherings; the relative want of any privacy; the unceasing stimulus of the air as of the human type there prevalent, – all these things, attractive as they are, make it also almost impossible there to keep it up. So that I am open to doubt whether the actual artistic output of New York is at all formidable. (*NYNA* 117)

Ford goes on to say that it will soon be Provence from where he contemplates New York. 'Oh, with all the nostalgia in the world, I grant you. But I still want to write one good book' (*NYNA* 118). Earlier, he has said he will take the departure 'in order to recover from too much delight' (*NYNA* 75).

I would not want to claim that *New York Is Not America* is one of Ford Madox Ford's very best works, but there is much to be enjoyed even in what must be judged middling Ford. Writing of New York, as he says in the italicised 'Advertisement', '*as he would talk to his mother or his mistress*' (*NYNA* 7), that is, impressionistically, he creates a convincing portrait of the city and of the country to which it is attached and opposed. In 'L'Envoi', sitting in Provence he thinks of what New York has meant to the world:

> New York believes that the Good Time is not only desirable, but to be obtained this side of cloud-cuckoo land. Here we believe that it is not. Nevertheless we have assimilated jazz-dancing and jazz-music. Nothing more innocent, frugal and beautiful was ever given to the disillusioned by those full of hope. In the mediæval times the most that the poor could hope for was one day to get justice in heaven, to-day they dance inexpensively from the Lizard to Caucasus. . . . That is the doing of Gotham. Against that you may set all the Puritanisms, crassnesses, wants of artistry, ignorances and presumptions committed by individuals in the United States and chronicled by my friends Messrs. Mencken, Pound & Co., by the Master of Y . . . , the Dean of X . . . and the British poet who smelt the stockyards in the foyer of the Chicago Opera House, and they will not come to a feather's weight in the golden scales of the recording angel. (*NYNA* 243-4)

This member of the Brooklyn diaspora already believed that, but I think *New York Is Not America* can convince others as well.

NOTES

1   Ford Madox Ford, *New York Is Not America*, London: Duckworth, 1927 –
    hereafter *NYNA*; pp. 17-18.
2   Ford Madox Hueffer, 'On Impressionism', *Poetry and Drama*, II (June-Dec.
    1914); rpt. in *Critical Writings of Ford Madox Ford*, ed. Frank MacShane,
    Lincoln: University of Nebraska Press, 1964, pp. 47-8.

NEW YORK MINUTES:
FORD'S NOTES ON THE CITY

Michele Gemelos

Introduction

In 1664, the English seized the City of New Amsterdam, extended its boundaries to include all of Manhattan Island, and gave this still miniscule area of land the grand name 'City of New York'. After a public vote in 1898, Manhattan's centrality, which was cemented by the area's English rule, remained intact. The area's governance and that of its surrounding counties and boroughs were consolidated and modern 'Greater' New York City was created. These Anglo-American amalgamations foreshadowed the microcosmic and summarizing ability of this irregular land-mass that would become the subject of prolific commentary.

'New' New York City replaced an old, sprawling, and fragmented world. While its geographic features and population have been variously limited and compartmentalised, the immense diversity contained in the finite space has been celebrated. Even prior to 1898, observers of the city explored this tension between variety and homogeneity. Over one hundred years of reportage and imaginative impressions of New York have been recorded by various writers who assign the city the role of national representative, omnipotent protagonist or who use it as an 'unsettled setting'. The city has served as both a productive context for the writers, and the explicit subject of the writing. Long-term residents and émigrés as well as passers-by have participated in the stenography that has yielded a flood of New York minutes: notes on a city that has recalibrated our sense of identity, space and time.

Ford Madox Ford's engagement with New York City as an early twentieth-century microcosm and megalopolis was not dissimilar to the ways in which literary travellers in the mid-nineteenth century, such as Charles Dickens and Anthony Trollope, visited the burgeoning metropolis, collected impressions and gave them multiple expression in various publications.[1] Rather than conforming to and praising their nineteenth-century trends of condescension or flouting and rejecting their generalization, however, Ford experimented with forms and styles, vacillating between artistic and journalistic approaches and creating hybrids of fact and fiction. His New York writings are more than catalogues of newsworthy events or impressionistic moments; they probe for the reasons why visitors in the early decades of the twentieth-century may have struggled to find the diction and the form for what seemed like an unreadable and illegible environment. As Henry James lamented in *The American Scene* (1906) – his proud but poignant record of an uneasy homecoming – the metamorphic city-scape and shifting crowds constituted 'that concert of the expensively provisional into which your supreme sense of New York resolves itself'.[2] Resolutions about New York abound; however, Ford, like James, constantly amended his thoughts, studying the city in search of ultimately elusive truths. Unlike James, Ford enthusiastically accepted what the city could offer: tentative impressions. Moreover, he main-tained that '[...] for me New York is so intimately and solely the few miles of which I have so often spoken [...] along Fifth Avenue and Broadway from the Battery!'[3]

It is my aim to begin an overdue investigation of Ford and New York City. Within the scope of this essay I will suggest ways in which Ford's view of the city as both a sensory and social maelstrom and as a creative sanctuary developed. To chart this, in section I, I have focused on some of the literary influences on and antecedents of Ford's New York writing, such as James, H. G. Wells and the journalist W. T. Stead. Ford brought New York into focus in his contemporaneous discussions about the state of England. Non-fiction works such as the three texts comprising *England and the English* (1907, American edition) provide evidence of how his literary and professional activities shaped his ideas about Englishness, national identity and cosmopolitanism, and they all find outlets in his New York writing. In *An English Girl,* published by Methuen in 1907 (*EG*), Ford experimented with the paradoxical effects of New York on identity and an individual's sense of duty both to family and 'nation'. By reflecting in sections II and III on that work's genesis, reception, themes and character sketches, I will show how the novel points to Ford's later thoughts on the city.

Ford's New York texts can also more generally be read as responses to British approaches to writing about America, as he moves away from the acceptable nineteenth-century synecdoche of the city for the entire nation. New York City's status in his *oeuvre* has previously been addressed simply in terms of a fixed scene that Ford occupied rather than as a force that shaped his work or as a general site for his commentary on American civilization. Perhaps the relative lack of supplementary resources (letters, newspaper articles, notebook entries) in which Ford directly addresses New York has discouraged all but a few scholars from investigating the city's role in his work.[4]

Ford participated in the ongoing interrogation of interlocking concepts such as modernity, identity and urbanism that preoccupied Edwardian writers. American and European approaches to urbanism fluctuated between devotion to national archetypes on the one hand and iconoclasm and rejection of traditions on the other. Ford's writing on cities is aware of the contemporary revolutions in thinking about cities and in thinking about identity. In the same year as New York City's consolidation, Ford had an illustrative conversation about nationality with E. V. Lucas, who observed glibly that Ford could not be English because he was not devoted to the magazine *Punch*. Ford's reaction, whilst being a touch dismissive, promotes a fluid sense of identity:

> Till that day in 1898 I had never given the matter of my own nationality a thought. I gave it very little after that. There remained in my subconsciousness a conviction that must have grown stronger – that I was not English. Not English at all, not merely 'not really English.' I never had much sense of nationality. Wherever there were creative thinkers was my country.[5]

It might be objected that focusing on Ford's 'Englishness' within a consideration of Ford and multicultural New York City obscures his important interactions with other European and American writers. On the contrary, Ford's reaction to Lucas underscores the importance of the debate about Ford's nationality, not only because the reaction is a suspiciously easy dismissal of the author's own conundrum and of the concept of modern nationality, but also because it is precisely this satisfied disavowal of nationality that is disrupted by Ford's encounters with New York. A close reading of Ford's New York writings serves to identify this youthful repudiation of Englishness and nationality as preoccupations, while finding evidence of his desire to belong to (if not to lead) a 'republic of letters'. Moreover, Ford's desire to belong is fulfilled if we view British 'New York' writing and his contributions to it as constituting a virtual and mostly unwitting 'republic' – an intertextual space in which ideas bump democratically, if chaotically, into each other. Even though Ford's heart was firmly placed in Provence by the time he engaged literarily with New York, he 'held his "courts" of literature in the U.S.A. which became his new horizon for the republic of letters'.[6]

Ford further revises his early declaration of 'un-Englishness' in a response that coincided with the publication of his collection of essays entitled *New York is Not America* in 1927. In a review of contemporary novelists, an American interviewer suggested that Ford might be a German or American citizen. Ford was moved to correct him in a letter to the New York *Herald Tribune*: 'I never became a German for legal or illegal reasons or for any reason. I should be flattered to be included among your countrymen, but I always was and shall always be a British subject'.[7]

Ford's sense of Englishness and his version of New York evolved considerably and in tandem during his lifetime. These changes can be traced throughout his writings on New York, which have previously been read in different contexts (i.e. in terms of genre, in terms of biography). Just like his fictional protagonists, Ford discovered firsthand that twentieth-century New York was not static and had not become knowable. The provisional quality of the City lends his project of writing New York as well as his image as a transatlantic literary figure an unfinished and temporal quality.

Influences and Antecedents

From puritanical preaching to nostalgic elegy to nightmarish prophesy, the plethora of thematic, formal and stylistic choices presented to Ford as a reader and writer of cosmopolitan commentary melded into a broader platform from which he launched his opinions. Ford's New York was a catalyst for commentary on modernity and identity; in particular, he sought to articulate its tendency to obscure and elide. New York was both a 'city of good times' and the 'city of dreadful night', a habitat and a hell, but even a quick look at Ford's city-centred novels and essays show that he hoped to present a balanced but personal portrait of a place that evolved through his meditation on it and through his wide reading and great awareness of other practitioners of city commentary.

In his founding of *The English Review* (1908), with its echo of Matthew Arnold's commitment to promoting 'culture' in criticism, Ford also echoed the mission of W. T. Stead, a vocal commentator on New York's civic culture. Stead was a target of Arnold's vitriol about journalistic sensationalism in the latter's essay 'Up to Easter' (1887). The melding of polar viewpoints, in this case Arnold's and Stead's, is something Ford often achieved in his literary projects, though the views he drew upon were not always fully acknowledged.[8]

A prominent Victorian reformer, avid internationalist and spiritualist, Stead was the editor of the *Pall Mall Gazette*, which he later left in order to establish the highly-influential *Review of Reviews*, a monthly forum for commentary on the best written work published in the English language. Stead also published a controversial study of New York in a Christmas edition of *Review* entitled *Satan's Invisible World Displayed, or Despairing Democracy: A Study of Greater New York* (1898).[9] Although Ford did not, as far as I know, acknowledge Stead's editorial or literary work when he founded the *English Review*, he was probably aware of the Victorian's far-reaching projects – including dramatic crusades against child prostitution and in support of internationalist policies, his scathing critiques of Tory politics as well as his paradoxical friendships with industrialists and imperialists such as Andrew Carnegie and Cecil Rhodes. Stead's tragic death on the *Titanic* filled the omnipresent British press with voluble reminiscences from both high-status supporters and opponents.

Ford's editorial mission departs from that of the *Review of Reviews* in that he did not manifest Stead's beliefs in a civic form of Christianity as panacea for social ills or in 'government by newspaper'. However, other goals for their respective *Reviews* were similar: creating an outlet for the very best contemporary writing in the English language, which would serve, in Ford's terms, to 'enjoin upon the Englishman a critical attitude' in a climate where critics seemed 'extraordinarily rare'.[10] But Ford was wary of the appropriation of his writings as platforms for social, political and moral reform, and Stead's work on New York is a model which Ford may have had in mind when rejecting that kind of overt moralising. Nevertheless, *Satan's Invisible World Displayed* plays with allegory, character profiles and point of view, employing techniques that blurred the boundaries between fact and fiction – boundaries that Ford also challenged in his literary treatment of the city (and, through impressionism, elsewhere in his writing too).

In looking for a yet more apposite model for his type of New York commentary, Ford turned to his contemporary H. G. Wells, who in turn acknowledged Ford's trip to America at the end of his own study of *The Future in America* (1906).[11] Partially secularising the eschatological elements of 'sage-writing' so well illustrated by Stead's work, Wells presented New York as a manifestation of a nightmarish but ultimately redeemable future. Wells stressed the apocalyptic ability of the city, observing the potential destruction that could result from its invincible growth, its 'threatening promise, growth going on under a pressure that increases, and amidst a hungry uproar of effort' but also its redemption through careful consideration of what 'Progress' should mean, rather than progress for progress's sake.[12]

Similarly, in his 1908 novel *The War in the Air*, Wells employed an inquiring Englishman, Bert Smallways, as his messenger of New York's destruction. A series of accidents allows Smallways to witness a German aerial bombardment on New York, which 'had long ousted London from her pride of place as the modern Babylon [...] and men likened her to the apocalyptic cities of the ancient prophets.'[13] In short, Smallways unsuspectingly contributes to a Teutonic display of 'air power' that asserts technical prowess as they attack the city for its sentimentality, hubris and heterogeneity. However prescient the work, it is also sensitive to the longstanding tensions between imagination and reality, degeneration and progress, emotion and reason. These are further interrogated throughout Wells's body of work, and once again against the backdrop of New York in *The Shape of Things to Come* (1933), which yields a more pessimistic view of human interaction with the cityscape than his earlier works.

Of all of Ford's literary predecessors and contemporaries, none had as direct and problematic an influence on his New York writings as Henry James, a native New Yorker who became a British subject just a few months before his death in 1916. Reviewers freely acknowledged Ford's aesthetic debt to James, especially in *An English Girl*. In 1913 Ford published what can be read as a response to those observations: in *Henry James*, Ford both praises James's power of observation and tries to assert his independence from his influence. The six years that passed between the publication of *An English Girl* (1907) and *Henry James* (1913) allowed Ford to eschew imitation for a more complex relationship with the Anglo-American writer. Ford's non-fiction writing on England (such as *The Spirit of the People*, also published in 1907, the same year as *An English Girl*) can be viewed as the media in which he began to distance himself from Jamesian pastiche.[14]

In light of this, it is difficult to state without qualification that James's *The American Scene* – written after his visit to America in 1904 following an absence of over twenty years – influenced Ford's outlook on New York. Ford read the book in September 1907 whilst completing the non-fiction trilogy reflecting on England's past, present and future.[15] These volumes were first published separately as *The Soul of London* (1905), *The Heart of the Country* (1906), and *The Spirit of the People* (1907) in England and subsequently published in America in a New York omnibus edition by McClure, Phillips, entitled *England and the English*. James's restless analysis of the twentieth-century hub of modernity is performed by contrasting the nation of his youth and early manhood with the turn-of-the-century chaotic agglomeration of peoples and features – not dissimilar to the scope and angle of the composite texts of *England and the English*. Finding distance from James on the elder writer's literary 'property' was a task that seemed to haunt most of Ford's writing on New York.

W. H. Auden's intuitive introduction to the 1947 edition of James's elegiac text unearths concerns and paradoxes about 'writing America' and travel writing in general, with which Ford would have empathized:

> Of all possible subjects, travel is the most difficult for an artist, as it is the easiest for a journalist. For the latter, the interesting event is the new, the extraordinary, the comic, the shocking, and all that the peripatetic journalist requires is a flair for being on the spot where and when such events happen – the rest is merely passive typewriter thumping: meaning, relation, importance, are not his quarry. The artist, on the other hand, is deprived of his most treasured liberty, the freedom to invent; successfully to extract importance from historical personal events without ever departing from them, free only to select and never to modify or to add, calls for imagination of a very high order.[16]

In Auden's judgment, James is the inventor of a dominant literary image of 'America', who has lost control of the events that play out in his old scenes but who cannot stand idly by and watch without protesting. James resists the journalistic demands that New York City makes on his observations, as the city forces him to remark on the present, pulling him away from the past. Like Auden, I do not see this as a failing; rather, James's deprivation and discomfort are signs of his significant engagement with the troubling subject of modernity as presented and governed by New York.

Although James describes scenes outside of New York City, four chapters of the book (approximately one hundred pages) are devoted to the city. Throughout the rest of James's commentary on the future of America, New York is never far from view.[17] Dismayed by his hometown's relentless urbanism, James laments the devaluation of history and of his authority over the space.

Progressive-era New York is also central to Wells's argument that society should not resist widespread mechanisation, which would obliterate the past that stands in the way of a utopian future. In fact, Wells was still working on his non-fiction impressions while reading James's magazine instalments of what would become *The American Scene*.[18] As Wells and James approach America differently, with the former describing himself as 'a go-ahead Englishman,' *The Future in America* and *The American Scene* were probably seen by Ford as contentious archetypes as well as

> companion texts [that] offer marked comparisons; the former is prescriptive, the latter descriptive. In part, this derives from Wells's vocation as prophet, whereas James was elegiac about his native land [. . . .] Focus differs, as does tone; the voyagers arrive at polar 'new found lands'.[19]

Visible and vocal presences on the English literary scene, Stead, Wells and James presented options for Ford's approach to New York, some of which are markedly shaped by the threat, realities and spectre of European war and exile. As I have briefly noted, this trio – and others such as G. K. Chesterton, Rupert Brooke and the journalist Stephen Graham – directly and obliquely influenced his thematic, formal and stylistic decisions. Arriving at the subject of New York, Ford encountered a landscape that accommodated the polar and unstable visions of his literary predecessors.

Author's Notes: Ford's First Impressions

Ford had wanted *England and the English* to be titled *The Anglo-Saxons,* perhaps as a gesture towards the cultural and political bond between the two nations, and to make his work seem, paradoxically, less bounded by one country.[20] As assemblages of prose poetry, historical reminiscence, and modern prophecy, these volumes can be viewed as models for Ford's New York City writing. Presented to an American audience as a compilation of contemporary views on Englishness, *England and the English* is preceded by an Author's Note that curiously lists questions about New York and its function in shaping the way Ford viewed London and the English nation. He identifies two that arose while he walked in St. James's Park: Why is New York so unlike London? and why should a Londoner feel so at

home in New York? The 'two statements from which the two
questions arise' seem to him to:

> be so mutually contradictory that, as it were, there appeared to be no answer to
> either. For New York is unlike London – and the Londoner – the *true*
> Londoner – does feel at home in New York. I think he feels there more at
> home than in Manchester: I am certain that there he feels more at home than
> in Boston or Philadelphia. (*EE* xx)

This paragraph, and the entire 'Author's Note', can be read as the
earliest formal articulation of Ford's need to use New York City as
'shorthand' for the conundrums and contradictions of modern cosmopolitan life. Ford draws attention to the paradoxical feelings that
accompany his encounter: of strangeness and alienation versus the
familiarity of a shared language; of authority to navigate the landscape
and of paralysis felt when confronted by alien, shifting sounds and
sights. Ford acknowledges the mystery surrounding the place as part
of a shared phenomenon – with Londoners here but expanded to all
Englanders in *An English Girl* and to a universe of English-speaking
Anglo-Saxons in *New York is Not America*.[21]

The publication dates of *England and the English* and *An
English Girl* (as said, both 1907) deserve especially to be noted when
considering Ford's attempts to increase his American readership.
Judging from the generic and thematic variety of Ford's writing in the
first decade of the twentieth century, these years marked a significant
confluence and entanglement of questions in Ford's mind about the
state of England, the idea of New York and his potential career in
America.

Transatlantic Impressionism: *An English Girl*
An English Girl considers not only the conflict between blood and
social ties but also between impressions and facts. The protagonist –
millionaire heir Don Collar Kelleg – is the son of British parents who
emigrated to America, where the senior Mr Kelleg ruthlessly amassed
the family fortune. Despite Don's English public school education and
established position in London social circles, he is troubled about his
identity and purpose. After receiving news of his father's death, Don
departs for New York – what he calls 'the field of battle' (*EG* 214) –
in order to restore dignity to the family by destroying its links to the
avaricious Trusts that control New York City's financial and political
prospects. Don's reflections on his duty to and place in society

endanger his fragile relationships with the legitimately 'English' Eleanor Greville, her father and her aunt, all of whom follow him to the city on various journeys of reconciliation.

A nearly complete version of the work was initially entitled 'The Reformers', and Don's ethical and philosophical dilemmas do come to dominate the published novel.[22] Don adopts some Victorian attitudes towards metropolitan life, while trying desperately to save his artistic inclination from the banality of an overly realist perspective. Criticism of the novel has often privileged Don's development as a character over Ford's portrayal of Eleanor's relationship with the city, which merits greater consideration. Indeed, the title of the novel reminds readers that Eleanor's experience is as central to the development of the narrative as Don's bitter homecoming. Its structure serves as a series of parallel encounters that reform how we view what has been called the 'tragedy of [Don's] fluid temperament': a popular Edwardian theme that develops in *An English Girl* against the backdrop of New York City.[23]

Don's pessimism and frustration towards New York's social ills are complicated by his desire to reform the behaviour and aspirations of the locals. In contrast, Eleanor is happy to have attained a 'sort of irresponsibility' in having left England to tour New York. She feels responsible, however, for reconciling Don to America. Soon both she and her father realize that Don's reformist visions actually blind him to the 'trend of time and a nation like this'; as a result he will never 'appreciate what [he] can't like' (*EG* 235-6). Don's personal and public conflicts are contrasted continually with Eleanor's nervous but increasingly comfortable impressionistic experience of the city, facilitated by her employment of a stenographer: the 'half Irish, half Manhattan Dutch' Miss Dubosc. Dubosc serves as a 'native' guide and an empathetic companion for Eleanor as she negotiates interviews with the 'high society' press corps, hungry as it is for her impressions of the metropolis (*EG* 259).

Methods for 'coping' or 'dealing' with New York life are dissected, but Eleanor's self-assured impressionism is presented as the more successful strategy for surviving the onslaught of social stimuli and self-preservation. Don's fluid temperament has been viewed as tragic because it paralyses him in every environment, whether native or adopted. In contrast, Ford seems to champion Eleanor's solid 'Englishness'. Her self-assuredness allows her to perceive the spirit of New York as that which 'makes things happen,' whereas Don likens it to 'rigging' – specifically that of the market but, when extended, 'rigging' implies widespread fallaciousness and entrapment rather than true progress (*EG* 262-3, 255).

Stasis is held up as a virtue by both Don and his unlikely ally, Mr Greville, who exclaims to Eleanor that Don is

> 'like me in being hopelessly out of date with his time [. . . .] Don is acting precisely as I've acted all my life. He hates modern circumstances. I don't say that he wants what *I* want. He doesn't. He isn't for the Tory Party right or wrong. But he *is* for Aestheticism right or wrong. He *does*, really, want the American people to go in for certain European virtues – for Poetry and the Higher Thought and Rational dress. Well, they can't! How can they? America is made up of men who've fled from him just as much as they've fled from me [. . . .] The point is that Don isn't, really, any more the proper person to regenerate New York than I'm the person to regenerate London [. . . .]' (*EG* 268, 270)

Don supports Mr Greville's presentation of his state of mind and this bolsters the joint attack on Eleanor's optimism. Ironically and cruelly, she is first persuaded by her father to encourage Don's reformism and later berated for it. Confident of his authority in commentating, Mr Greville declares the futility of their collective exercise of learning about New York, which he conflates with America:

> 'How could any one ever understand America or the future of America? You can't tell anything about it [. . . .] the best thing [Don] could do – the most heroic action – is to have the self-restraint to abstain from muddling.' (*EG* 270)

Just as James mourned the loss of the old city in *The American Scene*, Ford's male protagonists in *An English Girl* question to what extent the cult of change in America has eroded sanity, morality and judgment. Thwarted in his attempts to make amends and frustrated by the growing philistinism of American society as presented to him by the New York press and financial institutions, Don resolves (in Mr Greville's words) to 'abdicate' (*EG* 268) to England to live as a 'gentleman-artist'. He concludes that America 'couldn't use him as an artist' (*EG* 258), whereas he declares that Eleanor sees 'a poetry in these things that [he doesn't] see [...]' (*EG* 266), in the simplicity of the sensory pleasures of New York that he finds bewildering and horrifying:

> He had been simply appalled at New York – at its squalid back streets, at its hard voices, at its hideous language, at its physical recklessness, and at the

fact that he hadn't discovered, anywhere, a trace of desire for anything
morally better. (*EG* 271)

In an attempt to repair his relationship with Eleanor, he nevertheless
seems to be placing blame for his failure to conquer or connect with
New York on her:

> 'Why,' he began again suddenly, tenderly and humorously: 'what a folly to
> think that you could teach me to love New York? [. . . .] Wasn't it you who've
> made me yearn for spirit and fineness? Wasn't it you?' (*EG* 287)

In a reversal of his presentation of this strong, assured witness to
events, Ford highlights Eleanor's main 'virtue' just as all three visitors
prepare to leave New York. He has her articulate her belief that
'tenderly nurtured Englishwomen' must 'be ready to make the best of
things [...]' (*EG* 288). She likens the regretful departure – which takes
place in the aptly-titled section 'Thicker Than Water' – to the passing
of a friend: 'a frail, small, chattering, fluttering, bright person that has
died and that one regrets' (*EG* 295). Once back in England, Eleanor
notes with a mixture of defeat and renewed understanding of the
impact of place that New York City's surplus of humanity hid its
surfeit of 'tenderness, a sort of humility', a quality that she feels is in
abundance in London (*EG* 295). Although she stops short of
championing one city over another, the moment instils in her alone the
ability to love New York and admire her own country equally and
without paradox.

Conclusion

From *An English Girl* to his 1927 non-fiction collection *New York is
Not America* to his novels *When the Wicked Man* (1931) and *The Rash
Act* (1933), Ford's treatment of New York City underwent shifts
determined by the Great War, changes in Anglo-American relations,
and debates about aesthetic principles and the writer's profession with
his collaborators. Ford's New York was transformed from a fearsome
frontier or 'field of battle' into a 'charmed circle of Gotham' (*NYNA*
viii). The inclusiveness of this chosen shape for the 1920s city
signifies his increased comfort in the city that became another one of
his foreign homes. Alluding to the magicians' community, Ford also
acknowledges his privileged access as well as the extraordinary value

and power of the information he has acquired by observing the transitions of the enchanted city.

Although Ford insisted in the 'Author's Note' to the English edition of *When the Wicked Man* (published first in America) that it is not a novel of New York or American manners,[24] that text and *The Rash Act* contain allegories about the dangers of the American financial and publicity machines that run off the energy of New York. Both novels also trace the impact of the city on identity and destiny, especially in their treatment of the fluid nature of self as suggested by doppelgängers. New York City, as presented in *The Rash Act*, dismantles ethnic differences, scrambling the truths about individuals. As Paul Wiley has noted, Ford's late work presents American scenes and central characters in a more tolerant, disinterested way, compared with his treatments of them in *An English Girl*, *The Good Soldier*, and his war period writings. This shift might be explained by Ford's desire both to 'extend the international mode in fiction' and as a 'bid for an American audience'.[25]

Without the complication of Ford's direct denial of New York's significance in *An English Girl*, one can approach that novel as an example of 'New York fiction' with more confidence – if not with the assurance of a generic definition. Answering the question 'What is New York literature?' is not the aim of this essay but the analyses contained here indicate that Ford grappled with it directly and creatively and with an awareness of the British writers who walked the same streets before him and alongside him.

NOTES

1 For example, *American Notes for General Circulation* (1842) and *The Life and Adventures of Martin Chuzzlewit* (1844) by Charles Dickens; *North America* by Anthony Trollope (1862).

2 Henry James, *The American Scene, Together with Three Essays from 'Portrait of Places'*, New York: Charles Scribner's Sons, 1946, p. 77.

3 Ford Madox Ford, *New York is Not America*, New York: Albert and Charles Boni, 1927 – hereafter cited as *NYNA*, p. 133. Note: throughout this essay all ellipses in brackets are mine; all others are Ford's or the quoted author's.

4 Ford did, however, include detailed accounts of his life in New York City when writing to Stella Bowen in Paris. These letters give a sense of Ford's schedule, the company he kept, and his opinion of the contemporary cultural scene. For more on

these accounts, see Sondra Stang and Karen Cochran, eds, *The Correspondence of Ford Madox Ford and Stella Bowen*, Bloomington and Indianapolis: Indiana University Press, 1994.

5 Ford Madox Ford, 'Not Really English,' *Your Mirror to My Times: The Selected Autobiography and Impressions of Ford Madox Ford*, ed. M. Killigrew, New York: Holt, 1971, p. 274.

6 Dominique Lemarchal, 'Ford Madox Ford's Moveable Provence', Conference Abstract for 'Ford Madox Ford and The Republic of Letters', Bologna, 11-14 January 2000. For more on Ford's engagement with England and America, see Sergio Perosa, 'Ford, England and the American Scene' in Vita Fortunati and Elena Lamberti, eds, *Ford Madox Ford and the Republic of Letters*, Bologna: Clueb, 2002, pp. 131-41.

7 Letter to the Editor of the New York *Herald Tribune Books* (15 February 1927), *Letters of Ford Madox Ford*, ed. Richard M. Ludwig, Princeton, NJ: Princeton University Press, 1965 – hereafter cited as *LF*; p. 172.

8 For more on Arnold's attack on sensational journalism, see Matthew Arnold, 'Up to Easter,' *The Nineteenth Century* CXXIII (May 1887), 629-643. For more on Ford's engagement with Matthew Arnold's philosophy and its impact on *The English Review* see Paul Peppis, 'Conjuring new character: *The English Review*, Wyndham Lewis and the reconstruction of Englishness', *Literature, Politics and the English Avant-Garde*, New York: Cambridge University Press, 2000.

9 There are no lengthy treatments of Stead's writing on New York but for a consideration of his earlier journalist crusade in Chicago that prompted him to continue eastward, see Joseph O. Baylen, 'A Victorian's "Crusade" in Chicago, 1892-1894', *Journal of American History,* 51 (December 1964), 418-34.

10 Ford Madox Ford, *The Critical Attitude*, London: Duckworth, 1911, p. 5.

11 H. G. Wells, *The Future in America: A Search After Realities*, New York: Harper and Brothers, 1906. Wells writes in 'The Envoy':
My friend Mr. F. Madox Hueffer was here a day or so ago to say good-bye; he starts for America as I write here, to get *his* vision. As I have been writing these papers I have also been reading, instalment by instalment [sic], the subtle, fine renderings of America revisited by Mr. Henry James. We work in shoals, great and small together, one trial thought following another. We are getting the world presented. It is not simply America that we swarm over and build up into a conceivable process, into something understandable and negotiable by the mind [. . . .] Collectively, this literature of facts and theories and impressions is of immense importance. Things are done in the light, more and more are they done in the light. The world perceives and thinks... (pp. 256-7).

12 Wells, *The Future in America*, p. 36.

13 H. G. Wells, *The War in the Air* (1908), London: Penguin, 1976, p. 120.

14 For more on Ford's negotiations with James's models see Kathryn Curle Rentz, 'Ford Madox Ford and the Jamesian Influence,' Doctoral Dissertation, Univ. of Illinois at Urbana-Champaign, 1986, Chapter 3.

15 Max Saunders, *Ford Madox Ford: A Dual Life*, Oxford: Oxford University Press, 1996, Vol. 1, p. 230.

16 W. H. Auden, Introduction to *The American Scene, Together with Three Essays from 'Portrait of Places'* by Henry James, New York: Charles Scribner's Sons, 1946, p. v.

17 For a reading of James's *The American Scene* in the greater context of city literature, see Jeremy Tambling, *Lost in the City: Dickens, James and Kafka*, London: Palgrave, 2001, especially Chapter 7.

18 Harold Beaver, 'In the land of acquisition', *Times Literary Supplement*, September 18-24, 1987, 1020-1021.

19 Beaver, 1020; Nicholas Delbanco, *Group Portrait: Joseph Conrad, Stephen Crane, Ford Madox Ford, Henry James, H. G. Wells*, London: Faber, 1982, p. 151.

20 In a letter to James B. Pinker in August 1906 Ford mentions how he proposed to his publishers (McClure, Phillips and Co.) that they should publish the three volumes in one 'called, say, *The Anglo-Saxons*'; *LF* 23-24.

21 Going beyond my consideration here of New York City's influence on Ford, Harriet Y. Cooper suggests that *England and the English* may have influenced the American playwright Israel Zangwill's use of the term 'melting pot' – Zangwill has long been credited with coining this term. For more on this see Cooper's essay, 'The Duality of Ford's Historical Imagination', *History and Representation in Ford Madox Ford's Writings*, ed. Joseph Wiesenfarth, Amsterdam, New York: Rodopi, 2004, pp. 189-99.

22 David Dow Harvey, *Ford Madox Ford 1873-1939: A Bibliography of Works and Criticism*, Princeton, NJ: Princeton University Press, 1962, p. 108.

23 Sandra Kemp, Charlotte Mitchell and David Trotter, eds. *The Oxford Companion to Edwardian Fiction*, Oxford: Oxford University Press, 2002, pp. 117-18.

24 Ford, *When the Wicked Man*, London: Jonathan Cape, 1932, p. 9.

25 Paul L. Wiley, *Novelist of Three Worlds: Ford Madox Ford*, Syracuse, N.Y.: Syracuse University Pres, 1962, p. 250. Wiley also goes on to say that Ford is not concerned with local events by the 1930s; rather, he is concerned with the placement of America within the large scale cultural map that to the end of his life he was striving to design, for which reason in the late novels American scene and character tend increasingly to occupy an orbit which includes that part of the continent of Europe which Ford thought worth salvaging from the waste land. The rescue of an 'ersatz-civilization' from further ruin makes necessary the creation of a bond between America, as the new leader of Anglo-Saxondom, and the remaining vestiges of a Provencal Mediterranean tradition (p. 252).

'SPEAK UP, FORDIE!': HOW SOME PEOPLE WANT TO GO TO CARCASSONNE

Paul Skinner

There is a story that Ford Madox Ford tells of walking up and down in a Greenwich Village apartment, looking at a bookshelf and taking out 'a dullish-backed book at random', remembering then his reading Kipling on a train running into Rye station forty years before.[1] Elsewhere, he recalls lying on his back on the downs above Lewes, watching dandelion seeds drift across 'the crystalline blue of the sky', before noting that it wasn't his experience and that he had never been on that particular down. He was remembering a passage from a book by W. H. Hudson, and remarked that it had become a part of his life. 'It is as much part of my life as my first sight of the German lines from a down behind Albert in 1916...which is about the most unforgettable of my own experiences in the flesh. . . . So Mr. Hudson has given me a part of my life . . .'.[2]

Reading; place; memory of the place read about and of the place in which a book was read: these things do indeed become part of our lives, their precise history and chronology difficult to disentangle. I myself can hardly remember when it was that I first went – if only in imagination – to the Ancient Town of Carcassonne, which fell after a two-week siege on 15 August 1209, during a crusade against the Albigensians launched by the inappropriately named Pope Innocent III. Because I too have taken down from a shelf a dullish-backed book at random, and seen, near the top of a page, the words: 'I just wanted to marry her as some people want to go to Carcassonne'.

The first time I read those words, and indeed, the second and perhaps third times, I thought of that flatness of tone, that strange equation of the two things – wanting to marry the loved person and wanting to visit a place – as merely illustrating what many readers have seen as the odd, even pathological nature of the narrator's character. But I always read on: 'Do you understand the feeling that you must get certain matters out of the way, smooth out certain fairly negligible complications before you can go to a place that has, during all your life, been a sort of dream city?' (*GS* 84).

To Ford, London was long a city of ease and freedom, which changed utterly after the war, as he recalled in *It Was the Nightingale*; Paris, where he spent a great deal of time, he claimed, not altogether convincingly, never to have liked very much;[3] New York, yes, with some reservations. All very real places, in which one lived, worked, loved, wrote and suffered. But what of Carcassonne?

'I just wanted to marry her as some people want to go to Carcassonne.' How *do* some people want such things? Faintly or passionately? Casually or with intense longing? One clue is perhaps, as not unusually in Ford's writings, in that word 'just'. Try this: 'I loved Edward Ashburnham – and . . . I love him because he was just myself' (*GS* 161).[4] 'Just' meaning, among other things, only, merely, precisely, a perfect fit, an exact equivalent, punishment to crime, cost to value, desire to object of desire, word to thing.

It is fatally easy to write about *The Good Soldier*. There have been many ingenious analyses, though there is always the temptation to leave Occam's Barber Shop somewhat abruptly, still with a full beard. As with Pound's *Hugh Selwyn Mauberley*, there are strong currents pulling simultaneously in opposite directions, and siren voices whisper of the desirability of recklessness.

But I merely want to think about one of the ways in which Ford seems to tease us: and I say 'seems' because it's not always clear whether this is deliberate – and therefore teasing – or not. He gets facts exactly wrong, confuses stories, imports bits of one into another. Some critics complain that he never gets things right or simply lies – others point out that there is always a kernel of fact in even the most fantastic inventions. And sometimes he's exactly right. He referred more than once to *The Good Soldier* having hatched within him for a decade before he wrote it, and being based on a true story.[5] Ford was uncommonly fond of decades. In *Provence*, he remembered a snowstorm in Carcassonne, 'snowstorms happening there once every forty years or so. That was in 1913, when I was refreshing my memory as to the Albigeois martyrs of that city...' (*Provence* 154).[6] Every forty years or so. Exactly the span of Ford's life at that date. 'I had always entertained the idea that . . . I at least should not be able to write a novel by which I should care to stand before reaching the age of forty. . . .' And again: 'on the day I was forty I sat down to show what I could do – and *The Good Soldier* resulted' ('Dedicatory Letter', *GS* 3). It was during 1913, of course, that he published his fortieth book.[7]

I should mention here that, firstly, I use 'Provence' quite loosely, unencumbered by geographical niceties and governed by Ford in this; secondly, that there is no doubt about Ford's later feelings for Provence, which he came to regard as an earthly paradise. Weather, landscape, cuisine, people, their attitudes to the arts and to the artist, all these became a large part of his vision which, to reduce it to crude essentials, set the life-giving south against the north from which death came: coldness, militarism and the chill of capitalist mass-production. The war affected this, as it affected so much else. Suffering, and surviving, that war, learning to live again and – crucially – to write again, gave him a heightened sense of the elemental, of the paradoxical richness of life lived – literally – close to the earth.

But now, thinking about 1913-14, we have, I think, to consider simultaneously 1903-4, as, of course, other readers have done. This means, unavoidably, rehearsing what may be familiar details but, since (at least apparent) repetition and familiarity are central to my *sense* of Ford, I may be forgiven. Ford's personal situation, then, in the later year – the hopeless love affair, the trip to Germany in autumn 1913 – must surely have brought back to him, with unwelcome vividness, that earlier time, which he once called 'the most terrible period' of his life (*JC* 212).

The 'germ' of *The Good Soldier*, if we want to call it that, appears in *The Spirit of the People*, published in 1907, the events presumably having occurred a few years before that. A man who has fallen in love with his ward drives her to the station, taking Ford along for company and, implicitly, to make sure he doesn't crack and tell the girl how he feels. In bidding her farewell, the man doesn't even speak: but the internal strain reveals itself in his completely forgetting about Ford and driving off without him. Ford, in his telling of the story, seeming both admiring and appalled, mentions that the girl died shortly thereafter and that the man spent the next three years on the Continent, undergoing various 'nerve cures' (*SP* 148-151). So go back ten years from 1913-14, when Ford was writing *The Good Soldier*. From the late summer of 1904 he was in Germany; in fact, he left England for Germany almost exactly ten years before the outbreak of war, a tidy span that may have occurred to this connoisseur of decades once or twice thereafter. One of his uncles was dying and Ford wrote that it shocked him to see his uncle 'quite blind and impotent', a striking phrase.[8] It strikes me partly because, though acquainted with the fact of death, Ford may have been a little less familiar with the

process of dying. It was dying that would engage him later: Edward
Ashburnham was so in love with Nancy Rufford, he said, that he was
dying of it (*GS* 158). In May 1914, Ford apparently wrote to his
daughter Christina that he himself was 'dying' (Moser 120). He was,
as Max Saunders notes, 'always imagining his own death'.[9] And it
strikes me that such terms as 'blind' and 'impotent', among many
others, have been applied to Ford's narrator, John Dowell, by critics
either exasperated by a profusion of possibilities or feverish with
certainties.[10]

     In 1904, Ford was, in fact, suffering a nervous breakdown:
that's why he was in Germany, seeking the cure. A quarter of a
century later, he recalled the efforts of various doctors to prove that
his troubles had 'an obscure sexual origin'. Everyone, he wrote,
'diagnosed my trouble as agoraphobia; *sixteen or seventeen of them*
[my emphasis, to ensure that this is savoured] attributed it to sexual
abnormalities and treated me for them.' 'Those were the early days,'
Ford adds, 'of that mania that has since beset the entire habitable
globe' (*RY*, 267, 269). Well, if that happens to be your attitude, if you
find it extremely distasteful to discuss your most intimate affairs with
a stranger, I think we could term that talking to 'an unsympathetic
listener'. And the emphasis on sexuality is certainly a feature of *The
Good Soldier*. So move forward in time again to 1913, when Violet
Hunt carries her report of the *Throne* trial to Ford at Boulogne. Ford
was stricken by the news, of course; everybody would be talking
about his affairs and he couldn't answer them back. He was ill; he had
– literally – lost his voice. Voice is such a Fordian thing: several
acquaintances remarked on his tendency to speak indistinctly,
compelling them to lean towards him to catch his words, while one of
his anecdotes about his childhood centres on his father calling from
the audience, 'Speak up, Fordie!', as Ford reluctantly performed a
minor role in a Greek play.[11] And in 1913-14, there was a great deal of
noise. Blasts, Futurism, Vorticism, Marinetti, Wyndham Lewis, Ezra
Pound. Madame Strindberg's Cave of the Golden Calf. Ford wrote 'a
shadow play' to be performed there – voiceless indeed. The Rebel Art
Centre, lecturing: Lewis's canvas, *Plan of War*, with improbable
symbolic aptness, falling on his head. Speak up, Fordie!

     And Ford's preoccupations, as suggested by the columns he was
writing in the *Outlook*, where he *could* speak up, if, sometimes, a little
obliquely, included, of course, the desired form of the novel, famously
described as 'a book so quiet in tone, so clearly and unobtrusively

worded, that it should give the effect of a long monologue spoken by a
lover at a little distance from his mistress' ear'.[12] Elsewhere, he
remarks, à propos of Gerhart Hauptmann: '. . . I am not sure that there
is not something after all in the English-German idea that if one saw
the whole truth of things – being English-German oneself – one would
go mad'. And a little later:

> . . . whereas England is the very worst place in which to suffer from any form
> of nervous complaint, Germany is the best of all asylums for the really
> neurasthenic. In England you find practically nobody to understand how you
> could possibly be in a bad way if you don't happen to be in the divorce court,
> bankruptcy court, or upon the operating-table.'[13]

He was thinking of Maupassant, whose novel *Fort comme la mort* he
claimed to wish to emulate, and who had, Ford remembered, 'died
mad' (and, of course, syphilitic: Ford probably knew of Violet Hunt's
condition before this).[14] And he was thinking of Arthur Symons, who
had written a book called *The Knave of Hearts* – which cannot have
failed to bring to mind once again his beloved Ford Madox Brown,
whose appearance he had likened to that of the King of Hearts. Who
would play the knave to *that* king? But, more than this, Ford would
have known that the poems in Symons' book, proof-read by Yeats and
published in November 1913, had all been written between 1894 and
1908; that Symons had suffered a major nervous breakdown in 1908,
had been declared insane and briefly confined to Brooke House in
East London.[15] In his review, Ford reflected that he had barely read
Symons, because he'd thought he knew what kind of writer Symons
was and could thus ignore him. He goes on: 'I think that is a sad
history of the evil hearts of men. I think it is the saddest history that
can be told...'.[16] Well. Perhaps one reason why that seems to Ford to
be 'the saddest history' is that Ford himself is thinking – or at least,
writing – about giving up imaginative literature.[17] He has written forty
books, some of them well-received; he has edited, albeit briefly, a
famous review; his name has been associated with a celebrated
novelist. Yet he can't make a decent living; he has problems with
publishers; he knows that his critical reputation isn't what he'd like it
to be. In a review of Dostoievsky, he remarks: 'And I suppose that
what is at the bottom of my feeling of weariness, of my aversion from
Dostoievsky, is just the feeling of Bertin, the painter of *Fort comme la
mort*. It is the feeling that one is getting on in life, and that one's
successors must be upon the horizon'.[18] Exactly a month before the

outbreak of war, writing about Wyndham Lewis – and, by extension, all those successors on the horizon – he referred to himself as 'I who am, relatively speaking, about to die …'.[19]

He was thinking, then, of madness, of death, of literary obscurity or supercession, of the form of a novel by which he might care to stand. Yet, as always, he was constantly writing. In 1913, he published over thirty essays and reviews, two novels and his *Collected Poems*, wrote *Henry James*, and began *The Good Soldier*.

And to John Dowell, narrator of that novel, Carcassonne is 'a sort of dream city'. Why is this? In the context of the novel, linked, most specifically, with the Provençal troubadour Peire Vidal, it stands as the symbol of a civilization, a way of life, that has been extinguished. Some criticism of *The Good Soldier* has focused on this, pointing out that Leonora can be seen as representing the orthodox and repressive tendencies of the established – Catholic – church. The views of life, often characterized as 'pagan', which were destroyed by the Inquisition, are thus aligned with Edward Ashburnham, whose suicide makes a kind of sense in view of the Albigensian or Cathar tolerance of suicide as a means of escape from the body, though his amorous involvement with various other bodies doesn't quite seem to fit.[20]

In a sense, though, the dream city is, precisely, death: those 'certain matters' to be got out of the way, those 'certain fairly negligible complications' which must be smoothed out seem like nothing more – or less – than the ordinary business of living, of being in the world, of dealing with the complexities and responsibilities that this entails.

'My job in life as I have conceived it', Ford once wrote, 'has always been to record as passionlessly as possible my impressions of my own times and the places in which I have worked'. He noted that his impressions were happiest when he was merely glancing aside from something, adding: 'Thus Carcassonne has for me an extraordinary life because I wrote practically the whole of a book there' (*NYNA* 18).

That book must have been *The Young Lovell*, the last novel Ford wrote before beginning *The Good Soldier*. It exhibits many familiar Fordian motifs and themes but, more to the point, perhaps, the story ends with the hero's death – or rather, the separation of body from spirit, Lovell's earthly body being walled up in a hermit's kennel while his spirit conducts courtly battles in a heavenly valley on an island ruled over by the goddess Venus, who in fact presides over the whole novel. But it ends with a death, and a comparable one to that which ends *The Good Soldier*.

Although Ford seems to have spent only about ten days in Carcassonne in early 1913, Carcassonne's centrality may have been to do with the other places that he and Violet Hunt visited: of Montpellier, Hunt recalled that it was 'a wash out'; of Les Baux, that it 'depressed us immeasurably', of St Rémy that the mistral cut with 'its knife-blade of cold'. Of Carcassonne, she notes that 'rabies was raging' and that she was nearly bitten by a mad dog which was killed soon afterwards. Her sympathies, she says, were 'too much with the dog, wild, maddened', and notes that she had 'read John Galsworthy's story in the *English Review* – perhaps the dog was only being driven mad by agony?'.[21]

Ford had known of Carcassonne, and of Peire Vidal, from his father's book on the Troubadours, from Ezra Pound's poem, 'Peire Vidal Old', and probably from Pound's unpublished manuscript 'Gironde' which Ford read – and severely criticized – in 1912. From the walls of Carcassonne, Pound wrote in one of his surviving notebooks, 'one looks out to Penaultier which may have been Loba's' – that is, the lady beloved by Peire Vidal.[22] And in 1913, Ford was writing his tribute to Henry James. In *A Little Tour in France*, James noted that he had spent 'only a few hours' at Carcassonne, but Ford rather immoderately praised his 'rendering' of the city, while acknowledging that it was 'archaeologically inferior to any one-franc guide's'. Carcassonne is not a dream city but a real one, yet remains inescapably connected with dreams. 'In the warm southern dusk,' James wrote of it, 'it looked more than ever like a city in a fairy-tale'.[23]

The story of Peire Vidal, always connected by Ford with Carcassonne, and so important in *The Good Soldier*, recurs in Ford's later book on *Provence*, where Ford tells the story twice and also links Vidal to Christina Rossetti, just as he links his memory of studying the archives of the city of Carcassonne to a dispute with his grandfather, which clearly afflicts him with guilt, still, more than forty years later (*Provence*, 65-66, 176, 145, 133-138).

And why Vidal? In *The Good Soldier*, the main point of his story is surely its mixture of absurdity and tragedy: thus it represents, on its smaller scale, the novel that contains it. Indeed, Vidal is a good example, for Ford, of the man who suffers and the artist who creates, with joy and grief woven quite together, not separated, just as, in Ford's telling, the arts in Provence are not screened off in museums and universities but are part of the very stuff of life. In Vidal's character, Ford's father Francis Hueffer wrote, '[h]igh gifts and wildest eccentricities are strangely mixed up'.[24]

And in Provence, John Dowell remarks, 'even the saddest stories are gay' (*GS* 15). Does that mean stories that emanate from Provence or stories told to those in Provence? And what of stories told to us when we are not in Provence but wish to be? Because, hearing that story, are we not – in part – in that Provence, as we are – in part – in that country cottage where Dowell talks on and on in a low voice?

Vidal's dressing in wolf-skins, maddened by love for the Lady Loba ('She-Wolf') of Penaultier, mistaken for a real wolf and beaten by shepherds, this twelfth-century scenario is, of course, a kind of burlesque of the Diana-Actaeon myth. We are already immeasurably far from the world of Greek gods and goddesses. As for wolves . . . 'Homo homini lupus' – man is a wolf to his fellow-men – was one of Ford's favourite tags: as late as the 1930s, he wrote: 'I can still see the shadows of wolves if I lie awake in bed with a fire in the room' (*RY* 72).[25]

Though Edward Ashburnham has sometimes been identified with the figure of Peire Vidal, the doubling that is everywhere in the novel resists this degree of straightforwardness.[26] Looking at the split between the man who acts out his desires and the man who observes and tells the story, we are pointed towards the figure in whom both functions are inextricable: the artist, as Ford conceives him. A purely passive observer leads to Hugh Selwyn Mauberley syndrome – or John Dowell. Man of action leads to the posturing often detectable in Kipling and Henley. Clearly, both are needed; or rather, the observer who has *been* a man of action, in Ford's telling of it: Conrad or Crane, or Hudson, who comes from life among the gauchos to study birds or to observe thistledown drifting above a hill. In *The Good Soldier*, John Dowell reflects:

> But, as soon as I came out of my catalepsy, I seemed to perceive that [. . .] what I had to do to prepare myself for getting into contact with her, was just to get back into contact with life [. . .] I [. . .] had to do [. . .] a little fighting with real life [. . .] something harsh, something masculine. I didn't want to present myself to Nancy Rufford as a sort of an old maid. (*GS* 84)

In *Hugh Selwyn Mauberley*, Ezra Pound describes the minor poet that he might have been or remained – without Imagism, Vorticism, Fenollosa and others, including Ford Madox Ford – and both completes and demonstrates his escape from that role through and by the writing of *Mauberley*. Ford's case is a little different. He had published many books; had been almost famous; had achieved, in *Ladies Whose Bright Eyes* and *The Young Lovell*, a kind of intensity which was still muffled, still split. There is a sense in which this split is healed by *The Good Soldier*: resolved not in the novel but by it, just as, at the other end of the war, Ford, in writing about his inability to write, the split between the mind of the writer and that of the soldier, involved in the most extraordinary experiences of his life yet unable to transmute them into the medium of which he is master, comes through it, in and by the writing of *No Enemy*.

So John Dowell has been seen as a buffoon, a pathological case, a eunuch, even a lunatic. Perhaps he *is* mad. The nature of the novel ensures that we can prove and disprove nothing. Can we be sure he's not? Has he been driven mad by love? He tries to interpret, to explain the unfathomable events which have turned his world to dust – he dresses up, let us say, as a critic. Ford would say of a student audience at the University of Jena that their 'avidity for facts, dates and factual meticulousnesses . . . was like the hunger of wolves'.[27] And critics were always coloured for Ford by his memories of the *Athenaeum*, where lapses of factual accuracy were lambasted in the review columns (*RY* 183, *LF* 110-111). So Dowell, dressed as a wolf, is savaged, first in the novel by those who abuse and deceive him, then by those real wolves, who snap at his chronological inaccuracies and inconsistencies, who hunger for definition and closure. And it's a nice touch that when Dowell recalls arriving in England and being met by Edward Ashburnham, he remarks: 'The girl was out with the hounds, I think' (*GS* 21).

Indeed, when we open *No Enemy*, written for the most part in 1919, we meet Gringoire – which is not the poet's real name but the name of the poet to whom Alphonse Daudet's story, 'Le Chèvre de M. Séguin', is addressed. Ford often cited this story, which, a footnote in *No Enemy* tells us, is meant to show that 'though a poet may struggle all his life against poverty, in the end the wolf, starvation, will get him' (*NE* 19).[28]

But in the meantime? Provence might awaken you 'from a dream of immortality to the realisation of what is earthly permanence'.

Tolerance, warmth, even amidst the eternal worries, the compensat-
ions of bright sunlight, grey rock, an inescapable slowness and ease.
And, perhaps most tellingly: 'It is thus, you see, difficult to sin in
Provence' (*Provence* 90, 83).

To Dowell, in *The Good Soldier*,

> the world is full of places to which I want to return [. . . .] Not one of them did
> we see more than once so that the whole world for me is like spots of colour
> on an immense canvas. Perhaps if it weren't so I should have something to
> catch hold of now. (*GS* 16-17)

And Valentine Wannop, on Armistice Day, 11 November 1918, who
has missed the moment of the war's ending because she was called to
the telephone to speak to Lady Macmaster, thinks that might be 'an
omen that she might miss some universal and necessary experience!
Never see Carcassonne, the French said...'.[29]

The Good Soldier – a narrator, perhaps blind, perhaps impotent,
talking on and on, in a quiet voice, to a sympathetic listener. Dowell's
– or Ford's? For Dowell: probably Nancy, some of that time – she
doesn't answer back much. Shuttlecocks! For Ford: Conrad, perhaps,
in imagination. Hilda Doolittle and, certainly, Brigit Patmore; even
Richard Aldington. And us, surely. Someone who knows what it is,
what it takes, to be the suffering teller of a tale: to make art, to fiddle
with it and make it seem quite careless. John Dowell – so nearly John
Doe: and nearly John Do-well. What does John do well, to lift him
from the John Doe realm? He talks. 'Good prose is just your
conversation'.[30] Is this a conversation? Or just talk? Your body in one
place and your mind in another. Memories of a clamorous world
coming apart at the seams, that season of 1914. Closer than that. If
Ford's fears included ruin, scandal and the failure of his art, they also
included suicide and madness. He feared them and was fascinated by
them, as so many artists are. Ezra Pound remarked that 'Villon's verse
was real because he lived it; as Bertran de Born . . . as that mad poseur
Vidal, he lived it'.[31] And, when his patron Alfonso of Aragon died,
Vidal wrote, in a song addressed to Alfonso's son: 'Certainly, I should
not live if suicide were not a sin'.[32] Ford has Edward Ashburnham act
out that feared fantasy of suicide – does he have John Dowell act out a
kind of madness? In any event, he was having his say. 'I have rushed
through all Provence – and all Provence no longer matters' (*GS* 149).
That was as high as he could pitch it. When Dowell talks about how
he will tell the story, he pictures himself and his listener stepping

outside and comparing the brightness with that of Provence. Provence the measure. And Carcassonne, that double city, where two important thoroughfares intersect, north to south and east to west. Carcassonne was besieged, fell, and Troubadour culture foundered. A breaking relationship, a creaking civilization. What might you feel that you might miss? 'Never see Carcassonne, the French said . . . .' Ford had seen it – but it had been, so to speak, glancing aside from his story of sexual enchantment and death, and in the midst of a snowstorm, in any case. In *Provence*, he would comment: 'And I am hardly exaggerating when I say that all my travelling has always been one long planning to return' (*Provence* 59). Carcassonne may have stood for – what? All that he feared he might not see, do, achieve? Forty years – and what if? If it happened – and you were remembered as a minor poet, an editor of brief tenure, a writer of a few historical novels, a pastiche or two. The last chance? I am straying here into one of the most vexed questions: the dates of *The Good Soldier*'s writing. In the face of such rich uncertainty, let me be arbitrary. I have no new insight into why and when he picked August 4th as his recurrent date – unless some anniversary in his largely hopeless love for Brigit Patmore?

Or perhaps this, a fancy which pleases me more: in that dark spring of 1904, Ford wrote to W. H. Hudson, asking for advice about places to which he might escape from his situation in London. Hudson proposed Brockenhurst, 'the best country in England', and Ford went first to Setley (just outside Brockenhurst), where the Hueffers' maid Johanna, the children and, a little later, Elsie Hueffer, joined him; and then to Bridge House at Winterborne Stoke, near Salisbury, three miles from Stonehenge.[33] He met and walked with Hudson, and later remembered standing with him for half an hour, watching a rookery near Broad Chalke, where Maurice Hewlett lived in the Old Rectory (once the home of John Aubrey). Ford 'saw a good deal of him [Hewlett] in his beautiful mediaeval manor at Broad Chalke at a time when Hudson had his hiding hole in the valley behind – the valley with the rooks' nests' (*RY* 290).[34] Later still, he would remark of Hudson: 'he was a healer who brought you good luck merely by looking at you. . . .'.[35] Hudson's given names were William Henry but he was sometimes called, by his Spanish neighbours in Argentina, Dominic. This was because his birthday was the feast-day of St Dominic, who preached against the Albigensians: his followers hunted in packs and earned the nickname 'the hounds of the Lord'.

Hudson's birthday was 4th August.

In any case, I plump for what is now, perhaps, the majority view – that Ford began the novel more or less when he said he did; that he added to or emphasized that remarkable concurrence with history after the war began, and completed the novel – a little later than he said he did. He may well not yet have made the decision to enlist but, one way or another, all manner of endings seemed nearer, even, in some moods, desirable. So – the last chance?
Speak up, Fordie!
'*This* is the saddest story I have ever heard.'

NOTES

1   Ford, *Return to Yesterday*, London: Victor Gollancz, 1931 – hereafter cited as *RY*, p. 3.

2   Ford, *Thus to Revisit*, London: Chapman & Hall, 1921, p. 77. Cf. Ford's 'Preface' to *The Nature of a Crime* (London: Duckworth, 1924, p. 8), where, surely remembering his amnesia in 1916, he remarks: 'At a given point in my life I forgot, literally, all the books I had ever written; but, if nowadays I reread one of them, though I possess next to none and have reread few, nearly all the phrases come back startlingly to my memory, and I see glimpses of Kent, of Sussex, of Carcassonne – of New York, even; and fragments of furniture, mirrors, who knows what?' For a similar sentiment concerning Conrad, see 'Joseph Conrad', *English Review*, X (December 1911), 78, on *Lord Jim*: 'it is a part of me. Yes, it is a part of my soul, of my life'.

3   See Ford, *New York is Not America*, London: Duckworth, 1927 – hereafter cited as *NYNA*; p. 118; *It Was the Nightingale*, London: William Heinemann, 1934 – hereafter cited as *IWN*, p. 202, but see also p. 253.

4   The word 'just' occurs 183 times in the book.

5   'Dedicatory Letter to Stella Ford', *The Good Soldier*, ed. Martin Stannard, New York and London: W. W. Norton & Company, 1995 – hereafter cited as *GS*, p. 5; 'Publicity Notes from Albert & Charles Boni', dated 6th April 1926, cited in Max Saunders, *Ford Madox Ford: A Dual Life*, Oxford: Oxford University Press, 1996 – hereafter cited as Saunders; volume 1, p. 601 n. 100.

6   On the matter of decades, Sondra Stang has pointed out that the dates of the Tietjens novels (1924-8) followed the war (1914-18) by exactly ten years: *Ford Madox Ford*, New York: Frederick Ungar Publishing Co., 1977, p. 95.

7   Excluding *The Desirable Alien*, of which Ford wrote only two chapters (and many footnotes), this would have been *The Young Lovell*, his last novel before *The Good Soldier*. Note that Ford's 'oldest literary recollection' (already cited), that of reading Kipling on a train when he was eighteen, could be dated to exactly forty years before his recording of the fact, in 1931 (*RY* 3-4).

8   Ford to Olive Garnett (8 August 1904), quoted by Saunders, vol. 1, 173.

9   Saunders, vol. 1, 443. See, for example, 'Literary Portraits – XXXVI. Les Jeunes and "Des Imagistes" (Second Notice)', *Outlook*, 33 (16 May 1914), 683: 'one frequently wishes one were dead, and so on', and 'Literary Portraits – XLIX. A Causerie', *Outlook*, 34 (15 August 1914), 207: 'though it is my ambition to be dead by that date [1922]…' See also Ford's 'Immortality' in *Ford Madox Ford: Selected Poems*, ed. Max Saunders, Manchester: Carcanet Press, 1997, pp. 111-14.

10 See, for example, Theodore Dreiser, 'blind as a bat', in *Ford Madox Ford: The Critical Heritage*, ed. Frank MacShane, London: Routledge and Kegan Paul, 1972, p. 49; Bruce Bassoff, 'impotent', 'Oedipal Fantasy and Arrested Development in *The Good Soldier*', *Twentieth Century Literature*, 34:1 (Spring 1988), 45.

11 *Memories and Impressions*, New York: Harper & Brothers, 1911, pp. 114-15.

12 'Literary Portraits – XXIII. Fydor Dostoievsky and "The Idiot"', *Outlook* 33 (14 February 1914), 207.

13 'Literary Portraits – XIX. Gerhart Hauptmann and "Atlantis"', *Outlook* 33 (17 January 1914), 77, 78.

14 'Literary Portraits – XXXIV. Miss May Sinclair and "The Judgement of Eve"', *Outlook* 33 (2 May 1914), 599.

15 Karl Beckson, *Arthur Symons: A Life*, Oxford: Oxford University Press, 1987, pp. 261-3.

16 'Literary Portraits – XVI. Mr. Arthur Symons and "The Knave of Hearts"', *Outlook* 31 (27 December 1913), 891.

17 'On Impressionism (Second Article)', *Poetry and Drama*, 2 (December 1914), 326.

18 'Literary Portraits – XXIII. Fydor Dostoievsky and "The Idiot"', 206.

19 'Literary Portraits – XLIII. Mr. Wyndham Lewis and "Blast"', *Outlook* 34 (4 July 1914), 16.

20 See, for instance, Daniel R. Barnes, 'Ford and the "Slaughtered Saints": A New Reading of *The Good Soldier*', *Modern Fiction Studies*, 14:2 (Summer 1968), 157-70.

21 Violet Hunt, *The Flurried Years*, London: Hurst & Blackett, 1926, pp. 234-6.

22 Richard Sieburth ed., *A Walking Tour in Southern France: Ezra Pound Among the Troubadours*, New York: New Directions, 1992, p. 53. For Ford's criticism of 'Gironde', see Omar Pound and A. Walton Litz eds, *Ezra Pound and Dorothy Shakespear – Their Letters: 1909-1914*, London: Faber, 1985, p. 155.

23 Henry James, *A Little Tour in France*, London: Home & Van Thal, 1949, pp. 134, 145. For Ford on James, see Ford, *Henry James*, London: Martin Secker, 1913, p. 104. Ford remarked that James's quarrel with Flaubert arose from James's criticisms of Prosper Mérimée. Did Ford know that, when it was decreed in 1850 that all fortifications at Carcassonne were to be destroyed, the concerted action of three men helped prevent it: the scholar Jean-Pierre Cros Mayrevielle, the architect Viollet-le-Duc and – Prosper Mérimée?

24 Francis Hueffer, *The Troubadours*, London: Chatto & Windus, 1878, p. 169.

25 See also 'Literary Portraits – XVII. Nineteen-Thirteen and the Futurists', *Outlook*, 33 (3 January 1914), 15; 'From China to Peru', reprinted in Stang's Ford *Reader*, p. 186; 'Women and Men: I', *Little Review*, 4:9 (January 1918), 27; Ford, *No Enemy*, Manchester: Carcanet, 2002 – hereafter cited as *NE*, p. 124; Ford, *The Marsden Case*, London: Duckworth, 1923, p. 165; *IWN* 64. Pound borrows the phrase in 'Revolt of Intelligence: IX', *New Age*, 26:19 (11 March 1920), 301.

26 See particularly James Trammell Cox, 'Ford's "Passion for Provence"', *ELH*, 28:1 (March 1961), 383-98 – and Joseph Wiesenfarth's comments in 'Criticism and the Semiosis of *The Good Soldier'*, *Modern Fiction Studies*, 9:1 (Spring 1963), 42n.; on Ford and Vidal, see also Stuart Y. McDougal, '"Where Even the Saddest Stories are Gay": Provence and *The Good Soldier'*, *Journal of Modern Literature*, 7:3 (1979), 552-554. Perhaps the crucial words on the matter are these: 'Vidal was, you see, a great poet and it was not proper to treat a great poet with indifference', in *GS* 19.

27 'Literary Portraits – LIV. The Classic Muse', *Outlook*, 34 (19 September 1914), 368.

28 See also *NE* 150, 223, 227; and Ford, *A Mirror to France*, London: Duckworth, 1926, p. 52. Recalling one period of financial crisis, Janice Biala phrases it thus: 'Once the wolf nearly got us . . .' (*The Presence of Ford Madox Ford*, ed. Sondra J. Stang, Philadelphia, PA: University of Pennsylvania Press, 1981, p. 198).

29 Ford Madox Ford, *Parade's End*, London: Penguin, 2002, pp. 506, 812.

30 Pound (quoting Ford), 'Affirmations ... VI. Analysis of This Decade', *New Age*, 16:15 (11 February 1915), reprinted in *Gaudier-Brzeska*, New York: New Directions, 1974, p. 115.

31 Pound, *The Spirit of Romance*, New York: New Directions, 1968, p. 178.

32 Hueffer, *The Troubadours*, p. 181.

33 Hudson's letters to Ford are in Douglas Goldring, *The Last Pre-Raphaelite: A Record of the Life and Writings of Ford Madox Ford*, London: Macdonald, 1948, pp. 119-24. See also Saunders, vol. 1, 169-71 and Ruth Tomalin, *W. H. Hudson: A Biography*, Oxford: Oxford University Press, 1984, pp. 184, 209 (where she claims that when Ford saw the rookery with Hudson, he was staying with Hewlett).

34 Ezra Pound would go to Broad Chalke for Christmas in 1911, a journey poignantly remembered in Canto 80: see Pound, *The Cantos*, Fourth Collected Edition, London: Faber, 1987, p. 515.

35 Ford, *Portraits from Life,* Boston: Houghton Mifflin, 1937, p. 54.

PORTRAITS OF CITIES

Ford Madox Ford

Three Essays From An Unfinished Work,
Edited by Sara Haslam and Max Saunders

Editorial Note

In the last three years of his life Ford began work on a book that was
to have been the third volume of a trilogy, the other two being
Provence and *Great Trade Route*. At first he thought of it as continuing the exploration of the 'Great Trade Route' idea, 'taking in the
parts of it which I have not hitherto treated'. It was to include 'the
English South Coast, the U. S. Deep SOUTH and back by way of the
Azores, Tangiers, Jaffa and the Mediterranean shores'.[1] Another
projection in 1936 added Burgundy, North France, and Marseilles.[2] In
the following year he was calling it 'Portraits of Cities'. It was to be a
collaboration with his partner, the artist Janice Biala, who had
illustrated the other two books, and who was to provide drawings of
each city. Indeed, in June 1937 he was describing it as primarily
Biala's project: 'a book of drawings [. . .] text by myself'. He was then
thinking of a book mainly on American cities (Boston, New York,
Washington, Natchez, New Orleans, Chicago, Detroit, Denver, Salt
Lake City, Los Angeles, and San Francisco), which would have taken
him to the West Coast, and then via the Panama canal and Cuba back
across the Atlantic and back to Europe (Marseilles, Dijon, Paris,
Strasbourg, and London).[3]

But the list of cities to be included continued to change,
reflecting not only Ford's and Biala's travels and travel-plans, but also
his developing thoughts about civilisation and politics. In the autumn
of 1938 he was talking of writing 'a book on the international situation

---

1 Ford to Stanley Unwin, 3 Nov. 1936: quoted Max Saunders, *Ford Madox Ford: A
   Dual Life,* 2 vols, Oxford: Oxford University Press, 1996 – henceforth 'Saunders';
   vol. 2, pp. 659-60.
2 Ford to [G. F. J.] Cumberlege, 27 Oct. 1936: *Letters of Ford Madox Ford,* ed.
   Richard Ludwig, Princeton: Princeton University Press, 1965 – henceforth *LF*; p.
   264.
3 Ford to Ferris Greenslet of Houghton Mifflin, 12 June 1937: *LF* 279.

from my rather aloof – nowadays distinctly very left – point of view',
but according to Arthur Mizener, he decided to incorporate such
material into this third volume of the 'Great Trade Route' trilogy.[4]

In an undated synopsis, provisionally titled 'A Little Tour at
Home', the cities are almost exclusively American, and include
Boston, Detroit, Chicago, Denver, Kansas City, Pittsburgh, Richmond
(Virginia), Washington, Charleston, Baltimore, and New York.[5] But
they are framed between an account of the voyage from Naples, 'in
which comparisons will be made between various types of highly
cultured civilizations' from Periclean Athens onwards, and a final
chapter ('How to be happy though human'[6]) set on the boat returning
to the Mediterranean.

Only four chapters appear to have been written, all in 1937, and
all on the U. S. A.: 'The Athens of the South' (on Nashville, where
they had visited Allen Tate and Caroline Gordon in the spring and
again in the summer of 1937); 'Boston' (Ford was there in May 1937);
'From Boston to Denver'; and 'Denver' (where he and Biala had gone
for an exhibition of her pictures in August 1937). Perhaps it was the
drafting of these essays that had led him to reconceive the book as
more exclusively American in focus. The typescripts of all four essays
are at Cornell University. Only the first of these was published, as
'Take Me Back to Tennessee', *Vogue* (New York) (1 Oct. 1937), 104-
05, 134, 138, 140. The editor of *The American Mercury* was interested
in publishing the essays, but in the spring of 1938 Ford told him: 'I
simply found that I have not got either the material or the frame of
mind to write them seriously enough really to adorn your pages'; and
that though he had been able to make 'graceful comments' around
Biala's drawings, 'when I tried to write something that would stand up
by itself I just found I couldn't do it'.[7] This was scarcely surprising,
since he had been ill that winter, and was writing under pressure to
finish his colossal survey *The March of Literature*. But it also suggests
how he still thought of the book as a collaboration, and was not
prepared to publish any of it without the illustrations. Certainly once

---

4   Arthur Mizener, *The Saddest Story*, London: The Bodley Head, 1972, p. 456; also
    see pp. 439, 453, and 598n20, for further comments and redesigning of the
    project.
5   'A Little Tour at Home', Typescript, Carl A. Kroch Library, Cornell University.
6   Ford proposed a work of this title to his agent, George T. Bye, in a letter of 14
    April 1939 (Cornell), but there is no other evidence that it was written.
7   Ford to Paul Palmer, 19 Apr. 1938: Carl A. Kroch Library, Cornell University.

The March of Literature was out in the autumn, he began thinking about the book on cities again. He told his agent, George Bye, that it now had 'The quite provisional title, *Forty (?) Years of Travel in America*', and he added the cities of St. Louis, Lexington (Virginia), and Grand Rapids (Michigan) to the itinerary.[8]

Sometimes Ford's self-deprecating descriptions of the project make it sound like an excuse for rambling, as if the cities serve only as a pretext for free association:

> It will show the writer moving from Boston via New York to Washington, D.C.; Nashville, Tennessee; Denver, Colorado; St. Louis, Chicago, Detroit, and not so much commenting on those places as sitting down in those places and thinking about anything under the sun. (*Reader* 507)

Yet there was a coherent aim of both the book and of the whole trilogy. 'It is in short', he said, 'what in the old days would have been called humane literature'. As Ford put it, describing himself in some draft publicity material for *Great Trade Route*:

> he deals with a certain erudition of most of the things that made for the happiness of mankind . . . cooking, reading, farming, fighting, the Fine Arts, the Stage . . . how they all – and particularly politicians – should be handled if the civilization which we know and which is founded on the civilization of the Mediterranean is to have any chance of continuing. (*LF* 264)

But by 1939, when such a message was needed more urgently than ever, Ford was also working on a new novel, and wrote no more 'Portraits of Cities' before his death that summer in France.

The essay 'From Boston to Denver' is not published here. Though it includes interesting discussions of poverty, newspapers, food, and travel, it is only obliquely concerned with the idea of the city. The others are published with the kind permission of Michael Schmidt, the executor of the Ford estate, and the Carl A. Kroch Library, Cornell University. The text of 'Take me Back to Tennessee' follows that of its first publication; the essays on 'Boston' and 'Denver' have been transcribed from the Cornell typescripts, and include Ford's autograph corrections where legible. Editorial conjectures appear in square brackets. All the footnotes are editorial. Typographical errors have been silently corrected.

---

8   Ford to George Bye 29 Nov 1938: *The Ford Madox Ford Reader*, ed. Sondra J. Stang, Manchester: Carcanet, 1986 – henceforth '*Reader*'; pp. 506-8.

1) BOSTON

I

The true portrait of Boston would show a man who would be what the heralds call dimidiated – split in half from crown to toe and stuck together, each half differently clothed. To make it pretty one half should be in scarlet – cardinal's scarlet and with a cardinal's hat. The other would be black ... with the mortar board of the university don and his black gown to match the cardinal's scarlet one.

Spiritually and materially Boston is split in half and stuck together again like that.

In whatever part of the city you find yourself sooner or later you will hear – usually angrily uttered – the words: 'But there is *another* Boston!'

On a prim, old, red brick street with bulging, purplish window panes and steeply descending red brick sidewalks you meet a strayed champion of Big Boston Business. 'How charming all this is!', you say. His face becomes suffused with red, he makes a sweeping gesture and exclaims: 'But there is *another* Boston!'

You feel foolish. You remember that you belong to a century where special prices are not given for corner lots and battlefields. You remember that at the last census Boston 'together with Suffolk County' had a wholesale trade valued at two thousand four hundred million dollars – or, if you prefer it that way: $2,409,048,284. And all that stretches out, wheel-like, round that red-bricked paved hub[9]... in an extraordinary ordinariness of chimneys, gasometers, wool-warehouses, leather factories, slums, tenements, rusty cans – stretching out for miles beyond the horizon. You might be anywhere ... New York, London, Detroit, Paris, Chicago ... or Constantinople under Khemal Pasha. All cities today have identical approaches.

But if between an incinerator and a dripping housewall on a rainy day with the water of the gutters over your shoe-tops you there meet a thin, hawk-eyed man, with high features and silver-rimmed spectacles – if that is to say you there meet a strayed scholar and remark to him: 'It is rather – er, ornery isn't it?', he will insert his thin, scholarly hand under your arm and say in your ear: 'But there *is*

---

9 'The Hub' is a common nickname for Boston, though opinions vary as to whether it is the hub of New England, the U. S. A., or the universe.

another Boston ... Not, eh, so inexorably governed from the Bahamas by the red Cardinal'. He will add: 'Too *much* governed ..... Municipally ... But not so supine beneath the spiritual yoke ... You get my meaning?'

But it isn't our affair – to get his meaning. We are making only a portrait – of externals. Only one gathers that the eternal struggle between Rome and not-Rome goes on in the city of the red-bricked hub.... It goes on with varying fortunes, taking up and dropping municipal statemen [*sic*] with names of ringing Irish and concerning itself less perhaps with the saving of souls than with economies on town drains and the consequent rake-offs that may be made in the overflowings of gutters. And I imagine, having seen His Eminence the Cardinal Archbishop of Boston at his receiving of the red hat years ago, that that massive churchman must make a pretty formidable figure in any municipal mêlée even though he be retired from the streets of his metropolitan city to the smooth-climated Bahamas.[10] And, judging both by the state of the gutters – on the Hill[11] or off – in any sort of rainy weather and by a glimpse that I had of the municipal taxes on quite a small Boston property – well, someone must be living pretty comfortably.

But the rest of us have to have wet feet and trouser-legs and skirts and mud-spattered waists and shoulders and faces as the heavy trucks spatter through the street-lakes.

Because of that for thirty years I have really hated a city that I happened only to have seen in winter days – grim, with its dripping, black, naked trees over a windswept Common, with the rain hurling itself against you in handfuls as if of peas.... It seemed the very city of Irish-directed grafter-gangsters with the Hill a faded, shrunken wen of intellectual anglo-maniacs peering dimly out through their purplish, puffy window panes on the gusts of rain and the bare trees of their backyards.

But now, having reached it at dawn, by sea, to see the full rush and sunlight of the spring sweeping over the green-tasselled elms and beeches and locust trees of the Common above which peep house-fronts and chapel and church spires and the innumerable bright

---

10 The autocratic Cardinal William Henry O'Connell (1859-1944) kept a winter home in the Bahamas. Ford had seen him when, improbably, reporting from Rome on 'The Investiture of the American Cardinals', for *Collier's*, 48 (16 December 1911), 10-12.
11 Beacon Hill.

infantry squadrons of tulips in the public gardens... and the little old
streets all bright sun on the one side, and shining windows and clean
steps, and all soothing, deep shadow on the other.... Well, who could
hate that?

It is a compact and, if you will, miniature beauty, that which
begins with Commonwealth Avenue, with its brick bowed fronts,
broad with the trees between, swinging their boughs, and [runs] up to
the Common.... a planned approach to a city treasure such as you will
find in profusion in Paris, in greater but rather too uniform profusion
[i]n Washington D. C. and very seldom in London – though [illegible
autograph addition here] approach the suburb of Hampstead in
London, with its red brick and white window frames is the very spit of
the Hill at Boston.... Or it might be politer to say that the Hill is the
very spit of Well Walk Hampstead.

And the resemblance is even the greater since the suburb of
Hampstead in London is the Hub of the intellect of the other half of
Anglo-Saxondom, all professors, scholars, judges and the learned
dwelling there and innumerable poets and critics from Keats and
Coleridge and A. E. Housman and Mr H. G. Wells having done so as
Emerson and Holmes and Alcott have left here their shadows with
those of Adams' galore and all the Names that went up to make up the
New England Conscience.... We shall have to search for that in a
moment or two.

But for the minute in the young sunlight, we don't have, thank
goodness, to think of shadows or consciences.... or even Cardinals.
The impression is one of sheer gaiety. There can't be a pleasanter
street in the world than Beacon Street as it runs up its hill. With the
trees on the one hand it has the youth of the rue de Rivoli in Paris of a
spring morning.... Or, Heavens, isn't it exactly Constitution Hill
running up to Piccadilly, with the bow-windowed houses to the left
and to the right the Green Park with all the tramps of several counties
stretched out on the grass in the sunlight? You would swear that in ten
minutes a Coronation Procession will be debouching into it with the
heralds and kettledrummers and Guardsmen in scarlet with bright
t[r]im waistcoats and helmets and nodding plumes.

And your gaiety will be heightened for you – or it certainly has
been for me – by having eaten the best food I have ever eaten on this
continent – consistently best in both quality and cooking, though to
mitigate the jealousy of other cities and places where they eat I will
say that the service has not always been impeccable even in the

Ritziest locales…. But even that fact may be excused when you learn that the – very slightly – offending waiters are Harvard students making their livings whilst they study.

In short the lobsters were the best I have ever eaten; other sea-food perfect; French-made dishes not as good as you would get them at Larue's or Drouant's in Paris but good enough for any ordinary mortal and roasts again perfect. But Boston has always been memorable to me for its roast meats. I remember thirty years ago and more eating here one of the three most admirable slices of roast sirloin that I have ever eaten, the other two having been respectively at Gloucester, England in 1894 and the third in Chicago in 1927…. In short of eleven meals we partook of in public restaurants in the course of a week in the Hub only one – in a very gilded hotel – was the usual, rather avoidable, cosmopolitan Grand Hotel type which is the same the world over though here redeemed by the quality and freshness of the food served and only one – a Teutonic concoction of *sauerkraut mit eisbein* was poor even of its kind.

Boston, in fact, admirably situated between the fish-filled sea and innumerable trunk-gardens is better situated than almost any other city of this country in the matter of food and that may well account for the maintained intellectual superiority of its inhabitants. So that when I commission my half-cardinal, half-professor portrait-statuette of this city I shall see to it that the artist puts a basting ladle in the one hand and a roasting spit in the other – and that both the dimidiated faces shall be bright, masterful, slightly chubby and intelligent – as it were a real Prince Cardinal and a University Dean of the Golden Stalls.

II

You would say that the impact of both Papist and New England Puritanisms in one place – as if an irresistible ram should meet an immoveable post – would result in a moral vacuum such as should make human life impossible. We Catholics – like everyone else – when we are in a religious minority and therefore on our p's and q's become Puritan beyond anything conceived of by the Pilgrim Fathers who, once they were assured of being in a state of Grace, could find time for a sufficiency of carnal weaknesses. But, possibly because His Eminence's sheep are here more nearly in a majority than in most places, and so can unbend and be genial, the note of Boston seems much more un-threatening than it did before the Cardinal had his red hat. Or it is possibly because since the days of the slightly morose orthodoxies of the Concord School – who gave poor Mark Twain such a hell of a time for just once poking fun at them – since those days the intellectual leaders of the Hill and the Campus have had to react in the direction of a certain freedom of thought.

They had to react towards looseness because it was impossible to go any further in the direction of prohibiting things. When I was young in this city it was impossible to know what did not offend ... not so much the law as Good Taste. I would say to a Young Thing in a Beacon Street or a Cambridge drawing room that I *did* like raspberry tarts, or free-wheel bicycles, or the study of biology or the writings of William – or Henry – James ... It was all one what I liked. The Young Thing, gazing at me with her veiled, aloof eyes would exclaim: 'Well, you see *I* have the New England Conscience.'... And that suppressed you and your tastes ... whatever they were ... It never occurred to me till this minute to say that I *did* like the New England Conscience ... What would that Young Thing have found to answer to that?... Except perhaps that that was so sudden!

That is all changed now. Those who were girls and boys when I was a boy today preside – sedately enough – at cocktail, not tea, tables and speculate as to birth-control and Trotzky-ism and – to the disgust of their sons and daughters – declare that it is a scandal – in the interests of the sanctity of divorce – that Mrs Warfield[12] does not sit on the Throne whose tea their ancestors threw into the Harbor.

The sons and daughters on the other hand – as far as I could tell from conversations with them – hold opinions that would have been reactionary in the days of Pres[ident] John Quincy Adams. Whilst their parents and professors carry on with their conscientious progressivenesses, they stand in corners pishing and pshawing ... except of course when they – some of them – with the sudden fever of spring coursing through their veins, block up the streets with collapsed automobiles, bonnet the cops with bags filled with tap water and very splendidly carry on the traditions of the Town and Gown riots of Oxford across the Herring Pond that stretches to their doors.

Then Town meets Gown in the open – the scarlet against the black. Say the magistrates, rigid with indignation on their thrones:

---

12 Presumably Wallis Warfield Simpson (1896-1986), later Duchess of Windsor. However, although she had been married twice before meeting Edward VIII, Warfield was in fact her maiden name.

'This must be stopped. And pronto-pronto. Is it thinkable that in this twentieth century our right-thinking Hibernian police should be mishandled by a licentious, ribald and blasphemous studentry?'

To which, lolling benignly in their presidential fauteuils and twiddling their pince-nez between thumb and forefinger the University Presidents reply:

'Why don't their fat and incompetent Irish cops keep their noses and stomachs out of the very proper Walpurgis Nights of our lusty Agnostic-Unitarian lads – and lasses?'

In the meantime, the morning after the students are moaning:

'Oh, hell, why do we do such stupid things?'... and determine, in repentant compliment to Professor T. S. Eliot, to join the Church of England.

Conscience in New England has, as you see, become a very parti-coloured affair.... Even in the idle rich Youth of the Back Bay and beyond the North Shore. Of them I can't be expected to know much. But the patient New Yorker[13] who guides my culinary wanderings across this Continent and being younger sees Youth more from the inside.... that patient, observant and veracious being assures me that the remoter and wealthier Massachusetts beaches and capes are covered with bronze-limbed, sparsely clothed young men. Each one, between Old-Fashioneds, groans lamentably beside the wife of some other bronze-limbed, sparsely clothed one! But, says the patient but mildly incredulous Manhattanhite, the intentions of every one of them are strictly correct. They groan beside the even bronzeder and less clad young matrons to get them the more quickly to divorce their still more bronzed, nearly more nudist, even more Old-Fashioned-pickled, young spouses.... So that they may reconstitute for themselves, for a further year or so, an honorable estate of matrimony. And as I heard the eighty-two year old Mrs Wertheimer[14] once sigh – I suppose it does not matter as long as they really love one another.

---

13 'Ford also used the strange device of inventing a male character, "the Patient New Yorker", and dividing Biala's role in both *Provence* and *Great Trade Route* between her propria persona and this fictionalized alter ego': Saunders, vol. 2, 628-9.

14 Possibly the Flora Wertheimer painted twice by John Singer Sargent. She married the London art dealer Asher Wertheimer around 1873 and died in 1922. See Richard Ormond and Elaine Kilmurray, *John Singer Sargent:Complete Painings*, 3 vols, New Haven, Yale University Press, 1998-2003; Vol. 2, *Portraits of the 1890s* (2002), no. 348, pp. 134-5. The editors are grateful to Leonée Ormond for this reference.

Perhaps really to appreciate the City and Port of Boston you should enter it at dawn from the sea. Then with the new sun-rays upon it, from miles away, it resembles any other port of Romance ... Yes, from the sea it resembles Tunis seen from Algeciras ... shining, pinkly white, with pinkish-white vertical shafts, like minarets....

One almost invariably forgets that all [the] greatest cities are really also Ports upon which their true glories have been founded..... Boston according to the guide books is the greatest wool market of these States and the leather-trade center of the entire world. Give that glory to your scarlet half-robe. It is also distinguished for the x-score and then some Universities, Colleges, Seminaries, Technological Institutes, Libraries[,] Museums and shrines of the Concord School which give it its world fame ... because you don't get much fame out of wool and leather ... That fame, then, will give you your black half-gown for your spit-and-ladled portrait.

And I think it should, finally, stand upon an anchor ... in memory of what made the Hub the Hub ... and in token of Hope.

2) DENVER

I astounded myself by saying:
'Gawd, give us a skyscraper!'
We were entering the city of Denver on a sort of elevated Pulaski highway,[15] up in the air. Behind us the Rocky Mountains ran away like a pink, scalloped cake set on a department store counter ... set flat down on the alluvial plateau. And flat down, too, the city stretched itself out, in the mists of a thermometrical effect of 97° in the shade, below us. It had, like so many of the indistinguishable plain cities that for months and months we had zigzagged through between the Atlantic and the Mountains, the effect of a doormat that someone had thrown, for beating, into a front yard. Some cities like Detroit had given the effect of ten doormats, others like Terre Haute or Rochford, Ill. – of one. Denver looked like perhaps four. She pressed herself flat down to the plain ... as if in fear of the appalling catastrophes and panics that in those boundless solitudes the skies can produce.

We had expected something different of Denver. Life-long we had expected something different of her. She has historic distinctions; she was born in gold rushes, with their horrors, hysterias, crowd-madnesses, pestilences – as in the case of any ancient European city. We had expected to see at least half-ton nuggets on the tops of spires and monumental records to long-since-played poker hands that should never be forgotten ... with over all in the sky the mirage of a bucking broncho kicking perhaps a gold prospector's cradle to the limits of the welkin. Because today tourists [and] sugar beet farmers have chased away the gold-washers – not to mention the buffaloes, the Ute[16] braves and the few Mexicans who were the earlier owners of those plateaux.

But we might have been running down into any old Middle Western town on any old Middle Western plain ... any old place that exists not because of any special features but because railway systems there intersect.

And although we hadn't expected, yet certainly after those small town flat months we had hoped to find crowds in streams, with

---

15 Part of Route 40 in Maryland and also Delaware, where it was known locally as the 'Delaware Drag Strip'.
16 A native American people inhabiting parts of Colorado, Utah, and New Mexico.

clinking purses, jostling before the lit windows of department stores and uttering agreeable outcries and jocularities as in the shadows stream met and jostled with stream.... The things that go on on the sidewalks beneath sky-scrapers and only there. Why shouldn't we have expected that? Wasn't this Denver of the Gold?

But, seen from that aspect, it was as if Denver desired to prove that, herself a Ghost City, she was the fittest of all jumping off places for tourists visiting the deserted mining camps that, according to legend, surround her. She had the air of a city long abandoned; she might have been Central City[17] itself if she had had a canyon or two about her outskirts.

And yet, when by that road you find yourself, without any intermission, bewildered and moving in the midst of a perfect maze of triumphal arches, white Ionic pillars, capitol-domes, statues actually of bucking bronchos, captured field guns. They suddenly rise up around you without any apparent arrangement as if some giant had shovelled a fragment of Washington D. C. into a sack and had then haphazardly emptied that sack into the Center of the city.

It would appear that Denver had once a three times elected mayor who was determined to give her everything that she wanted. When she hungered he distributed meat and bread by the car-load; when she sizzled in too prolonged [tropic] heats, freight trains of ice; in winters of disaster whole mountain ranges of coal.

Then one day he found that his lieges wanted signs of cultural magnificence. Immediately he ordered all those architectural splendours ... Even to the presentation of the bucking broncho!... And in addition an art gallery with an admirably selected if small collection of modern paintings and sculpture.... And a Greek Theatre! Yet what can Hecuba have been to that Mayor?

And they look, all those white pillared buildings and arches of triumph like the pieces of furniture of a multibillionaire's apartment when he has just moved in and they are not arranged.... Sort of shy! For after all what must a Greek Theatre feel, suddenly dumped down there where the air is so rarefied by the altitude that, if you try to raise your voice, you fall to panting like a carp on a pond bank. You are five thousand feet high there – and don't you forget it!

That perhaps accounts for the ghostlinesses. Perhaps everything here has died for want of oxygen – except for the administrators and

---

17 Colorado.

professional men, and such a city is a ghost. You go into the classical restaurant here and it is full of lusty pink-cheeked men, all in the prime, and all, in that torrid heat, wearing English Harris tweeds – which proves they must be some fellows. And you ask who they are and you are told that the first is a high railroad official; and the next a dentist; and then four lawyers; two doctors; a museum curator; two publishers; two federal judges; a county court judge; the Chief of Police.... All, you see, administrators. And the waiter knocks with one elbow the soup into one of your ladies' lap and, with the other, the hat off the lady of the other party.... And only grins. So you gather that there ladies are not invited. Of course Administrators do not like Ladies. Yet Denver started her career and was world famous as being the centre of attraction of the most hideous world epidemic of human greed of all there have been.

There have been Crusades; pilgrims have rushed shoulder to shoulder like buffaloes in stampeding millions that formerly covered these Plains – pilgrims stampeding to Bethlehem, to Mecca, in search of holiness – and being properly swindled by the tourist agencies of the day.... And there have been other gold-rushes.

But no other gold-rush equalled for its horrors that of Colorado. Partly because it came very late.... Mrs Tabor died only last year, still watching her hopeless mine.[18] Partly because it came too early – there was no supervision of the tourist agencies that poured thousands of unequipped, penniless men onto the edge of the desert.... And relatively perfected rail and steam transport permitted them to pour all those rachitic[19] nitwits along with the worst toughs of Central Europe and the entire world out here.... And innumerable women – virtuous ones – with children at the breast, ready to rock them in the creeping wagons – supposing only that their menfolk had had foresight to provide them with wagons.... But innumerable people, mostly aliens, died along the roadsides. Some got home again never having so much

---

18 When Horace Tabor bought the 'Matchless Mine' in Leadville, Colorado, it was notoriously unproductive. Yet he found a rich seam of silver ore, and became a millionaire. As the price of silver fell, he lost his fortune; but as he died in 1899 was said to have urged his wife, Baby Doe, to hold on to the mine because it would pay again. She did, until her death in 1935, but it didn't. The mine is now a museum.

19 Suffering from the disease rickets.

as seen Pike's Peak[20] .... the agents having sold them worthless transport vouchers.

The stronger women who got through kept post offices, boarding-houses. They ran tiny grocery stores grubstaking the prospectors; they raised innumerable children; fed, when they could, the starving; wrestled with the food profiteers; backed their men in their wildest enterprises – and lost their figures, their complexions and their men's affections.... That is almost the most frequent note in the city's contemporary chronicles.

But there were enough strong notes. You figure for yourself the first dancing saloon to go up; a vast, garish shed, festooned with scarlet [p]lush; with drop-glass chandeliers sparkling and dropping grease on the clients.... And the bewhiskered scoundrels, or mere toughs, grasping small sacks and revolving to the sounds of ophiclides,[21] trombones, percussion cymbals and steam organs – and of course now and then a shot – revolving round the planturous,[22] much-bosomed, Strange Women – themselves in scarlet plush to match the internal decorations. But of course the shots were not as frequent there as you might well wish.... An English Lady of Quality, visiting Denver in quite early days, complains that she heard no shot at all in ten days....

And then, in an open-sided lean to, against one extremity of the dancing shed, with the thermometer thirty below zero, without lights or bedclothes or sanitation, as many as seven men – all it would hold – naked because their clothes have been stolen, dying, six of small-pox and one, incomprehensibly, of cholera – each one beneath a single blanket supplied by the Charitable. The poor, devoted Charitable – mostly from San Francisco suffered nearly as much as their charges.

But the profligacies of Denver were less egregious than in the mining camps – the now Ghost Cities, that at present in the august silences of the Rocky Mountains form an annexe to Coney Island. For a short time colour was found in the streams round Denver herself –

20 This imposing mountain close to the edge of the Great Plains was named after the explorer Lt. Zebulon Pike; though 'Zebulon's Peak' would have been more appropriately sublime and less jingly as its name. . . It was the first landmark seen by the wagon trains in search of new fortunes; hence the mid nineteenth-century expression 'Pikes Peak or Bust'.
21 Usually spelt 'ophicleide' or 'ophicleid': a wind-instrument, a development of the ancient 'serpent', consisting of a conical brass tube bent double, with keys.
22 This appears to be Ford's coinage, from the French *plantureux/euse*: 'une femme plantureuse' is large and fleshly.

enough to give a [Czecho]-Slovakian prospector seven cents a day after a day's heavy work with the rocking cradles – so that the [Czecho]-Slovakians became dish-washers and prospered. So, quite early on, the city had settled down to be merely a Center for the camps that half-encircled her... Before the 'nineties visiting tourist ladies were, as we have hinted, complaining like ourselves just now that Denver was far too dim – and decorous.

She so remains – a Center and disillusioningly quiet for visitors from the East. We tried for three weeks there and in the neighbourhood to raise a game of Poker – and it could not be done. We were perhaps alarming in aspect!... Yet for at least half a century of her career, Denver was the Mecca of Poker.

Yes, certainly in that respect, Denver is today a Ghost City whilst the original ghost cities, remaining on the sites of the mining camps for which Denver was originally the centre have become on occasion at least as crowded and as noisy as the first camps can have been. The outraged silences of the great mountains look down on old noises in new forms – even to the performances of Ibsen in the Theayters. And the roads going up into the mountains are as crowded as they can ever have been in the days of the old covered wagons that crept over the bouldered roads... But today they are solid with automobiles and charabancs, going hell for leather over roads like billiard tables, their wheels almost locking... up to altitudes of fifteen thousand feet or so. You cannot get out to change a tyre because the next car, coming round a bend, would throw you into the watercourses miles below ... and follow you like as not. And the august mountains, except for patches here and there of the beautifully criss-crossing pines have their surfaces completely obscured by cafes imitating in their architectures every kind of flash building in the world... And by crowds of rodeo-cowboys with their made-up faces, red scarlet satin shirt-waists, multi-gallon comic hats and sheepskin pants... And to keep you thoroughly in with the spirit of the place the seats in the cafes are in the form of merry-go-round horses with protuberant eyes... And to end the day Ibsen's *Ghosts*!

And in Denver you walk the grey, empty streets with the rare pedestrians moving with extraordinary slowness.... What we had wanted after months of the baking solitudes of the plains[,] what we had wanted was that Denver of the Gold should provide for us Fifth

Avenue by day and by night the Great White Way[23].... But the most emotional moments you achieve there are when you shiver internally because a hard faced man has fixed on you a glance that penetrates to your backbone. They still raise some Gold round Denver and she is the Center, not merely of the Tourist Trade but that of the national I. G. B. – illicit gold buying. And you must not have gold in Denver. You must not have it anywhere else but most particularly you must not have it there because a considerable portion of her population is made up of G men[24]....

And of course we had wanted to see, all round Denver, the great dry solitudes aching beneath the sunshine... Solitudes... with the few Mexicans in their adobe huts, the Ute Indian or two in the silent canyons and the millionfold herds of buffaloes gazing at us, as we rode by, with heavy, resentful eyes. Yes, of course, like everybody else, we had wanted to see the plains around Denver, in the pre-gold days of romance.

What a hope!.... The only buffaloes for hundreds of miles round are cooped up in a tiny paddock in that sweltering city where the dusty hair drops away in rags from their parched sides.... Do they really have to do those things? It is bad enough in other cities – but there in the land of which those prisoners were once the lords!....

It is better, if you want vestiges of that Past, to go to the art Museum and see the wonderfully beautiful pieces of New Mexican Art that they have there got together with infinite pains. It is a primitive, Latin art astoundingly like all the other primitive Latin Arts – the Italian, the South French, the Spanish... paintings of saints and martyrs, and crucifixes and descents from the cross carved in wood, with such sincerity and earnestness.... More educative really than buffaloes dissolving under your eyes into tallow; more precious both literally and metaphorically, than gold.... Yes, you should see Denver.

---

23 Broadway.
24 F.B.I. agents. James Cagney had starred in the successful film *G Men* in 1935.

3) TAKE ME BACK TO TENNESSEE:[25]
[NASHVILLE]

The chief glory of Nashville, Tennessee is in her hair – in the really incomparable beauty of the deep foliage which hides her suburbs. You can not indeed match, in its own English way, anywhere on this continent the showering greennesses of the bowl in the hills that surrounds the Athens of the South. If Shakespeare and the Elizabethan lyric writers should there be reborn, they would go on writing about the darling buds of May and the doxy over the dale as if they had never stopped doing so, and if you there let loose a nightingale it could sing its head off as if no Atlantic spread itself between there and the dingles of Warwickshire. And there the sunlight falls peacefully and you sit in the shade and watch the garden paths winding away into green secrecies.

She has even a sky-line like that of fabled cities. If you look for it carefully, at a given spot on the Clarksville new road, on the bridge over the Cumberland, you will see the Capitol stand up on a cliff, the fortifications running away, square like the lines of Ehrenbreitstein,[26] on a ridge of fortified earth from which you might think you could assault high Heaven itself. And towards it the white road runs with expectant enthusiasm so that you would swear you saw there on it all the Pilgrims of Chaucer on the road that bobbed up and down to Canterbury. And, as if it were Nuremberg, or Toledo, or Rome, or perhaps New York, or even Athens, you step on it like mad, desiring without delay to see from its ridge the golden glories of the Parthenon, the frowning menace of its Castle, the venerable cloisters of its Colleges, the mellow lichens of its venerable tombs.

---

25 A song with this title was recorded by Fiddlin' Arthur Smith between 1937 and 1940. In *Great Trade Route*, London: Allen and Unwin, 1937, pp. 339-40, Ford recalls his Welsh battalion bursting out singing about getting back to Tennessee during the Battle of the Somme.

26 David Garnett remembers Ford telling him stories of his youth, including one about staying when a small boy with his grandmother, 'who lived in a house on the end of the bridge, by the fortress of Ehrenbreitstein'. On this occasion Garnett stayed with Ford and Hunt near the fortress, at Assmanshäusen, in Germany, late in the summer of 1910. See Saunders, Vol. 1, p. 313, on this example of Ford's 'humorous, fantastical romances upon history'.

For miles and miles back upon the truly bobbing up and down road, chaste posters have been telling you that you *must* visit Nashville's Parthenon, her Castle and her Colleges – and that she is the Athens of the South.

Of those, there are I wonder how many in the world . . . Charleston, South Carolina, calls herself, one knows, the social Athens of the continent; Boston is the Athens of the North.... So is Edinburgh. Heidelberg is the Athens of the Reich; Berkeley, California, of the Coast. And, of course, there is also Athens. But she is rather forgotten. If she turned up at a Congress of all the Athens of the World, she would probably be jailed as an imposter or confined as having *Chiropteræ*[27] in her Parthenon.

It is perhaps the story of her monuments that makes Athens, Tennessee, singular amongst the cities of that name. You enter Nashville by a road that bobs its houses up and down more precipitously than is the case with any town that I know, through a coloured quarter that, except in its hill-climbing, resembles all the other coloured quarters of the South; you pass a coloured University, spick and span and scarlet, picked out with black faces and the white corneas of scholastic enthusiasms. For they say that the enthusiasms of all the other educational establishments of this city pale to ineffectualness before those of Fiske University. In compensation, the white professors of the institution are not received in Society – but, in recompensation, they are paid living wages suitable for learned persons.

You plunge then violently down between printing-houses, railroad shops, roasted coffee-factories, shoe-, stove-, structural steel-factories; fertilizer-, hosiery-, textile-, and men's clothing-factories. You are then flung violently upwards between men's clothing-, textile-, hosiery-factories and between structural steel-, stove-, shoe-, and roasted coffee-factories. You would never think you were in a 'centre' of the finest stock-raising, dairy, and specialty farming in the country. You would think you were in a world stretching forever between clothing-, stove-, structural steel-, fertilizer-, and all the other factories. If you happen to have been gassed in the late War, your lungs distend and close like old bellows with the sulphur in the air.[28] You sway and bump through the district known as Black Bottom – the

---

27 *Cheiroptera*: the order of mammals including bats.
28 Ford himself had, of course, been injured in this way.

'original' Black Bottom you are warned to remember that it is![29] – and you marvel that blackness can be so black. Then you perceive that nearly all the once red brick houses of the town are as black as the Negro shacks of the Bottom. You will be told that so prosperous is this Athens and so much soft coal is there consumed, that in winter the soot is three inches deep on the house-fronts. If you go there eleven times you will be told it eleven times or more, each time in tones of pride and veracity, and if you are told a thing eleven times, however great its exaggeration may seem, you will believe something of it. I begin myself to believe that the winter soot must be at least two inches and a third deep on the house-fronts – and of course in the lungs of the Southern Athenians.

In your exhaustion you pant up a last hill and arrive in front of the thousand and first white angel-cake Municipal edifice that you have seen. For there are miles and miles of them in Washington, some be-columned, some not, and leagues in the Parisian suburbs, and the Tower of London is buried under them, and Rome takes from them her modern colour…. So the little, charming, red brick cupola'd new market beside that white enormousness is a relief to eye and mind; and you sink onto the benches of the steak house where they offer you consistently as good porterhouse steaks as you could desire. And the place will not be too full and the voices will not be too grating…. And you will listen to the story of the Monuments…. For the eleventh time if you have visited the city eleven times…. But of course you may be told it as many as three times on one visit.

In the old days, then, S. Athens, Tennessee, boasted of a financier who built a railway with his fiddle, a park commissioner who did not like the violinist-financier, and a race-horse owner who knew nothing of either. The financier who built the railway with his fiddle did so because the park commissioner put so much opposition against the financier's railway – wanting to build a railway of his own – that the financier had to take his railway entirely around the city to find a way in for his line. So the park commissioner called him a thief. I don't know why he called him a thief – but he is said to have done so, and it is an integral part of this story that he should have done so. In the meantime, the park commissioner's opposition had cost the

---

29 The dance 'the Black Bottom' rivalled the Charleston in the 1920s. Though it was introduced to white audiences in Nashville by Perry Bradford's 1919 song 'The Black Bottom Dance', it is also claimed to originate from the town Black Bottom near Detroit, Michigan. See www.streetswing.com

financier so much money that his finances were unable to pay for the construction of the railway. On most days of the week, the men who worked for him would not work, and the men who should have supplied him with materials would not supply. So, mornings, the financier who was an incomparable fiddler; fiddling so that he could make you wear out all your shoes with dancing and your eyes with weeping – the fiddler-financier would take his fiddle down to where the permanent way had stopped and the men leaned on their tools and shouted for pay…. Then he would put his fiddle end underneath his chin, and in five minutes they would all be dancing, dancing as if they had been on the very Bridge of Avignon. And so they danced back to their shovels and picks and cranes and sleepers and – to use a Latin phrase which should be permissible in a city of colleges – *solutum est saltando*.[30] The railway was finished, and the park commissioner foiled.

Years then passed. The commissioner went on with his parks; the race-horse owner went on entering his horses for races; the financier, his finances prospering and his fiddle-playing growing daily sweeter, became dearer and ever more dear to the hearts of his fellow citizens. He, indeed, was not such a one as to play his fiddle while Athens burned.

So, when he died, his fellow citizens set up to him the stately effigy in sounding bronze that Biala will have immortalized somewhere in these pages.[31] And on it could be inscribed his even more sounding words: 'That I love my country the marks that I have left on it testify….' as who should say, remembering once more that we are in Athens of the Parthenon: '*Si monumentum queris circumspice*'… especially as his railway goes right round Nashville, the Latin being translatable by: 'If you seek my memorial, look all around you.'

The race-horse owner, who must not be forgotten, had some years before purchased a Derby favourite, and when that noble animal breathed its last – having sired Heaven knows how many of the

---

30 'It is resolved by dancing'. The editors are grateful to Rachel Collier for advice on this translation.

31 The financier was Jere Baxter, the organizer of the Tennessee Central Railroad, who had died in 1904. His statue was the first commission for seventeen-year-old sculptress Belle Kinney (1890-1959). Originally it stood at the intersection of Broadway and Sixteenth, but was later moved to Gallatin Road to stand in front of Jere Baxter School.

steeplechasers for which the Blue Grass country around the Southern Athens is famous.... The Derby favourite, then being dead and the monument erected to the fiddler-financier, nothing would suit the race-horse owner but that his favourite, too, must have its monument.... So said, so done. The monument to the race-horse was erected and still stands for all to see.

But then, into this idyll must creep the snake – in the form of the commissioner of parks. 'Ha! Ha!', hisses he between his teeth, whilst rubbing his hands in triumph. 'Now I hold them in the hollow of my palm!' Though of course, rightly speaking, snakes have neither teeth nor palms.... 'Listen then', cries that snake to the *patres conscripti* – which really should be the *patres et conscripti*[32].... (We are nearly through with the Classics now!) 'Listen then', cries the snake to gentle and simple of the good town of S. Athens, Tenn. 'You have now a monument to a horse and to a thief. I will now give you one to a horse-thief.' And in his park he erected the monument that you may see to this day – though not in the park.[33] For even park commissioners are mortal, and last year a new commissioner removed the memorial and placed it in some one's back-yard.

....It has been objected by the sort of person who likes to spoil good stories that Murrell,[34] to whom the monument was erected, was not a horse-thief. That is not true. Murrell is most famous because he was the gentleman who planned the uprising of all the slaves in the South who should murder their masters – no, I am not thinking of John Brown.... And when the slaves had massacred all the masters, Mr Murrell and his friends were to murder all the slaves. So they

---

32 Roman senators: 'When certain new senators were first enrolled with the "fathers" the body was called Patres et Conscripti; afterward all were called Patres conscripti': *Webster's Revised Unabridged Dictionary*, 1913.

33 Like many of Ford's stories, this is truer than it might sound. When Baxter's statue was unveiled in 1907, Eugene C. Lewis, who was a president of the rival Louisville and Nashville Railroad, as well as a member of the City Park Commission, 'arranged for a marker to be erected in Centennial Park honouring one John Murrell, a legendary horse and slave thief in early Tennessee, who compared favorably, Lewis thought, with the man who sold the city one million dollars of near-worthless railroad stock': Don H. Doyle, *Nashville in the New South, 1880-1930*, Knoxville: University of Tennessee Press, 1985, pp. 31-2.

34 John Murrell was indeed notorious not only as a robber and horse-thief but also for his plot to take over New Orleans. He appears in Chapter 29 of Mark Twain's *Life on the Mississippi*, as well as in Eudora Welty's story 'A Still Moment', from *The Wide Net* (1943), which imagines an encounter between Murrell and the naturalist John James Audubon.

would become, he, Emperor, and his friendly buccaneers, state governors or something of the sort, over all the South. Unfortunately, the coloured nursery maid of Mrs. Latham of Beattie's Bluff was overheard, whilst holding her mistress's baby, to say: 'But this is such'n a pretty one. You'all ought to know I would never kill she.'... And her interlocutor answering: 'Us got to kill'n. Us got to kill 'em all....' The plot was discovered, and Murrell duly hung.... Such wild stories there are in the hinterlands of this Athens.... Nevertheless, in his beginnings, the famous Mr. Murrell was nothing better than a horse-thief, his first exploit, I am told, having been to steal three mules somewhere between Knoxville and Athens.

So much then for Music in the Southern Athens. Let us consider the other Arts – for in Athens, the Arts should be uppermost in your minds.

In, then, the quiet place of reflection where you can rest from the sun and consume such admirable steaks and deep apple-pies, there will gradually drift in huge, well-covered, silver-haired, pink-faced men – eight or ten of them, like powerful, massive rams, clothed in white from head to foot, with pale neckties and distant gazes.... Magnificent specimens of the Aryan Quinquagenarian type. Anglo-Saxons to the last hair. And your informant – or your several informants, if you go to that place several times – will whisper to you behind the back of his hand that those are the famous Silver Knights who are sworn to restore West Tennessee to its former state of purity.[35]

So, rising on tiptoes and stealing out of that place, not without fearful side-glances at those shining figures – stealing as Shakespeare has said 'out of God's blessing into the hot sun'[36].... For, of course, in Athens you must quote Shakespeare at least once!... you step like Hell on the gas and get to the Hermitage in fifteen minutes.

---

35 This is almost certainly a reference to the Ku Klux Klan, a still powerful force at that time in the southern states. Members are more often also known as the White Knights, but high ranking 'officers' wore silver trimmed costumes.

36 'Thou out of heaven's benediction com'st / To the warm sun' is the form Shakespeare uses in *The Tragedy of King Lear*, Act 2 Scene 2, ll. 152-3: William Shakespeare, *The Complete Works*, ed. Stanley Wells and Gary Taylor, Oxford: Clarendon Press, 1986. In the form given by Ford, the expression is proverbial, meaning 'from better to worse'. See *The Oxford Dictionary of English Proverbs*, Oxford, The Clarendon Press, 1975, p. 602.

The Hermitage was the last house – another having just a hundred years ago been burned down – to shelter the nearly always on the verge of bankrupt, and always tortured, career of the ex-President as real estate speculator.[37] It is a post-colonial, not quite planter's mansion, with the usual white brick walls and white colonnade. It is nothing like as fine as the near-by house of the kind Judge Overton who was forever picking up the ex-President when he fell…. But it contains one thing – the sole work of art that you will be able to find in all S. Athens…. The sole Primitive work of art, perhaps it would be more accurate to say…. Primitive New York art.

Biala made a sketch of it. It represents two children named for the President and his Rachel…. I understand that they will shoot you on sight if you merely look as if you were thinking that his Rachel was not all…. But one had better not complete the sentence. And, in fact, Rachel deserves every one's sympathies.[38] The picture, if you could see it in colour, would have all the un-blasé, touching colour and feeling of a really primitive art.

Otherwise, as I have said, you will find it extremely difficult to find any specimens of the Fine Arts in S. Athens. There are said to be some paintings in a cellar in the Parthenon. But the janitor when you go there says: Pictures! What do you want to see pictures for? There are hundreds of millions of pictures in the world. But there is only one Parthenon…. And he would be so hurt, if you insisted on seeing the pictures, that you don't.

The Parthenon itself is an exact replica of the forgotten one in Athens, GR.[39] That is to say, it would have been exact but for a proud S. Athenian gesture. Tennessee marble, beautiful as it is, is so plentiful

---

37 Andrew Jackson, 7th President of the USA (1829-37). It is Jackson's 'Indian Removal Policy' for which his presidency is most known. Exploitative treaties were forced on various Native American tribes as part of their removal west of the Mississippi River, enabling whites to buy their land. The policy resulted in great loss of life. The re-chartering of the US Bank was the other major issue of this administration. Jackson believed the bank held too much power and was a threat to national security. The Hermitage was the mansion Jackson commissioned on his Tennessee land in 1819. It is just outside Nashville.

38 Rachel Jackson married Andrew Jackson twice. Their marriage became a scandal during the 1828 Presidential Campaign when it was discovered that they had married before her divorce was finalised. When it was finalised, they married again. She died a few weeks after he became President.

39 It is indeed a full-scale replica, and is the centrepiece of Centennial Park, Nashville.

and so cheap, that they built their Parthenon out of the more costly cement. Except, in fact, for the rather grim quays and the rather gay vessel said to be the last showboat, the note of S. Athens is not the picturesque. It is tense, it is nervous, it is austere, filled even on market-days with people too anxious and too baked by the fierce sun that is so cruel alike to them and to their crops. The only touch of the picturesque, of the coloured, animated and self-abandoned, is conveyed by the coloured people. They say that a hunt-ball is not colourful because, the men's coats being scarlet, there is no black to show off the colours of the ladies' frocks. But there are about seventy thousand Negroes in Nashville, so what colour there is, is enforced enough. I saw a white – that is to say an orange – man standing in front of three pure Negroes the other day. His cap was a streak of light yellow, his baked face a patch of the orange of fishing-boat sails, his jersey a patch of light yellow, his pants two vertical streaks of fishing-boat orange. He just blazed. He would have been dull enough against a ploughed field....

So, for Heaven's sake, let us step on it and get to one of the kind green spots in the hair of this Athens of the South, and there with mint juleps or the better coke refresh ourselves to the sound of silver waters falling into the little stone fountains. You will find there kindness enough and talk of good runs with the hounds.... Or you can reflect that, after all, this is a little sort of an Athens in matters not thought of in markets. There was once here a small literary group whose work has penetrated to most parts of the civilized world. It centered, unusually, round the English classes of the University endowed by Cornelius Vanderbilt and bearing his name.[40]

When the concrete Parthenon has crumbled away and the last steeplechase shall have been run in the Blue Grass fields and the last pall of three-inch small-coal soot shall have descended from the proud chimneys of the Silver Knights, the betting is that the work of that band of writers shall still keep on the map the name of the Athens of the South.

---

40 Ford is probably referring to the 'Fugitives'. In April, 1922, a group of poets at Vanderbilt University began a small literary magazine, *The Fugitive*. It lasted only three and a half years, but scholars credit it with beginning the Southern Literary Renaissance. Allen Tate was a prominent Fugitive, and Caroline Gordon was a later Vanderbilt alumna.

CONTRIBUTORS

ASHLEY CHANTLER is Senior Lecturer in English at University College Chester, where he specialises in twentieth-century literature and creative writing. He has presented papers and written on Romanticism, and on Ford Madox Ford, Zbigniew Herbert, William Burroughs, and the theory and practice of textual editing. His poetry collection, *In Praise of Paving*, was published in 2003. He is the editor of *Prize Flights: Stories from the Cheshire Prize for Literature* (2004), and co-editor of a collection of essays on translation (forthcoming).

COLIN EDWARDS is Senior Lecturer in English and Creative Studies at Bath Spa University College. He has published articles on Ford Madox Ford, Ezra Pound and Wyndham Lewis; he writes, also, on early Gothic fiction.

NICK FREEMAN is Lecturer in English at the University of the West of England. His recent research has focused on late nineteenth- and early twentieth-century literature and culture, and this has resulted in several essays, including: 'Ballad of a Demon Barber: The Criminal Career of George Chapman, Serial Poisoner' in Andrew Maunder and Grace Moore, eds., *Crime, Madness and Sensation in Victorian Culture* (Ashgate 2004); '"Nothing of the wild Wood?": Pan, Paganism and Spiritual Confusion in E. F. Benson's "The Man Who Went Too Far"', *Literature & Theology*, 19:1 (March 2005); and 'Intentional Rudeness? Grant Allen and the Cultural Politics of 1895' in *Grant Allen: Literature & Politics in the Fin de Siècle* (Ashgate 2005). He has a particular interest in the representation of the Victorian city.

MICHELE GEMELOS is a doctoral candidate in English Literature at the University of Oxford, where she has received an M.Phil. in English Studies. Her doctoral thesis investigates late nineteenth- and early twentieth-century British writing about New York by W. T. Stead, H. G. Wells, Ford Madox Ford, and Malcolm Lowry. Since 2000, she has taught undergraduate tutorials on American literature, travel writing, and Modernism. Her interest in metropolitan writing led her to organise an international graduate conference at Oxford on 'The City in Literature' in 2003.

BRIAN IBBOTSON GROTH is an Associate Professor in the Department of Communication, Culture and Languages at the Norwegian School of Management BI in Oslo. Here he teaches and researches cross-cultural communication and negotiation with special emphasis on international negotiation. He wrote his master's thesis for the University of Oslo on the major female characters in Ford Madox Ford's *Parade's End* and has published its principal findings in 'The Dagger and the Sheath', *Modernism and the Individual Talent* (Münster, Hamburg, London: Lit Verlag, 2001).

SARA HASLAM is Lecturer in Literature at the Open University, England. She is the author of *Fragmenting Modernism: Ford Madox Ford, the Novel and the Great War* (Manchester University Press, 2002), and editor of Ford's *England and the English* (Carcanet Press, 2003). She has published articles on Ford, Henry James, and modernism, and current projects include an essay on *The Good Soldier*, forthcoming in the *Blackwell Companion to Modernist Literature and Culture*, and a book, *Victorian Inventions, Modernist Novels*. With pedagogy another of her interests, she has produced an interactive CD-ROM on the poetry of Thomas Hardy.

ELENA LAMBERTI completed her doctoral studies at the University of Bologna, where she teaches courses on literature, the arts, and the media. She is the author of *McLuhan: Tra letteratura, arte e media* (Milan: Mondadori, 2000), of articles on Ford, and co-editor (with Vita Fortunati) of a collection of Ford's critical essays: *Prove di un senso critica. Saggi di Ford Madox Ford* (Florence: Alinea, 2001). She has a special interest in English and Canadian literature, in Anglo-American Modernism, in literature and technology, and the innovative work of Marshall McLuhan.

ROBERT E. McDONOUGH is Professor of English at Cuyahoga Community College in Cleveland, OH. He has published one book of poems, *No Other World* (Cleveland State University Poetry Center), as well as articles on Ford Madox Ford. Current projects include a chapbook of poems, 'Greatest Hits'. A former president of the Poets'

League of Greater Cleveland, he moderates a monthly public poetry workshop for that organization. He leads discussions of crime fiction in public libraries in Ohio and in the Literary Center in Cleveland. He lives in an old farmhouse in Windham, OH.

CAROLINE PATEY is Assistant Professor of English Literature and Culture at the University of Milan. Her research has focused on two historical and cultural areas: Renaissance studies, leading to, among other publications, the volumes *Manierismo* (1996) and *Storie nella storia: Teatro e politica nell'Inghilterra rinascimentale* (2000); her interest in early and mature Modernism has resulted in *Tempi difficili: Su Proust e Joyce* (1991) as well as various essays on Ford Madox Ford, James Joyce, Ezra Pound, and T. S. Eliot. Recent publications include a book on Henry James and London (*Londra. Henry James e la capitale del moderno,* Milan, 2004); current projects include a volume of essays on James Joyce and memory.

MAX SAUNDERS is Professor of English at King's College London, where he teaches modern English, European, and American literature. He studied at the universities of Cambridge and Harvard, and was a Research Fellow and then College Lecturer at Selwyn College, Cambridge. He is the author of *Ford Madox Ford: A Dual Life*, 2 vols. (Oxford University Press, 1996), the editor of Ford's *Selected Poems, War Prose*, and (with Richard Stang) *Critical Essays* (Carcanet, 1997, 1999, 2002), and has published essays on Ford, Eliot, Joyce, Rosamond Lehmann, Richard Aldington, May Sinclair, Lawrence, Freud, Pound, Ruskin, and others.

SITA A. SCHUTT was until 2003 Assistant Professor in English at Bilkent University, Ankara. She has published various articles on French and English detective fiction and on Ford Madox Ford. She has edited H. G. Wells's *Ann Veronica* for Penguin (2005), and is currently writing a novel.

PAUL SKINNER has taught at the University of the West of England and the University of Bristol. His doctoral thesis was on Ford Madox Ford and Ezra Pound. He is editor of Ford's *No Enemy* (Carcanet, 2002) and has published articles on Ford, Pound and Rudyard Kipling. He lives in Bristol, where he works in publishing, and is slowly writing a book on Ford, centred on *Parade's End*.

JOSEPH WIESENFARTH is Professor Emeritus at the University of Wisconsin-Madison. He has written extensively on Ford and on the English novel. His book *Gothic Manners and the Classic English Novel* (Madison, Wisconsin: University of Wisconsin Press, 1989) includes a chapter on *Parade's End*. He was guest editor for the special Ford issue of *Contemporary Literature*, 30:2 (Summer 1989), and editor of *History and Representation in Ford Madox Ford's Writings* (2004), volume 3 of *International Ford Madox Ford Studies*. His most recent book is *Ford Madox Ford and the Regiment of Women: Violet Hunt, Jean Rhys, Stella Bowen, and Janice Biala* (University of Wisconsin Press, 2005).

ANGUS WRENN teaches Literature and Society at the London School of Economics (University of London), a course which focuses on twentieth-century British literature in its social and political context. His particular scholarly interests are Henry James and Ford Madox Ford. He has published an essay on both these writers, together with Rebecca West and H. G. Wells: 'The Mad Woman We Love', in *Ford Madox Ford and the Republic of Letters*, ed. Vita Fortunati and Elena Lamberti (Bologna: CLUEB, 2002); and 'Henry, Hueffer, Holbein, History and Representation', in *History and Representation in Ford Madox Ford's Writings* (2004). He has recently completed a book on Henry James and the Second Empire and the contributions on James, Paul Bourget and Proust in *The Reception of Henry James in Europe*, ed. Annick Duperray (London: Continuum, forthcoming).

ABSTRACTS

ASHLEY CHANTLER 'Ford's Pre-War Poetry and the "Rotting City".'
The chapter analyses Ford's use in his pre-First World War poetry of the 'rotting city' to critique the 'Spirit of the Age': the 'rotten age', in Ford's view, of religious, moral, social and political decay, of 'dead faiths' and 'dead loves', and of isolated selves within the city. The poems present various city-dwelling speakers, for example, the speaker of 'rot' (the 'sermon spinner', or the 'Reformer') who contributes to the 'Spirit of the Age', while the alienated speaker ponders where respite or redemption might be found. Concomitants of Ford's critique are meditations on schisms (religious, social and familial), suffering, death, desire, love, and uncertainty. The main texts analysed are: 'The Story of Simon Pierreauford', 'Faith' and 'Hope' from *The Questions at the Well* (1893); 'Grey Matter' and 'The Mother: A Song-Drama' from *The Face of the Night* (1904); and 'Süssmund's Address to an Unknown God' and 'To All the Dead' from *High Germany* (1912). Connections are made between the poems, Ford's novels and critical writings, and other contemporary, and earlier, authors.

COLIN EDWARDS 'City Burlesque: the Pleasures of Paranoia in Ford's *Mister Bosphorus and the Muses*.'
Ford's cinematographic stage imagery of the Victorian city is the visual counterpart of the poet Bosphorus' English gentility and the indigence in which he locates his mixed origins. Slothful, omniscient, lecherous: Bosphorus seems to veer between the twin poles of grandeur and abjection which paranoid narrators of the period alternately aspire, and succumb, to. Once established in France, Ford was to achieve a remarkable quality of 'slumberous consistency' at the centre of his epic style of war fiction: *Parade's End's* Christopher Tietjens keeps his own, and others', sanity by composing sonnets at the height of the German bombardment. His sufferings are infused with an artist's brand of désinvolture. 'City Burlesque' argues that Mr Bosphorus's quarrel – staged in the London style of Music Hall farce

– with his Northern Muse signals a deep-lying emotional accommodation with the country Ford was shortly to leave, in favour of Paris. *Mister Bosphorus and the Muses* is interpreted as a work of transition and preparation: a dream poem played out at pavement level.

FORD MADOX FORD 'Portraits of Cities'
Three essays, dating from 1937, from an unfinished book Ford planned as the third volume to complete a trilogy with *Provence* and *Great Trade Route*. The essays on Boston and Denver are published here for the first time. Ford portrays Boston in terms of the heraldic concept of a 'dimidiated' figure, divided down the middle, half in scarlet Cardinal's robes and half in black academic gown. The essay, which is itself bipartite, closes on a consideration of the New England Conscience. Denver is portrayed as a ghost city, haunted by its wild gold-rush history and oppressed by its heat and altitude. The third essay, on Nashville, was published in *Vogue*. Like the other two, it sets the scene by discussing the approach to the city, before exploring its history. Ford takes up its claim to be the 'Athens of the South', and relates the stories surrounding its monuments: not only its Centennial copy of the Parthenon, but the statues with which it portrays its own history.

NICK FREEMAN 'Not "accuracy" but "suggestiveness": Impressionism in *The Soul of London*.'
This chapter will examine the influence of Walter Pater and *avant garde* visual art on Ford's *The Soul of London* (1905). In rejecting the type of quasi-objective engagement with the city exemplified by the work of Sir Walter Besant and W. J. Loftie, Ford was aligning himself with a wider difficulty with facts in late Victorian and Edwardian writing. The discussion will consequently examine the congruences between the ideas of Ford and those of other radical writers and artists, including Monet, Henry James, and Arthur Symons in order to trace both the dissemination of impressionist ideas and their application to London at the beginning of the twentieth century.

MICHELE GEMELOS 'New York Minutes: Ford's Notes on the City.'

This chapter sets Ford's engagement with the city in the context of his writing about New York City in particular. By comparing Ford's professional agenda, methods, and conclusions with those of his contemporaries such as W. T. Stead, Henry James, and H. G. Wells, the essay suggests that Ford's New York texts represent a major shift in the way British literary visitors considered the city. He rejects the easy condescension of American civilization and the straightforward synecdoche of New York City for the United States. In doing so, Ford also experimented more broadly than his predecessors with forms and styles, vacillating between artistic and journalistic approaches and creating hybrids of fact and fiction. A biographical and historical interpretation of *An English Girl* (1907) provides evidence to support this characterization of Ford's New York writing.

BRIAN GROTH 'Ford's Saddest Journey: London to London 1909-1936.'
The city figures prominently in Ford's writing throughout his life. This chapter focuses on two of his 'city' essays, comparing and contrasting them. One is 'The Future in London' published in 1909, quite early in Ford's career; the second, 'London Re-visited' (1936) appeared not long before his death in 1939. The impressions Ford gives of England's capital are poles apart in the two works. The first essay bubbles with *joie de vivre* about the London of the present and what Ford predicts will be the London of the future; the second portrays a dull city lacking in energy mainly because its inhabitants in contrast have such a poor diet – especially when compared with those of Provence. Of course no-one can be sure why Ford's view of London changed so profoundly in the quarter of a century that separates the two essays, but this chapter attempts to provide plausible answers to that question.

ELENA LAMBERTI 'Real Cities and Virtual Communities: Ford and the International Republic of Letters.'
This essay considers the Fordian notion of the Republic of Letters, as developed in his critical essays, and central to his poetic. Although Ford did not operate as some utopian writers choose to, in providing a visual model of his ideal, there are real cities that can help us to imagine what it may have looked like, at different points in Ford's

career. Ideas connected with the modern virtual community are also shown to be significant in this respect. Both also assist in the discussion of the operation of the republic, a discussion that is broadened by application of Ford's thoughts on Plato's republic, as they appear particularly in his late work *The March of Literature*.

ROBERT E. McDONOUGH *'New York Is Not America*, But Then What Is?'
In this book, requested by his publisher, Ford uses his impressionistic narrative method to communicate a complex realization of New York and America. (Everything within the United States that is not part of Ford's New York is America.) With most of the text of the book set between an 'Author's Advertisement' and 'L'Envoi', which concern a voyage to Provence, the idea of the book might be phrased New-York-not-America-and-both-not-Europe. Ford's anecdotes contrast New York, the city of the Good Time, a kind of consummation of Europe, with puritanical, prohibitionist America. At the same time he recognizes that both New York and America change and predicts that America's change, as the Midwesterners with whom he had worked on the *transatlantic review* in Paris come to leadership, will be for the better.

CAROLINE PATEY 'Right Bank, Left Bank and an Island: Ford's Fragmented *Ville Lumière.*'
Though Ford's post-war Paris, located on the left bank of the river, revolves notoriously around the Contrescarpe of the *bal musette* and the Observatoire of La Closerie des Lilas, the chapter argues that the symbolic and literary geographies of the French capital combine in more complex ways in Ford's imagination and writings. A first paragraph assesses the weight, in Ford's reminiscences and narrative, of a previous Paris, the third-republic capital of Gustave Flaubert and Guy de Maupassant. The essay then moves to the location of the *transatlantic review*, the Saint Louis island embraced by the two arms of the Seine. The last section is dedicated to the feminine voices gravitating around Ford and represented in his work. Both Jean Rhys's and Stella Bowen's writings are connected to Ford's awareness of Paris' changing cultural tide. Through the editorship of the review, as well as the artistic encouragement offered to many women in search of

their personal and professional identity, Ford proved himself to be an acutely sensitive interpreter of the French capital and a prompt promoter of the expression and art of women. The essay finally argues that, though Ford's love for Paris and France never failed, the writer had the early and prophetic perception of the changing cultural hegemony and the mounting role of New York as a capital of culture.

MAX SAUNDERS 'Ford, the City, Impressionism and Modernism.' The importance of the city to literary modernism has been long familiar. The chapter aims to establish Ford's contribution. It concentrates on *The Soul of London*, showing how Ford develops an Impressionist aestheticization of urban scenes into a Modernist concern with energy, technology, movement, and fragmentation. It argues for Ford's awareness of how the modern city changes the perception of space and time. It considers the impact upon narrative of the geography, sociology, and communication technology of the modern city with reference to *A Call*. The chapter also briefly considers the role of the City in Ford's poetics, and his relation in this context to Pound and Eliot. It concludes with a brief discussion of Ford's subsequent treatments of the city.

SITA A. SCHUTT 'Close Up From a Distance.' The chapter explores the ways in which three turn-of-the-century writers, Bram Stoker, Conan Doyle, and Ford Madox Ford, evoke London and Englishness. Although they write in different genres, the chapter argues that they have much in common, notably in the ways in which definitions of strangers and 'Londoners' come into play in texts that have produced enduring representations of the city. This essay uncovers ways in which crime, foreignness and technology are motifs that contribute to the historical representation of London. They create a fixed sense of urban nostalgia, evoking the spirit of an age, and also look beyond, evoking the spirit of a place that lives on today.

PAUL SKINNER '"Speak Up, Fordie!": How Some People Want to Go To Carcassonne.' The city of Carcassonne, mentioned several times in Ford's *Provence* and in half a dozen of his other books, is often linked with the

Albigensian crusade and with the Troubadour poet Peire Vidal, who, despite the absurdities of his life and hopeless love affairs, produced good and lasting work. Ford uses Carcassonne most importantly in *The Good Soldier*, where it signifies both a kind of dream city and death. Ford's use of Vidal's story in that novel, together with many other indications of his writings of the 1913-14 period, point towards a situation paralleling that of 1903-4, the worst period of Ford's life. Fears of nervous breakdown, of suicide and artistic failure, all combined to exert enormous pressure on Ford and on the novel he was then writing. In these terms, *The Good Soldier* can be seen almost as a suicide note from what Ford called 'the writing self', a last chance to speak up against the destructive forces – personal, historical and artistic – which threatened it. Carcassonne comes to stand for all that Ford may not see, do and achieve. But, paradoxically, 'talking in a low voice', which is finally and emphatically his own, Ford comes through, in and by the writing of *The Good Soldier*.

JOSEPH WIESENFARTH 'Coda to the City.'
Ford's intense concern with war and civilization finds itself expressed in his poems as well as in novels like *Parade's End*. As early as *On Heaven and Poems Written on Active Service*, he writes about cities as well as soldiers: 'The Old Houses of Flanders' is a particularly poignant example of the destruction of religious, civic, and family life in the bombing of a city. He returns to this motif when he imagines the destruction of Paris in his last great poem, 'Coda'. In it, Paris, the home of lovers and artists, is also home to the civilizing process, for in art and love Ford finds not only hope for cities but for civilization itself.

ANGUS WRENN 'Angle of Elevation: Transport, Social Class, and Perception of the City in *The Soul of London*.'
The paper examines the formation of mental images of the modern city as described in *The Soul of London*. Much has been made of the ways in which Ford, writing in 1905, anticipates the mood conveyed in such classic modernist London texts as Eliot's *The Waste Land* and Woolf's *Mrs Dalloway*. These however did not emerge for another twenty years and come in the wake of the First World War. Ford shares with them a sense of emergence from recent psychological crisis, but the sense of violent fracture is not provided by war. Rather

the mental images of the city which Ford focuses on in *The Soul of London* are the product of social class, and also developments in modes of transport at the turn of the twentieth century. In addition to Ford's mental and personal crisis at this date the images evoked in this work must be seen in terms of specific contemporary technological developments in the urban landscape.

ABBREVIATIONS

The following abbreviations have been used for works cited several times, whether in the text or in the notes. The list is divided into two alphabetical sections: works by Ford and by others. A full list of abbreviations to be used in future volumes can be found on the Ford Society website.

(i) Works by Ford

AL   *Ancient Lights* (London: Chapman & Hall, 1911)

CE   *Critical Essays*, ed. Max Saunders and Richard Stang (Manchester: Carcanet, 2002)

CP   *The Cinque Ports* (Edinburgh and London: William Blackwood and Sons, 1900)

CW   *Critical Writings of Ford Madox Ford*, ed. Frank MacShane (Lincoln: University of Nebraska Press, 1964)

EE   *England and the English: An Interpretation* (New York: McClure, Phillips & Co., 1907); *England and the English*, ed. Sara Haslam (Manchester: Carcanet, 2003

FN   *The Face of the Night* (London: John Macqueen, 1904)

FQ   *The Fifth Queen* (London: Penguin, 1999)

GTR   *Great Trade Route* (New York: Oxford University Press, 1937)

HC   *The Heart of the Country* (London: Alston Rivers, 1906)

HG   *High Germany* (London: Duckworth, 1912)

HJ   *Henry James* (London: Martin Secker, 1913)

IWN   *It Was the Nightingale* (Philadelphia: J. B. Lippincott, 1933; London: William Heinemann, 1934)

LF   *Letters of Ford Madox Ford*, ed. Richard M. Ludwig (Princeton, NJ: Princeton University Press, 1965)

MF   *A Mirror to France* (London: Duckworth, 1926)

ML   *The March of Literature* (New York: Dial Press, 1938; London: Allen & Unwin, 1939)

MrB   *Mister Bosphorus and the Muses* (London: Duckworth, 1923)

NYNA   *New York is Not America* (London: Duckworth, 1927)

PE   *Parade's End* (London: Penguin, 2002)

QW   *The Questions at the Well*, pseud. 'Fenil Haig' (London: Digby, Long, 1893)

Reader   Sondra J. Stang (ed.), *The Ford Madox Ford Reader*, with Foreword by Graham Greene (Manchester: Carcanet, 1986)

RY   *Return to Yesterday* (London: Victor Gollancz, 1931)

SL   *The Soul of London* (London: Alston Rivers, 1905)

SP   *The Spirit of the People* (London: Alston Rivers, 1907)

(ii) Works by Others

Bowen   Stella Bowen, *Drawn from Life* (London: Collins, 1941)

Huntley   H. Robert Huntley, *The Alien Protagonist of Ford Madox Ford* (Chapel Hill, CL: The University of North Carolina Press, 1970)

Napoleon   G. K. Chesterton, *The Napoleon of Notting Hill* [1904], ed. Bernard Bergonzi (Oxford: Oxford University Press, 1998)

Saunders   Max Saunders, *Ford Madox Ford: A Dual Life*, Two Volumes (Oxford: Oxford University Press, 1996)

Stang and Cochran   Sondra J. Stang & Karen Cochran, *The Correspondence of Ford Madox Ford and Stella Bowen* (Bloomington and Indianapolis: Indiana University Press, 1994)

Toklas   Gertrude Stein, *The Autobiography of Alice B. Toklas* [1933] (Harmondsworth: Penguin, 1966)

THE
FORD
MADOX
FORD
SOCIETY

Ford c. 1915   ©Alfred Cohen, 2000   Registered Charity No. 1084040

This international society was founded in 1997 to promote knowledge of and interest in Ford. Honorary Members include Julian Barnes, A. S. Byatt, Hans-Magnus Enzensberger, Samuel Hynes, Alan Judd, Sir Frank Kermode, Ruth Rendell, Michael Schmidt, John Sutherland, and Gore Vidal. There are currently over one hundred members altogether, from more than ten countries. The Society continues to organize an active programme of events. Besides regular meetings in Britain, we have held conferences in Italy, Germany, and the U.S.A. Since 2002 we have published an annual series, International Ford Madox Ford Studies, distributed free to members. *Ford Madox Ford: A Reappraisal* (2002), *Ford Madox Ford's Modernity* (2003) and *History and Representation in Ford Madox Ford's Writings* (2004) are all still available. Future issues are planned on Ford and Englishness; Ford's Literary Contacts; and Ford and Cultural Transitions. If you are an admirer, an enthusiast, a reader, a scholar, or a student of anything Fordian, then this Society wants to hear from you, and welcomes your participation in its activities.

The Society normally organises two events each year, and publishes one or two Newsletters. A celebratory day on 'Ford Madox Ford: Writing and Painting', was staged in January 1998. In 1999 we participated in two conferences: one on Ford and Modernism held in Germany; the other in Kent on Ford, Conrad and James. For 1999-2000 we held a day conference in London on 'Ford and the City' and a Ford panel at the 2000 MLA convention in Washington. There were sizeable conferences at the Universities of Bologna in 2001 and Madison-Wisconsin in 2002. December 2004 saw a conference in Manchester on 'Ford and Englishness'. Future meetings are planned in Birmingham, Genoa, and Turku, Finland. The Society has also inaugurated a series of Ford Lectures, which have been given by Martin Stannard, Alan Judd, David Crane, Sergio Perosa, Oliver Soskice, and Nicholas Delbanco. To join, please see the website for details; or send your name and address (including an e-mail address if possible), and a cheque made payable to 'The Ford Madox Ford Society', to: Sara Haslam, Dept of Literature, Open University, Walton Hall, Milton Keynes, MK7 6AA.

Annual rates: **Pounds sterling:** Individuals: £12; Concessions £6; Member Organisations £17.50
          US Dollars: Any category: $25

For further information, either contact Sara Haslam (Treasurer) at the above address, or Max Saunders (Chairman) on e-mail at: max.saunders@kcl.ac.uk
The Society's Website is at: **www.rialto.com/fordmadoxford_society**

Innovation and Visualization
Trajectories, Strategies, and Myths

Amy Ione

Amsterdam/New York, NY 2005. 271 pp.
(Consciousness, Literature and the Arts 1)

ISBN: 90-420-1675-2   € 55,-/US $ 77.-

Amy Ione's *Innovation and Visualization* is the first in detail account that relates the development of visual images to innovations in art, communication, scientific research, and technological advance. Integrated case studies allow Ione to put aside C.P. Snow's "two culture" framework in favor of cross-disciplinary examples that refute the science/humanities dichotomy. The themes, which range from cognitive science to illuminated manuscripts and media studies, will appeal to specialists (artists, art historians, cognitive scientists, etc.) interested in comparing our image saturated culture with the environments of earlier eras. The scope of the examples will appeal to the generalist.

Amy Ione is currently the Director of The Diatrope Institute, a California-based group that disseminates information and engages in research exploring art, science and visual studies. She has published extensively on art, science and technology relationships. Ione's artwork has been exhibited in the United States and Europe, and is found in many collections.

USA/Canada: 906 Madison Avenue, UNION, NJ 07083, USA.
Call toll-free (USA only)1-800-225-3998, Tel. 908 206 1166, Fax 908-206-0820
All other countries: Tijnmuiden 7, 1046 AK Amsterdam, The Netherlands.
Tel. ++ 31 (0)20 611 48 21, Fax ++ 31 (0)20 447 29 79
Orders-queries@rodopi.nl   **www.rodopi.nl**
Please note that the exchange rate is subject to fluctuations

The Theater of Transformation
Postmodernism in American Drama

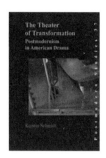

Kerstin Schmidt

Amsterdam/New York, NY 2005. 230 pp.
(Postmodern Studies 37)

ISBN: 90-420-1895-X   € 46,-/US $ 64.-

The Theater of Transformation: Postmodernism in American Drama offers a fresh and innovative reading of the contemporary experimental American theater scene and navigates through the contested and contentious relationship between postmodernism and contemporary drama. This book addresses gender and class as well as racial issues in the context of a theoretical discussion of dramatic texts, textuality, and performance. Transformation is contemporary drama's answer to the questions of postmodernism and a major technique in the development of a postmodern language for the stage. In order to demonstrate the multi-faceted nature of the postmodern theater of transformation, this study draws on a wide range of plays: from early experimental plays of the 1960s by Jean-Claude van Itallie through feminist plays by Megan Terry and Rochelle Owens to more recent drama by the African-American playwright Suzan-Lori Parks.

The Theater of Transformation: Postmodernism in American Drama is written for anyone interested in contemporary American drama and theater as well as in postmodernism and contemporary literary theory. It appeals even more broadly to a readership intrigued by the ubiquitous aspects of popular culture, by feminism and ethnicity, and by issues pertaining to the so-called 'society of spectacle' and the study of contemporary media.

Kerstin Schmidt is currently Assistant Professor of American Studies and Intercultural Anglophone Studies in the Department of English at the University of Bayreuth, Germany.

USA/Canada: 906 Madison Avenue, UNION, NJ 07083, USA.
Call toll-free (USA only)1-800-225-3998, Tel. 908 206 1166, Fax 908-206-0820
All other countries: Tijnmuiden 7, 1046 AK Amsterdam, The Netherlands.
Tel. ++ 31 (0)20 611 48 21, Fax ++ 31 (0)20 447 29 79
Orders-queries@rodopi.nl   **www.rodopi.nl**
Please note that the exchange rate is subject to fluctuations

EcoMedia.

Sean Cubitt

Amsterdam/New York, NY 2005. X, 168 pp.
(Contemporary Cinema 1)

ISBN: 90-420-1885-2   € 35,-/ US $ 44.-

For the last twenty years ecology, the last great political movement of the 20th century, has fired the imaginations not only of political activists but of popular movements throughout the industrialised world. *EcoMedia* is an enquiry into the popular mediations of environmental concerns in popular film and television since the 1980s. Arranged in a series of case studies on bio-security, relationships with animals, bioethics and biological sciences, over-fishing, eco-terrorism, genetic modification and global warming, *EcoMedia* offers close readings of Peter Jackson's *The Lord of the Rings*, Miyazake's *Princess Mononoke, The Perfect Storm, X-Men* and *X2, The Day After Tomorrow* and the BBC's drama *Edge of Darkness* and documentary *The Blue Planet*. Drawing on the thinking of Flusser, Luhmann, Latour, Agamben and Bookchin, *EcoMedia* discusses issues from whether animals can draw and why we like to draw animals, to how narrative films can imagine global processes, and whether wonder is still an ethical pleasure. Building on the thesis that popular film and television can tell us a great deal about the state of contemporary beliefs and anxieties, the book builds towards an argument that the *polis*, the human world, cannot survive without a three way partnership with *physis* and *techne*, the green world *and* the technological.

USA/Canada: 906 Madison Avenue, UNION, NJ 07083, USA.
Call toll-free (USA only)1-800-225-3998, Tel. 908 206 1166, Fax 908-206-0820
All other countries: Tijnmuiden 7, 1046 AK Amsterdam, The Netherlands.
Tel. ++ 31 (0)20 611 48 21, Fax ++ 31 (0)20 447 29 79
<u>Orders-queries@rodopi.nl</u>   <u>www.rodopi.nl</u>
Please note that the exchange rate is subject to fluctuations

Fiction after the Fatwa
Salman Rushdie and the Charm of Catastrophe

Madelena Gonzalez

Amsterdam/New York, NY 2004. 266 pp.
(Costerus NS 153)

ISBN: 90-420-1962-X   € 50,-/US $ 67.-

Fiction after the Fatwa: Salman Rushdie and the Charm of Catastrophe proposes for the first time an examination of what Rushdie has achieved as a·writer since the fourteenth of February 1989, the date of the fatwa. This study argues that his constant questioning of fictional form and the language used to articulate it have opened up new opportunities and further possibilities for writing in the late twentieth and early twenty-first centuries. Through close readings and intensive textual analysis, arranged chronologically, *Fiction after the Fatwa* provides a thought-provoking reflection on the writer's achievements over the last thirteen years. Aimed principally at academics and students, but also of interest to the general reader, it engages with the specific nature of the post-fatwa fiction as it moves from the fairy-tale world of *Haroun and the Sea of Stories* to the heartbreaking post-realism of *Fury*.

USA/Canada: 906 Madison Avenue, UNION, NJ 07083, USA
Call toll-free (USA only)1-800-225-3998, Tel. 908 206 1166, Fax 908-206-0820

All other countries: Tijnmuiden 7, 1046 AK Amsterdam, The Netherlands.
Tel. ++ 31 (0)20 611 48 21, Fax ++ 31 (0)20 447 29 79
Orders-queries@rodopi.nl   www.rodopi.nl
Please note that the exchange rate is subject to fluctuations

Extremely Common *Eloquence*
Constructing Scottish identity through narrative

Amsterdam/New York, NY 2005. 299 pp. (Scroll 3)

Ronald K. S. Macaulay

ISBN: 90-420-1764-3   € 60,-/US $ 81.-
ISBN: 90-420-1774-0 Textbook (minimum order 10 copies)   € 25,-/US $ 34.-

Extremely Common Eloquence presents a detailed analysis of the narrative and rhetorical skills employed by working-class Scots in talking about important aspects of their lives. The wide range of devices employed by the speakers and the high quality of the examples provide convincing evidence to reject any possible negative evaluation of working-class speech on the basis of details of non-standard pronunciation and grammar. In addition to this display of linguistic accomplishment the examples examined show how these skills are employed to communicate   important   aspects   of   Scottish   identity   and   culture. Although the political status of Scotland has fluctuated over the past four hundred years, the sense of Scottish identity has remained strong. Part of that sense of identity comes from a form of speech that remains markedly distinct from that of the dominant neighbour to the south. There are cultural attitudes that indicate a spirit of independence that is consistent with this linguistic difference. The ways in which the speakers in this book express themselves reveal their beliefs in egalitarianism, independence, and the value of hard work. *Extremely Common Eloquence* demonstrates how the methods of linguistic analysis can be combined with an   investigation   into   cultural   values.

Born and educated in Scotland, Ronald Macaulay taught for the British Council in Portugal and Argentina before going to California where he established the linguistics programme at the Claremont Colleges. He is now Emeritus Professor of Linguistics at Pitzer College. His books include: Language, Social Class, and Education: a Glasgow study, 1977 (Edinburgh University Press), Generally Speaking: How Children Learn Language, 1980 (Newbury House), Locating Dialect in Discourse: The Language of Honest Men and Bonnie Lasses in Ayr, 1991 (Oxford University Press). The Social Art: Language and its Uses, 1994 (Oxford University Press), Standards and Variation in Urban Speech: Examples from Lowland Scots, 1997 (John Benjamins), Talk that counts: Age, gender, and social class differences in discourse, 2004 (Oxford University Press).

USA/Canada: 906 Madison Avenue, UNION, NJ 07083, USA
Call toll-free (USA only)1-800-225-3998, Tel. 908 206 1166, Fax 908-206-0820

All other countries: Tijnmuiden 7, 1046 AK Amsterdam, The Netherlands.
Tel. ++ 31 (0)20 611 48 21, Fax ++ 31 (0)20 447 29 79
Orders-queries@rodopi.nl   www.rodopi.nl
Please note that the exchange rate is subject to fluctuations